Rh

A

DATE DUE

26972822		
2/24/7		

Demco, Inc. 38-293

FIRST EDITION

Published by
New River Press
645 Fairmount Street
Woonsocket, R.I.02895
(800) 244-1257
www.newriverpress.com

Printed in Canada

ISBN 1-891724-03-7

*In memory of my brother, Rev. Robert B. Eno SS, STD,
(1936-1997) whose love of history rubbed off -PFE*

*To my mother, Mildred Laxton Kelley, the historian
who was my guiding light -GVL*

Contents

Introduction

Albert T. Klyberg
Director Emeritus, Rhode Island Historical Society

The greatest crime a history teacher can commit is to bore students. And it takes real talent to do it. Now, math can be boring. Unless the lab ends up in smithereens, so can chemistry. Helminthology (the study of parasitic worms): Take it or leave it. But history — never!

This book is a tribute to that. How can it not be with a subject like Rhode Island! Ours is a state with more history than many places ten times its size, a state with more characters than a Dickens novel, a state with more heroes and villains than a TV cop show and, when it comes to politics, a state with more special effects than a Spielberg film.

And who better to tell the story in their own breezy way than two longtime Rhode Island journalists, both old friends of mine, who witnessed the latest years of that history firsthand, one from the newspaper end and one from in front of the news camera. They wrote this book not because they had some academic need to "publish or perish," but simply out of love for our state and its rich historical experience.

The core of the book is taken from the series of prize-winning newspaper articles Paul F. Eno wrote for the Rhode Island Historical Society to celebrate the state's 350th anniversary in 1986, while I was executive director there. Now revised and updated, they form the main chapter material. Emmy Award-winning journalist Glenn Laxton's contribution, a result of his long research and great respect for our common experience, helps us peer into corners of our history that even I had never heard of. Both authors bring a humanity to the tale that is too seldom seen even in popular historical writing.

So whether you're a native or a newcomer, read, learn and enjoy! You'll be surprised, enlightened and entertained. And if you happen to be a history teacher – this book is your big chance to avoid a life of crime.

-Lincoln, Rhode Island
2004

Foreword

Paul F. Eno & Glenn Laxton

This book is meant to be fun, a history book for those who don't usually read history. It can't help but be fun, because Rhode Island is to history what Garfield is to cartoon cats: independent, smart, resilient, proud, funny, and "in charge" in a canted sort of way.

Rhode Island: A Genial History certainly isn't meant to be scholarly or exhaustive, and we haven't covered everything, by a long shot. A truly complete work on the state's history would take volumes, and we list many fine books in our bibliography for readers who'd like to go deeper. We do hope that our book will be a friendly, entertaining and informative way for native Rhode Islanders to find out what *really* has been going on around here all these centuries, and for our state's many newcomers to find out what they've gotten themselves into.

The fact is that we live in a wonderful, welcoming place where anything can and does happen, and where we somehow manage to come out on top sooner or later. Because of this independent and resilient spirit, not in spite of it, our Rhode Island forbears pioneered crazy ideas like religious tolerance, freedom of thought, the rights of women and minorities, and all-around people power.

At the same time, some of Rhode Island's past is inexpressibly sordid. From the slave trade of the 18th century to the political corruption of the 19th and 20th, there's plenty *not* to be proud of.

There are two sides to every story, very often more than two. That's especially true when it comes to history. So we've added "You Decide" sections to some chapters that cover times in which there were really big national doings in which Rhode Island played a part – just to help keep the "big picture" in perspective and to stimulate discussion.

There's lots to love about Rhode Island history, lots to be proud of, and plenty to enjoy about our little corner of the world. So what are you waiting for? Start reading!

Woonsocket, Rhode Island
2004

Each section of this book ends with the initials of its author.

Most of Mr. Eno's material was originally written for the Rhode Island Historical Society and published in 1985 and 1986 as part of Rhode Island's 350th anniversary celebration. The authors thank the society for permission to reprint original elements of that material.

Chapter One

Born
⚓ of Rock and Ice ⚓

In the beginning, everybody lived in the sky. One day Great Sky Chief yanked up the Tree of Life and looked down through the hole. Calling Sky Queen, he told her to take a look and when she did, he gave her a push and down she went. Before she hit the world, which was nothing but water, two swans caught her. But neither they nor any other creature could hold her up for long. Finally, Turtle tried and had better luck. While he held Sky Queen on his back, the other creatures brought dirt from beneath the water and piled it on Turtle's back until Earth got bigger and bigger.

And that's how Rhode Island — and the world — were born.

Thus runs the story that has filtered down through thousands of years among members of the Narragansett Tribe. But regardless of Rhode Island's mythical origin, there were two mighty forces that gave the state the coastline and landscape it has today. One was what's known in geology as "plate tectonics" or "continental drift." According to this generally accepted idea, the continents literally float on the molten rock beneath the Earth's crust, drifting about over staggering periods of time. While the scenario is complex, the geological evidence, interpreted by the theory of "suspect terrane," indicates that Rhode Island and much of southeastern New

England were once part of islands off the coast of Europe. Geologists believe that this and other massive exchanges of land between what were to become Europe and North America took place between 250 and 400 million years ago.

The second major force was the vast ice sheet that moved from north to south through New England, beginning some 2 million years ago. One huge glacier apparently gouged the Blackstone Valley and Narragansett Bay, piling up hills and strewing rocks of every description from one end of the state to the other. There's evidence that another glacier carved out Mount Hope Bay and the bed of the Sakonnet River.

When the ice began to recede 15,000 to 20,000 years ago, Rhode Island was much larger than it is today because the sea level was lower. It was literally possible to walk to what would become Block Island across eighty miles of dry land. It was when the billions of tons of water from the melting glaciers poured into the seas, raising their level all over the world, that Rhode Island began to assume its current shape. The result was a stony, rolling land with vast forests filled with animals, and a great Bay and fresh waters teeming with fish. It was a rugged but bountiful land for the first people who made it their home.

Who those people were we can't be entirely sure. The scanty evidence indicates that people may have crossed from Siberia to Alaska about 12,000 years ago and gradually spread around North America. From these "paleo-hunters," most scientists believe, descended the many tribal civilizations that came to be known as the American Indians or Native Americans.

In Rhode Island, there is evidence of paleo-hunters beginning about 10,000 years ago. By the time the Europeans arrived, most of the small tribal groups had come to be known as the Narragansetts, who eventually rose to dominate the less powerful Wampanoags and often exercised great control over tribes elsewhere in southeastern New England.

Because they left no written records, and we have their folklore only in bits and pieces, we know very little about these Native Americans before the English arrived. We know something of their lifestyle from the artifacts we've found, such as spear points, bones and fishing implements. Like most New England Indians from all periods, they were semi-nomads, moving about within their territories according to seasonal food supplies. Of course, like all "primitive" peoples, they knew how to work with nature instead of against it, and they would have looked with horror on the way our civilization has ravaged the land. Things like private property and a year-round home were alien to their culture.

Even today, Rhode Island is filled with Native American place names. These not only designated a location, but almost always told what sort of place it was and what could be done there. Wabaquasset, in Providence, meant a place where women could find "flags or rushes for making mats." Azioquoneset, in the Bay, was "the small island where we get pitch," used to make torches for hunting sturgeon at night. Pawtucket is "place of big falls," Pawtuxet is "place of little falls," and Pawcatuck is "place of no falls at all."

These names literally made a map across the landscape that everyone could follow, and that could give entire Native American communities enough information to sustain themselves.

Just who the first Old World denizens to arrive in Rhode Island were is considered by some to be an open question. The Phoenicians, Egyptians, Romans and Celts all have been proposed as candidates at one time or another. One British author, Gavin Menzies, even suggests that the 15th century Chinese were among Rhode Island's first non-native explorers.

"There is a substantial body of evidence that the Chinese landed at Newport," Menzies states in his 2002 book *1421: The Year China Discovered America*. He cites Italian explorer Giovanni de Verrazano and his descriptions of people with Asian features he said he met on the Rhode Island coast in 1524.

This is all very intriguing. But aside from brief visits by Verrazano and, possibly, the Portuguese, the only pre-English visitors indicated by any substantial evidence are the Vikings. The establishment of at least one Viking settlement in Newfoundland, Canada, is beyond doubt. Some have asserted, though, that Norse adventurer Leif Ericsson or his brother Thorwald landed in New England.

In 1837, the distinguished Danish scholar Charles Christian Rafn published a huge volume in which, among other things, he said that Ericsson's "Vinland" was none other than the East Bay, Tiverton, and Fall River areas. As evidence, Rafn cited not only Norse descriptions of Vinland, but also the world-famous inscriptions on Dighton Rock in Massachusetts, which he claimed were in the Old Norse language, and a skeleton in armor reportedly dug up in Fall River in 1831. Rafn also pointed to the well known stone tower in Newport, popularly attributed to the Vikings even today, despite recent evidence to the contrary. In addition, it has been argued that many words in the native Algonquian language group (of which the Narragansetts are part) are derived from Norse words. Not too many years ago, coal samples discovered at Viking sites in Greenland reportedly turned out to be very similar to a unique type found near Newport.

Still, none of this proves that the fair-haired warriors indeed visited Rhode Island in the distant past. While it would be presumptuous to say they didn't, proof remains to be found.

Cloudy as it may be, Rhode Island's history before the coming of Roger Williams is long, fascinating, and may well provide many a surprise in the decades to come.

-PFE

Narragansett Bay's Mystery Rocks

With the possible exception of Plymouth Rock, perhaps no other large piece of the planet in America has inspired so much head scratching as Dighton Rock. To this day, people wonder who carved the designs, called "petroglyphs," on this rock, across the Taunton River from Dighton, Massachusetts. And no one has been able to figure out what they mean, at least not to everybody's satisfaction.

Although Dighton Rock gets much of the attention, the Narragansett Bay region has plenty of other rocks with mysterious carvings. All have been objects of local attention, often of the negative variety: People over the centuries have marred them with graffiti and other forms of vandalism. Nature hasn't helped. The hurricanes of 1815, 1938 and 1954, obliterating large areas of the shoreline, damaged or removed several carved rocks. In addition, because many of the carved surfaces are submerged at high tide, erosion has occurred. (Dighton Rock was saved from erosion when it was moved to higher ground in 1963.) Finally, over the years many carved rocks have no doubt been removed to make way for development.

Nevertheless, along with Dighton Rock, there survive at least three significant "mystery rocks" along our Bay shore.

MARK ROCK

To the few who have been able to find it, the aptly named Mark Rock, on the Bay shore at Warwick, kindles as much amazement as Dighton Rock. The rock actually is an uneven, sandstone ledge located near the mouth of developed but still picturesque Occupessatuxet Cove. At one time the ledge was huge: some seventy five feet long and fifty feet wide, but much of it was buried by the hurricane of 1938, when many of the carved designs were lost. But some petroglyphs still show.

The rock is covered with markings from the past three centuries, including what appear to be the emblems of four Native American leaders. One looks like the seal of Miantonomi, sachem of the Narragansetts and a friend of Roger Williams.

Among the inscriptions, one can see other, apparently older, carvings, including those of human figures, zigzag lines and spirals, and a flower-like design. There is even what looks like a four-wheeled vehicle or, perhaps, a star map: a system of circles with dots inside them, connected by straight lines.

As with most of the Narragansett Bay rocks, the scanty surviving Native American tradition indicates that, although the Indians were aware of the earliest Mark Rock carvings, they didn't know who had made them. The only legend associated with Mark Rock is one that has persisted since the 18th century: The ledge was marked by Vikings.

In the 1770s, Ezra Stiles, the Rhode Islander who later became president of Yale University, hunted for carved rocks along the shores of the Bay, but he missed Mark Rock. In 1835, a Dr. Webb reported to the Rhode Island Historical Society that he had tried in vain to find a rumored "inscription rock" on the Warwick shore. As far as we know, the earliest direct written mention of Mark Rock by European-Americans was not until March 1847, when it was named in a deed as indicating the southeast corner of land "at the shore near the marked rocks (so called)."

An 1889 local history mentions Mark Rock in passing; then, in 1917, historian Howard M. Chapin, after much time and trouble, managed to locate it. He drew a map that pinpointed it.

As far as we can tell, the first serious, on-site study of Mark Rock, as well as other Bay rocks with carvings, was conducted in the early 20th century by Edmund B. Delabarre, chairman of the Psychology Department at Brown University. Using Chapin's directions, Delabarre found Mark Rock, then documented and photographed its petroglyphs. Building on

Delabarre's work, local researcher Charles M. Devine documented the carvings that survived in the 1970s, when many had disappeared beneath the waves, then wrote about them in the journal of the New England Antiquities Research Association.

Would that the rock were as hard to find for vandals and curiosity seekers! By the middle of the 19th century, a tavern and a steamboat pier had been built a short distance north of the ledge. It became the popular thing among drunk and sober alike to contribute their scrawls to the venerable rock, often ruining the carvings of previous centuries. Even today, people scratch up this signpost to the mysterious past. Such graffiti, plus development of the nearby land over the past eighty years, make not only Mark Rock's past but its future a mystery.

THE MOUNT HOPE ROCK

On a stone-cluttered beach near the foot of Mount Hope, in Bristol, lies the Mount Hope Rock. Surrounded by boulders of every configuration, many graffiti-gouged, the large, low, flat-topped stone is about five feet wide and ten feet long. Like Mark Rock, it's most visible at low tide and, also like Mark Rock, the Mount Hope Rock has been "lost" and "found" several times.

The reputedly ancient design that has made the Mount Hope Rock famous, at least locally, is hard to spot amidst a junkyard of more recent carvings. But it's there: The clear figure of a boat or ship, surrounded by what are thought to be runes -- ancient Germanic, possibly Scandinavian, letters. Six house-like symbols nearby may indicate a village. The boat figure is only a few inches long, and the whole carving covers no more than two feet. It's visible on the rock's pointed end, nearest the water.

The rock apparently gained its other name -- the Northmen's Rock -- in a local monograph written in 1877. Many Bristol residents have embraced the monograph's view of the rock as a Viking relic. The rock received another name on June 13, 1919, in a ceremony devised by the Rhode Island Citizens Historical Association. With corn, wine and oil, in the manner of a Viking ship, the rock was christened "Lief's Rock." One cannot help wondering about this now-defunct group's command of history; among other things, the gallant Ericsson's name actually was spelled "Leif."

In the 1920s, linguists from local colleges suggested that the inscription around the boat figure was not in Old Norse, but in Cherokee. The Cherokees, however, didn't develop a written language until the 1830s. Whatever the language, the inscription is generally thought to be the signature of whomever made the carvings.

To honor the purported Norse visitors, Bristol officials named a street near the Mount Hope Rock "Viking Drive."

THE ARNOLD POINT CUP STONE

In Portsmouth, on the northwestern shore of Aquidneck Island, one can find the Arnold Point Cup Stone. When Delabarre saw it in 1920, it was on the water's edge at low tide, somewhat south of the spit of land called Arnold Point; at high tide, it was covered by water. Today, however, it's fifty yards farther south on the beach, away from the water, probably pushed there by the Hurricane of 1938.

The Arnold Point Cup Stone, also called the Portsmouth Cup Stone, is unique among the known inscribed rocks of Narragansett Bay. With its six deeply gouged, almost triangular, holes -- "cups" -- joined by shallower lines, it resembles a diagram of a constellation (Ursa Major — the Big Dipper — minus its seventh star, springs to mind). Cup stones are known to archaeologists in both the New and the Old Worlds; their purpose is thought to have been ceremonial. The Arnold Point Cup Stone, composed mostly of sandstone, is about five feet long and roughly three feet wide. Today, all but the stone's flattened top, with its "cups," is buried in the sand.

The earliest written reference to this carved rock was in 1910, when a David Hutcheson, of Washington, D.C., mentioned in a letter that a Portsmouth resident had led him to it. Hutcheson said that he had made a drawing of the carvings and had shown it to some Washington anthropologists, who "thought it was an Indian Cup Stone" -- something not uncommon in North America.

The Arnold Point Cup Stone, on the Narragansett Bay shore at Portsmouth.

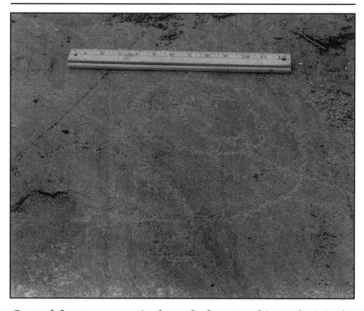

One of the strange spiral symbols carved into the Mark Rock ledge on the Warwick shore. The design appears to have been "pecked" by a stone or metal tool.

-Photos by Paul F. Eno

While there are all sorts of possible explanations for the carvings on these mystery rocks, most researchers think they are the work of Native Americans. The Indians themselves have disclaimed knowledge of who made the carvings, yet there is a chance that their distant ancestors — the ones who arrived just after the last ice age, about 10,000 years ago -- were the carvers.

Other researchers have thought that the carvings were the work of one or more pre-Columbian visitors, whose identity often seems to depend on the researcher's own ethnic background. The Phoenicians, the Egyptians, the Romans, the Celts, the Italians, the Portuguese, even the Chinese -- all these and others have at various times been nominated.

But the only long-term, pre-colonial, Old World visitors indicated by any real evidence are the Vikings. That they built at least one settlement in what is now Newfoundland, on Canada's east coast, is a fact. In 1837, the Danish scholar Charles Christian Rafn pointed out that Norse accounts of Vinland's pleasant climate and numerous grapes had stumped researchers, who thought that the Vikings had been referring to chilly Newfoundland. It all adds up for Rhode Island and southeastern New England, Rafn said, if you consider Rhode Island's climate and the wild grapes that thrive along the Bay.

Unfortunately for Rafn, most climatologists today are convinced that Newfoundland's climate in the 11th century was much milder than it is now -- mild enough for grapes and the other warm-weather delights the Vikings described.

In any case, Rafn was in touch with the Rhode Island Historical Society and with some of the people who had studied the Narragansett Bay mystery rocks. He was convinced that these rocks, too, were evidence of Viking visitors. It's worth noting -- especially with regard to Aquidneck Island's Arnold Point Cup Stone, which is located by an old coal mine — that coal from Viking sites in Greenland was determined in the 1970s to be similar to, if not the same as, a type found only on Aquidneck Island.

It's sad to say that, unless someone finances archaeological work at the sites of these mysterious carvings, and un-

less the state or the communities where they are located protect them, we probably will never learn the real story behind
the rocks.

-PFE

Chapter Two

The Republic
 # of Rejects

One minister called it "the sewer of New England." Another harrumphed that it was "a hive of hornets, and the sink into which the rest of the colonies empty their heretics." Neighboring residents blustered about that "asylum of evildoers."

These were among the thunderbolts hurled down upon "Rogue Island" by its neighbors for many decades after Roger Williams and others high-tailed it from the north to Narragansett Bay. From their own point of view, the critics were right: Rhode Island was a cesspool of malcontents, outcasts, bindlestiffs, and religious mavericks who were welcome nowhere else.

But from our point of view, colonial Rhode Island was the seedbed of some pretty revolutionary ideas — things the United States of America is supposed to be all about. Religious tolerance, the rights of women and, above all, the separation of church and state saw their first fruition on American soil right here in Rhode Island. All this became possible because of the unusual people who first came here. Rhode Island was indeed a sort of republic of rejects. More justly, Rhode Islanders often call their home the "independent state."

Rhode Island wasn't founded by any one person in any one

The statue of Roger Williams gazes from Providence's Prospect Terrace. There is no portrait of him from life, and nobody is sure just what he looked like.

-Photo by Paul F. Eno

year. Nor was it founded for entirely religious reasons, as is generally believed. To some degree, it was the largely accidental product of a long and complicated series of religious, economic and political events. For our purposes, these events began in Salem, Massachusetts, on a frigid January night in 1636 when Roger Williams, then about thirty-two years old, bid a bitter good-bye to his family, and set off into the wilderness. Considering his amazing life, we don't know much about this dreamy, courageous, God-intoxicated man. Interestingly, one of the clearest memories that has come down to us about Williams is that, for natives and newcomers alike, he was a lovable person, and a downright joy to be with.

Historians believe that Williams was born in London around 1693, the son of a tailor. He graduated from prestigious Cambridge University in 1626, and became deeply interested in theology. He turned up later as a minister in the Separatist or Puritan movement within the Church of England, and he built up a wide reputation as a preacher. But his ideas became more and more radical, as we shall see, and soon he was quite unpopular, even with his friends.

On a dreary day in February 1631, a small English ship dropped anchor in Boston Harbor. Among the immigrants who crowded the rails for a glimpse of this forbidding new land were Roger and Mary Williams.

The Puritans in Boston meant business. Sick of what they saw as a corrupt Church of England, and a society to match, 1,000 of them had landed there only a year before. They meant to establish a purified church and a society on the Old Testament model. As a matter of fact, they saw themselves in precisely the same situation as the ancient Hebrews in their exodus from Egypt. The name "New England" was no sentimental whim: These new Israelites were out to show England and the rest of Christendom how Christian life ought to be lived.

Roger Williams was the first really prominent Puritan immigrant, and his reputation as a terrific preacher had preceded him. Soon after he got to Boston, he was offered the job of second minister at the church there. He flummoxed everybody by refusing, because the group had not formally separated itself from the Church of England.

Purifying that church wasn't enough, Williams said; they had to start from scratch. He finally got a congregation in Salem to agree with him, and he became minister there. But this was only the beginning. Williams found himself at

sword's point with Puritan leaders with practically every sermon he preached. Among his outrageous ideas were: Government had no right to enforce church attendance, punish
blasphemy, or use tax money to support churches; that colonial charters were all wrong because the land belonged to
the natives and wasn't the King's to grant; and that churches
and governments ought to be free from each other's interfer-
ence. Indeed, Williams seemed more like a spokesman for
the American Civil Liberties Union than a Puritan minister.

Obviously, he was light years ahead of his time.

Believe it or not, most of Williams's ideas agreed with the
original intent of Puritanism. The trouble was that Williams
was the only Puritan Puritan enough to go that far. He refused to "go with the flow" more conventional Puritans had
set up in Massachusetts. By 1635, Puritan leaders had had it
with Roger Williams. On October 9th, the Massachusetts General Court (the legislature) found him guilty of heresy, and
gave him a one-way ticket back to England. But winter travel
was dangerous by land or sea, and lawmakers said Williams
could stay on until spring if only he would keep his mouth
shut.

Williams wouldn't be silent. So, having learned that officials planned to grab him and send him back on the next available ship, winter or not, he made his escape on that cold January night. He had only one companion on that dark journey,
a servant named Thomas Angell. Apparently, the two wan-
dered aimlessly for awhile, searching for food and shelter in
the wilderness. They ended up at Narragansett Bay and the
camp of some Wampanoags Williams had befriended while
preaching in the Plymouth Colony. There, in the vicinity of
what is now Warren, Roger Williams and his friends spent
the rest of a miserable winter.

As soon as Williams arrived on Narragansett Bay, one major reason that Rhode Island happened started to become
evident: The natives were restless. To the Wampanoags, Roger
Williams and the settlers they hoped would follow him would
create a buffer zone between themselves and their bitter enemies, the powerful Narragansetts, whose territory ended
roughly at the Seekonk River. Five followers and, shortly

thereafter, Williams's family, came to join him in the summer of 1636 on land the Wampanoags gave him on the banks of the Seekonk, in what is now East Providence. But no sooner had they begun digging in when Governor Edward Winslow of Plymouth began griping that they were on his turf, suggesting that they move "but over the river."

Even the Narragansetts welcomed Williams and his companions, giving them what is now the site of Providence, but the reasons are unclear. Maybe they liked the idea of friendly Englishmen on their eastern flank so they could concentrate on their enemies to the west, the Pequots, who lived in Connecticut. Thus began Williams's long and celebrated friendship with the Narragansett sachems Canonicus and Miantonomi. They gave land not only for Providence but, at Williams's request, sites for other Rhode Island towns. Roger Williams, armed with the respect of all his neighbors and an unabashed idealism, set out to establish a town — Providence — where no-one would be persecuted for his or her religious beliefs.

Williams had barely left Massachusetts when Puritan leaders were faced with yet another heretic, this time a woman. Anne Hutchinson was a sort of Puritan Joan of Arc. She was a stubborn, fiery mystic who claimed direct inspiration from God, and insisted that people didn't need clergymen to tell them what to do. While Roger Williams had enjoyed only a small following, those who agreed with Anne Hutchinson numbered several hundred. The Puritans dubbed them "Antinomians" ("those against law") because of their extreme individualism, and fought them as a major threat. In 1638, while Anne Hutchinson battled with Massachusetts authorities, some eighty of her followers headed for Narragansett Bay. Roger Williams got the Narragansetts to sell them Aquidneck Island, and the newcomers soon founded Pocasset, later to become Portsmouth. It was a supreme irony that their leader was William Coddington, one of the judges who had sent Roger Williams packing only two years before!

William Coddington was well off in three areas: money, good sense and ego. He led the Antinomians to Aquidneck not only because of religion but on account of the unique economic opportunities there. The Bay and its adjacent waterways couldn't be better as far as future shipping was concerned, and the numerous islands were outstanding for cattle and sheep because predators could be controlled easily there. Future years would prove him right.

In 1639, Coddington left Portsmouth with some of his disciples, went to the southern tip of Aquidneck Island (whose actual cognomen is the "Rhode Island" of our state's name) and founded Newport. His opposition to joining the island with Providence and the other "plantations" to form one colony would create endless headaches for Roger Williams, and inaugurate decades of rivalry between Newport and Providence.

The next major character on the scene was the cantankerous Samuel Gorton, who was so unorthodox that he was driven not only from Massachusetts and Plymouth but even from Providence and Portsmouth! He ended up becoming the founder of Warwick in 1642.

And so it went. Ahead lay years of internal bickering, attempts by other colonies to grab lands around the Bay, and occasional wars against one or another native tribe. It's rather surprising that the patchwork entity that came to be called Rhode Island and Providence Plantations survived at all. The single event that helped that survival most took place in 1663, when the colony was granted a Charter by King Charles II. In what must have been one of his more jocular moments, His Majesty granted Rhode Island an astonishing document that set up "a lively experiment," the modern world's first officially secular government. For the first time, it put the force of law behind freedom of religion and thought. It also made the colony virtually independent, politically as well as spiritually.

The Charter was so liberal and so ahead of its time that even Rhode Islanders agreed on it. Massachusetts, Connecticut and Plymouth were understandably aghast. The Charter worked so well that it was in force as the state constitution until 1842. Along with guaranteeing rights, setting boundaries, and laying out the fundamentals of the law, the Charter forbade other colonies to pick on Rhode Island, a prohibition that wasn't always obeyed.

While most of today's Rhode Islanders are no geniuses when it comes to our state's history, they might be surprised to learn how uncannily similar they are in general attitude, regardless of ethnic origin, to the early Rhode Islanders. The independent, contrary spirit of the founders has been very much with us all along. While even Roger Williams, Anne Hutchinson, Samuel Gorton and others would be horrified by certain tendencies in modern society, they probably would be quite proud of the way their "lively experiment" has turned out and of how much we all truly bear their stamp.

The old New England quip that Rhode Island is "the place where people are different" is as true today as ever!

-PFE

The Amazing
William Blackstone

Strange as it may seem, Roger Williams wasn't the first European to settle in Rhode Island. In 1635, a year before the father of Providence found his way to Narragansett Bay, a most exceptional man made his home on the banks of a river in what is now Cumberland. William Blackstone was a different sort of settler. A scholarly recluse who loved to read philosophy, and tend his apple trees and the rose bushes he had brought from England, Blackstone came here simply to get away from the Puritans who had moved in on him while he was living in what is now Boston.

While few Rhode Islanders know about William Blackstone, everybody from Providence to Woonsocket and on up to Worcester, Massachusetts, knows his last name, since all kinds of things in that area are named after him. These include the Blackstone River and its valley, Blackstone Boulevard and Blackstone Park in Providence, and the once busy Blackstone Canal. There have been a cigar, potato chips, a bank, and a number of other things and places in Rhode Island and Massachusetts called by that name. His name even finds its way into that of our own national park: The John H. Chafee Blackstone River Valley National Heritage Corridor.

We know so little about Blackstone largely because of the natives. This is both ironic and tragic, since his good relations with them rank second only to those of Roger Williams. A few days after Blackstone's death in 1675, a roving band of warriors then engaged in the brutal King Philip's War burned his house at Lonsdale, together with his library, the best in the colonies, and whatever writing he had done during his

*The William Blackstone Memorial on Broad Street,
Cumberland, claims to be his gravesite, but that's
unlikely.*

-Photo by Paul F. Eno

long life of seclusion. Blackstone is said to have owned 200 bound books and a number of pamphlets that today might be worth enough to fix all the roads in Rhode Island.

People sometimes say that an outstanding characteristic of true scholars is that they are clumsy in workaday affairs. This was hardly the case with Blackstone. Although a highly educated clergyman of the Church of England, he carved two separate homes out of the unforgiving New England wilderness with little or no help. He also kept a herd of cows, planted an orchard, and even saddle trained a bull because he didn't have a horse.

Blackstone was a promising young clergyman of twenty eight when, in 1623, he came to America with the Robert Gorges Expedition. Gorges had the idea of establishing an Anglican (Church of England) religious colony where Rhode Island is now. The group founded a small settlement on the present site of Boston but, before long, all but Blackstone and two other men gave up and went back to England. Blackstone stayed because he liked the solitude, and he may have had a missionary's eye on the natives.

Blackstone had some supplies the others left, including some cattle. He built a house on what is now Beacon Hill, pastured his cows on the forty six-acre clearing that later became Boston Common, and made friends with the natives. Everything probably was just the way Blackstone liked it until one fateful day in 1630. After seven years of undisputed solitude for him, nearly 1,000 Puritans from England suddenly began piling ashore, led by John Winthrop, who was to become the first governor of the Massachusetts Bay Colony.

The Puritans, of course, brought with them all the theological baggage that would make early Massachusetts famous. Worst of all, from William Blackstone's viewpoint, the Puritans promptly insisted that he accept their ideas. Pouring salt on the wound, the Puritans also refused to pay Blackstone for the land they took, even though he had been there first.

The stalwart Anglican stuck it out for five years and then, in 1635, decided that he couldn't deal with it anymore. He sold the Puritans what was left of his holdings, then moved to where he could live undisturbed once more, "each inhab-

itant paying him sixpence and some of them more."
Blackstone certainly couldn't have made much on the deal
and, even if he had, it wouldn't have done him much good
where he was going.

Perhaps from his own wanderings, perhaps from his friends
among the natives, Blackstone found out about the spot in
what is today Lonsdale in Cumberland, where he settled. It
was at a bend in the river that would someday bear his name.
The Ann & Hope and Building 19 department stores stood
there in 2000. Blackstone named it "Study Hill," and in his
time it was an elevation about a quarter-mile long, sloping
down to the river's edge and covered with chestnut trees.
There was a good spring and, across the river, the mouth of a
small brook. The fishing was great; herring and salmon ran
up the river in the spring to spawn, and the brooks were filled
with trout.

So, collecting his cattle in Boston, Blackstone marched
slowly along the rocky, native trail to Lonsdale with his cows,
his library, and some apple seeds and cuttings. Trotting
alongside was Blackstone's sole human companion, a "man
Friday" named Abbott, about whose origins we know practically nothing. It was May 1635.

Blackstone must have been a sight astride his "mouse-col-
ored," saddle-trained bull, his books and furniture strapped
on other cattle, proceeding down the leafy trails in that long-
ago spring. This prototype of Rhode Island's "Independent
Man" dwelt at Study Hill for forty years, studying philosophy, tending his beloved apple trees, and preaching to the
natives from time to time.

Reportedly, Blackstone's orchard was the first ever to bear
fruit in Rhode Island. In it were "the first of the sort called
yellow sweetings that were ever in the world, perhaps, the
richest and most delicious apple of the whole kind." It takes
no small ability to cross-breed apple trees, but this is the only
way Blackstone could have created this new variety. But educated hermits often are botanists, horticulturists or natural-
ists. As late as 1830, three of Blackstone's apple trees still
lived, and two bore fruit each year. Farmers would come from
all over Providence County and nearby Massachusetts to get

grafts from these trees because of their outstanding quality and historical significance.

After Roger Williams arrived in the area, he and William Blackstone became chums. When Williams had his trading post at Cocumscussoc, in the Narragansett Country, he got Blackstone down to conduct a service for the natives. This was the first Anglican service in Rhode Island. It must have amused the Narragansetts no end to see the clergyman lumbering along the Pequot Path on his bull! The story is that, after Blackstone's first trip, it became a monthly practice of his to make the long journey from Study Hill to Cocumscussoc. He later held services in Providence.

All this time Blackstone was a bachelor, though certainly not the complete hermit early historians made him out to be. Though it is known that he made occasional visits to Boston, how he got acquainted with the widow Sarah Stevenson of that town, we don't know. But in 1659, when Blackstone was sixty-four years old, he married Sarah and took her to Study Hill. The next year a son, John, was born. Today's growing crop of over-forty, first-time dads should count their blessings. William and Sarah lived together for sixteen years until his death in 1675. After King Philip's War, mother and son went back to Study Hill and rebuilt. In 1692, John sold the property and moved to Providence, where he became a shoemaker. Later Blackstones have made their homes at Branford, Connecticut, and in New York State, where some live today.

For a number of years there was an ancient oak tree encircled by an iron railing about 100 yards from the old Lonsdale railroad station, marking the traditional site of Blackstone's home. When ground was being cleared for the Ann & Hope Mill, later the department stores, there were two yellow stones found at the southern foot of the hill, where the stores' parking lot was to be. Traditionally, they marked the burial place of Blackstone and his faithful bull. The most common story has it that, under careful supervision, workers removed the stones and began digging. Some nails, bones and bits of decayed wood came to light. These supposedly were removed higher up the hill, with a monument to the memory of the scholarly parson that could be seen for many years on the south side of Broad Street, Cumberland, adjacent to the main entrance to the Ann & Hope parking lot.

In another version of the story, the bones were placed in a box and removed to parts unknown. In any case, in the 1990s, the stone monument was moved to a traffic island a short distance away, at the intersection of Broad and Mill Streets, then across Broad Street to its own little park. Surprisingly, the monument dubs Blackstone the "Founder of Boston," an allegation that probably would have amused him.

The fact that Rhode Island has become one of America's most densely populated places, and the possibility that he is buried near a busy parking lot, would undoubtedly draw some spicy comments from this unique and talented man, Rhode Island's first European settler.

-PFE

Rhode Island's
Joan of Arc

When it came to self-expression and freedom of thought, it took more than ordinary courage to stand up to Puritan authorities in 17th century New England. But for a woman, it took bravery so unique that we know of only a few who tried it. Certainly the most outstanding of these was Anne Hutchinson.

With some justification, Hutchinson can be called Rhode Island's Joan of Arc. A true mystic, she was convinced that she was directly inspired by God. Hutchinson also led hundreds of people in a battle against Puritan oppression, and became one of Rhode Island's founders, only to die a tragic death. The mother of fourteen children, Anne Hutchinson also has been called, accurately or inaccurately, America's first champion of women's rights, and the first to challenge the traditional prerogatives of men. Any parent must wonder where she found the time to accomplish all that she did.

The daughter of a stiff-necked Anglican clergyman, Anne Marbury was born in England about 1594, during the last years of the reign of Queen Elizabeth I. Marbury's first cousin was John Dryden, one of the most renowned poets in English literature. For her time, she was a remarkably educated and cultured woman. When Marbury was still a child, Queen Elizabeth died, and King James I, son of Mary Queen of Scots, ascended the throne. King James had an intense desire for "an ordered and obedient Church; its synods that met at the royal will, its courts that carried out the royal ordinances, its bishops that held themselves to be royal officers."

When the king started to push this idea that the church

should be, in effect, just another branch of the state, many religious people got nervous. Eventually, they congealed into the "Separatist" movement that sought to put the Church of England back on what they considered the right path. This was the group that would spawn the Puritan exiles who came to establish their "New Israel" in New England.

Being a churchman's daughter, Marbury undoubtedly absorbed much of what was going on. Everywhere people were studying the Bible, arguing religion, and rebelling against what they saw as the arbitrary dictates of the mainline church. She may well have witnessed many an act of persecution against Separatists. At any rate, she eventually became one, converted by an eloquent Puritan minister named John Cotton, to whom she grew very close and who would have a profound affect on her life.

Anne married William Hutchinson at an early age. While a successful merchant, he was described as a "very honest, peaceable man of good estate," and later was referred to by Massachusetts Governor John Winthrop as "a man of very mild temper and weak parts, and wholly guided by his wife."

When Cotton joined the Puritan exiles in Boston, Anne Hutchinson left England to follow him in 1634, accompanied by her husband and an already large brood of children. Fortunately for them, the Hutchinsons had pots of money. It has been recorded that the fortune they brought to America amounted to almost 1,000 guineas in gold (over half a million dollars in today's currency). Until the new Hutchinson home could be built in Boston, Anne and some of her children found shelter in the house of her idol, Rev. Cotton. For the three years the family stayed in Boston, their home was right across the street from Governor Winthrop's.

Hutchinson had a magnetic personality, and her fireside soon became the social center of Boston, still a small town. She proved to be not only a capable, energetic person but also a very good nurse. As she strode from home to home caring for the sick, all the young women gradually got to know and admire her. Both men and women agreed that she had a natural gift for leadership. As you can imagine, such attributes in a woman of that day led to trouble.

In 17th century New England, women participated in the endless church services, but they were excluded from certain religious meetings and from the government of both church and colony. Whether Anne Hutchinson resented this or just wanted to fill a vacuum, she started holding meetings for women at her house to pray, and to talk about John Cotton's twice-weekly sermons. At first, virtually everyone praised this novel idea. As many as 100 women would attend these meetings and, for awhile, Hutchinson led two each week. She certainly can be called the organizer of America's first women's organization.

How long it took Puritan authorities to start frowning on these gatherings isn't known, but by the end of Hutchinson's second year in Boston, she was branded a troublemaker. This wasn't because she organized women's meetings but because, after they got going, Hutchinson began spouting some decidedly peculiar ideas. Basically, she went much further than the ministers (except Cotton) in denying salvation through one's own works. She said that any effort at all to live a moral life was useless in attaining salvation. Hutchinson implied that ministers should preach, and people should live, only as the spirit moved them. She also denied that people should arbitrarily rule other people.

This is a good time to hit a critical point that some modern readers might either miss or ignore: Anne Hutchinson was not the 17th century's answer to Susan B. Anthony or Mary Ann Sorentino. In our "politically correct" times, it's tempting for anyone with a cause to make their points by saddling historical figures with 21st century attitudes and motives. This is bad historical scholarship that can cheat us out of a far richer understanding of other times and the loves, hopes and fears we really do share with the people of those times.

The fact is that Anne Hutchinson cannot be understood outside the context of her spiritual vision and sense of divine mission — no more so than can Joan of Arc. Her quest wasn't to free women from the bonds of men, but to free men and women together from the bonds of the church, which, in Massachusetts, also were the bonds of society. With the notable exception of the many women — and men – who devoted themselves to Goddess-oriented religions, most of the women's movement in the late 20th century was ferociously secular. You can bet your bottom dollar that Anne Hutchinson would have had nothing to do with it.

Among Hutchinson's many followers and fellow travelers were plenty of families and plenty of men, including William Coddington, a "male chauvinist" in today's sense if ever there was one. Why did so many men follow Anne Hutchinson in such a "sexist" society? Because even sexism (in the sense of subservient social roles for women) had a spiritual dimension in those days, one that in many ways placed women *above* men. Yes, women were kitchen slaves unless they were affluent, and there were plenty of abuses. But there also was a clear attitude that idealized women. Society — including women — believed that women belonged in the home not because they were considered nitwits or sex objects but because theirs was a God-given privilege. Involvement in politics and business would have demeaned them as the givers of life and primary molders of the next generation. Thus, when women turned up as prophets and spiritual leaders, as happened from time to time, people could readily accept that this had some spiritual foundation.

This hardly excuses the subjugation of women (for one can almost smell men's fear of strong women in those times and today) but it should help us understand where Anne Hutchinson was "coming from." The gist of the theological problem was this: Hutchinson didn't deny that people should obey moral and civil laws; she only said it wouldn't affect their salvation one way or the other. But Puritan authorities assumed that she *did* mean the denial of all laws. Hence, Hutchinson and her followers became known as the "Antinomians," meaning "those against law." Hutchinson called her inner-conversion idea the "Covenant of Grace," and started pointing fingers at ministers whom she thought preached the opposite, the "Covenant of Works."

To the alarm of the authorities, Anne Hutchinson's popular following increased dramatically in a very short time, bringing with it not only a theological but a political crisis. In 1636, the Antinomians even had one of their own elected governor over Winthrop, but he was turned out of office through Puritan intrigues the following year.

It wasn't long before the official boom was lowered. In 1637, Hutchinson was arrested on trumped-up charges of maligning ministers of the colony, holding improper meetings, and getting up a petition to defend a minister whose preaching had been declared seditious. She was tried and condemned by a church court, then tried and banished by the Massachusetts General Court, which had done the same thing to Roger Williams not long before. On March 28, 1638, Anne Hutchinson, her family, and about eighteen others left for Providence, that haven of those persecuted for thinking their own thoughts. There, America's first female activist was welcomed by the first advocate of religious freedom, Roger Williams himself.

In Providence, Hutchinson gathered a good following, including Baptists, who also were *persona non grata* in Massachusetts. Later, Governor Winthrop sent a message to say that if Hutchinson and the others would renounce their belief in the Covenant of Grace, they could return. This fell on deaf ears.

Hutchinson and her followers had intended to go all the way to Long Island to form a new colony, but Roger Williams talked her out of it. She decided to go to Aquidneck Island, where her richest and most prominent supporter, William Coddington, had led a large group of Antinomians, founding the town of Pocasset, later to become Portsmouth. It wasn't long before Coddington quarreled with Hutchinson and moved with his faction to the southern end of the island, founding Newport.

After William Hutchinson died in 1642, Anne and her family moved to what is now Westchester County, New York, where her life ended in tragedy. In August 1643, she and the fifteen members of her household, with one exception, were massacred by natives.

One of her few memorials is the name of the Hutchinson Parkway in the suburbs north of New York City, which passes the site of her death.

-PFE

The King
of Aquidneck Island

In some ways, Roger Williams felt about William Coddington the way other colonies often felt about Rhode Island. Even the tolerant Williams wrote that the founder of Portsmouth and Newport was "a worldly man, a selfish man, nothing for public, but all for himself and private."

While it's easy to notice Coddington's hard-driving quest for personal power, Roger Williams's measure of the man is hardly fair overall. Coddington was a capable leader and a man of deep religious faith. He also had good business sense and keen economic foresight. But the fact that Coddington happened to be one of the Massachusetts judges who condemned him to exile in 1636 may have influenced Williams's opinion.

William Coddington came to New England in 1630 with the crowd of Puritans that settled in Boston that year. A big cheese in the Massachusetts Bay Company, which had sponsored the infant colony, Coddington soon became a leader in the community. Before long, though, Coddington found himself in hot water when he sided with Anne Hutchinson and the Antinomians, who were challenging the religious and political authority of the Puritans.

In the 1636 election, the Antinomians managed to defeat John Winthrop and elect one of their own as governor. But, after what amounted to a *coup d'etat*, the mainline Puritans restored Winthrop the following year. In early 1638, facing exile, Coddington and about eighty other Antinomians found out that Aquidneck Island was vacant, and they moved there when Roger Williams convinced the Narragansetts to sell it to them.

On March 7, Coddington, William Aspinwall and John Coggeshall drew up a compact setting up a government for the settlement, which they called Pocasset. Later, it was re-named Portsmouth. Coddington was elected "judge" of the town and proceeded to set up an Old Testament regime, with himself at the helm as God-inspired ruler.

Meanwhile, Anne Hutchinson and her husband, William, turned up. Within a year, she and Coddington quarreled over religion and, with his popular support gone, Coddington took some followers and moved to the southern end of the island, where they settled at what is now Newport.

Coddington's economic dash came into play with the found-ing of what shortly was to become Rhode Island's most im-portant town. While he posed as a landed gentleman, Coddington actually was a frustrated merchant. The poten-tial of Newport's excellent harbor was high in his thoughts when he moved there.

It wasn't long before he and the other settlers began to ex-ploit the possibilities. Because he controlled most of the land titles there, Coddington forced Portsmouth to accept a com-mon government with Newport in 1649. What he really wanted was to have England make Aquidneck a separate colony, with himself as governor. Coddington did everything he could think of to derail Roger Williams's attempts to unite the towns around Narragansett Bay into a single colony, even after a colonial patent was granted to the "Province of Provi-dence Plantations in Narragansett in New England" in 1644.

Seven years later, in 1651, Coddington went to England and finagled his own patent, a preposterous document that ef-fectively made him dictator of Aquidneck for life. But the good folk of Aquidneck wouldn't buy it, and they got English au-thorities to revoke Coddington's patent the following year. Coddington himself had to flee to Boston from the ire of his own people.

By 1654, the towns around the Bay were organized enough to start acting like a single colony under the 1644 patent. In 1656, Coddington gave in, returned to Newport, and was for-given. He served in various offices and, under the Charter of

1663, was governor of Rhode Island for three terms. He died an honored man in 1678.

Whatever else can be said of William Coddington, he was an efficient leader, and his economic efforts helped make Aquidneck Island a leading agricultural and commercial center.

-PFE

The Cantankerous
Samuel Gorton

For a man of keen intelligence, the founder of Warwick embodied more contradictions than you would think could be crammed into one person.

In college, Samuel Gorton was what we would call a student radical. Yet he had a profound respect for English common law. A chronic troublemaker who was abrasive to anybody he didn't like, Gorton still established a strong religious following whose members considered him the virtual mouthpiece of God. A man of extraordinary piety, he still was so unorthodox that he maddened even the Job-like Roger Williams. While styling himself "Professor of the Mysteries of Christ," Gorton denied the authority of anybody, including himself, to establish a colony without having a charter from the king of England.

Gorton was born at Gorton (now part of Manchester), England, in 1592, the descendant of local gentry. Not long afterward, King James I, when he had succeeded his cousin, Queen Elizabeth I, started tightening his grip on the church, strangling the traditional rights of Englishmen along with it. Having no lack of money, Gorton received a superior education, though it was a time when student dissenters were protesting royal policy on campuses all over England. Gorton became an accomplished legal scholar, and he plunged into the protest movement with gusto.

In 1636, the same year Roger Williams was booted out of Massachusetts and founded Providence, Gorton, his wife and son appeared in Boston. As with Roger Williams, Gorton was disappointed not to find the religious liberty he had sought, and within two months left for the Plymouth Colony, where Puritan rule at the time was a little less stringent.

Shortly after Gorton's arrival, however, a new governor was elected whose oppressive policies put the Massachusetts Puritans to shame. Trouble wasn't long in coming for our Samuel. In 1638, the Gortons had arranged for a girl named Ellen Aldridge to come from England and work for them as a servant. Within a short time, Ellen was arrested for the heinous crime of smiling in church. With his world-class knowledge of English law, Gorton defended her in court with the not illogical argument that it wasn't against English law to smile in church. He was promptly cited for contempt of court. When Gorton tried to defend himself, the court accused him of sedition, and gave him two weeks to get out of Plymouth.

On December 4, 1638, Gorton left Plymouth, saying good-bye to his wife, children and friends. After surviving two weeks of great peril in the frozen wilderness, he found his way to the settlement at Pocasset, later Portsmouth, on Aquidneck Island.

Gorton arrived at one of those not infrequent times when the embryonic Rhode Island was in political chaos from one end to the other. In true Gorton style, he hurtled into the fray, siding with Anne Hutchinson's faction against that of Pocasset's elected "judge," William Coddington. This scrap was tailor-made for Gorton because, among other things, Coddington was trying to set up his own government on Aquidneck without a royal charter.

While the Hutchinson group eventually won that fight, at least in Pocasset, Gorton was forced out by Coddington in 1641 after a public whipping. Undaunted, Gorton made for Providence, where he at once began to vex Roger Williams, who also was operating an unchartered government. The exasperated Williams wrote: "Master Gorton, having foully abused high and low at Aquidneck, is now bewitching and bemaddening poor Providence both with his unclean and foul censures of all the ministers of this country...and also denying all visible and external ordinances."

Soon Providence was divided into three bickering factions: one led by Roger Williams, one by Gorton, and the other by

William and Benedict Arnold, who were trying to bring the Narragansett Bay towns under the sway of Massachusetts.

When the Arnolds seceded from Providence in 1642 and set up shop in Pawtuxet, submitting themselves to the authority of Massachusetts, Gorton and some followers hastily bought land from the Narragansetts, establishing a settlement not far away, at Shawomet, later to become Warwick, in 1643.

The result was pandemonium. The nearby Arnolds and others raised a storm, questioning the validity of the Gortonites' ownership of Shawomet. It seems that, because of the controversy over land titles in Providence, Massachusetts had gotten into the act and unilaterally forbidden the Narragansetts to sell any more land to anybody. The Arnolds appealed to Massachusetts, which immediately issued a summons to Gorton for trespassing on Massachusetts territory. Naturally, Gorton ignored this.

In October 1643, Massachusetts sent troops to arrest Gorton and everybody else at Shawomet. Gorton and his followers were hauled back to the Bay Colony for trial, and the "Professor of the Mysteries of Christ" was sentenced to six months at hard labor. When released and forbidden to return to Shawomet, Gorton went to England, where, with the help of the Earl of Warwick, an old family friend, he managed to obtain a charter in 1646. Returning triumphantly to Shawomet, Gorton renamed it Warwick. Even though Gorton continued to battle with everyone in sight, Warwick soon joined the other Providence Plantations under Roger Williams's patent of 1644.

Since he never was all that clear about it, it's difficult to tell just what Gorton's religious teachings were. Apparently, he believed in immortality but not in heaven or hell. The Gortonites had no organized church, and exerted no discipline on each other. In 1771, Gorton's last follower, John Angell of Providence, said simply that Gorton "lived and wrote in heaven," and that his teachings were above the understanding of us mere mortals.

It's clear that Gorton was one with Roger Williams in his attitude toward separation of church and state, but carried civil liberty to a degree that verged on anarchy. Nevertheless, despite his reputation as a colorful hellhound, Gorton was constantly in public life to the end of his days. His contributions to Rhode Island were many and unique. When he died in 1677, Rhode Island lost a staunch son and a true defender of human rights.

-PFE

The Other
Benedict Arnold

Rhode Island had its own Benedict Arnold, but history has been considerably kinder to him than to his great-grandson, the one who went back to the British during the American Revolution. Ours was the first governor of the Colony of Rhode Island and Providence Plantations under the Charter of 1663. Arnold wrote that he and his father, William Arnold, arrived in Providence on April 29, 1636. If he was right, which he almost certainly wasn't, it means the Arnolds got here at least two months before Roger Williams.

The Arnold family lived in Providence and Pawtuxet for many years, even though they often argued with Roger Williams over how the settlements ought to be run. During the early 1640s, Benedict Arnold often acted as an ambassador to the natives because he spoke the Narragansett dialect very well. Then, in 1645, the natives accused him of misquoting them and, for awhile, he couldn't go among them without an armed guard.

By 1651, when Arnold moved to Newport, he was quite rich and important. He at once became active in the government there, and served in many different offices. On August 3, 1657, while he was president of the Province of Providence Plantations under the 1644 patent, a ship docked in Newport with a band of Quaker missionaries.

The Puritan authorities who ran the Massachusetts Bay Colony had a cat fit, and they sent a letter to Arnold "requesting" that the Quakers be thrown out, and warning that none should be allowed to settle in Rhode Island. The Puritans carped that "noe care (is) too great to preserve us from such a pest." Even though they hinted that Massachusetts might take stronger action if Rhode Island didn't comply, Arnold stood up for the colony's ideal of religious freedom. He wrote:

And as concerning these quakers (so called), which are now among us, we have no law among us, whereby to punish any for only declaring by words, etc., their minds and understandings concerning the things and ways of God....

When King Charles II granted Rhode Island the remarkable Charter of 1663, he appointed Benedict Arnold governor until elections could be held. The following year, Arnold became the first elected governor. Once in charge, he pushed Rhode Island's claims for Westerly and the rest of South County against the territorial ambitions of Connecticut. He did much to earn Rhode Island some long overdue respect from its neighbors.

-PFE

A Second Look
at the Puritans

When most people, both New Englanders and otherwise, think of the Puritans, the vision arises of dry-mouthed old preachers, clad in starched black and white, scowling from the pulpits of their cold, barn-like churches.

In fact, the Puritans sometimes get a bum rap. There's no denying that their wildly unhistorical brand of Christianity, with its many fierce doctrines, all too often was based on fear rather than love. And they were no friends of tolerance or equality. But the Puritans had a bright side that few people today appreciate. They were great believers in education, founding both Harvard and Yale, and encouraged universal literacy. The New England town meeting was their brainchild, and they were the founders of rudimentary American democracy, albeit only for land-owning males.

Even Puritan theology had its bright moments.

Every student of American literature has, hopefully, read the frightful, 1741 sermon *Sinners in the Hands of an Angry God*, by Connecticut's Jonathan Edwards (1703-1758). Edwards was considered one of the greatest Puritan divines of his time — and New England has never forgiven him. This is unfortunate, because *Sinners* is quite untypical of his writings. If we read some other things Edwards wrote, such as *The End of Creation* or *True Virtue*, it becomes clear that he was a brilliant mystic whose life from an early age was shot through with a profound experience of God as a lover. His theology of beauty is particularly moving. Had he lived in a less restrictive religious environment, he could have grown into a true mystic in the tradition of Francis of Assisi or Julian of Norwich.

Despite their many faults, the Puritans laid the foundation of much that is best about America: the ethic of hard work, a spirit of independence, and a sense of community. In a modern society where selfishness often seems the rule, even the Puritans have something to teach us.

-PFE

Chapter Three

A Thriving

Economy
at Any Cost

Despite what some of us may have heard in school, Rhode Island's later colonial history didn't necessarily orbit around religion and high-minded virtues. Without a doubt, the most decisive element molding the colony and state was that most familiar of pastimes: the pursuit and capture of money. Thanks to a unique mixture of people, mild climate, good soil and Narragansett Bay, a successful, free economy got an early start in Rhode Island. At the same time, Rhode Island merchants sometimes got into some rather unorthodox — and often illegal — habits when it came to harvesting mammon through trade. To put it simply, they would do business with anybody, anytime: friend, enemy, and everything in between.

Rhode Island was so notorious that at one point, during the French and Indian Wars (which raged off and on from 1689-1763), Massachusetts Governor Sir Francis Barnard huffed in all seriousness, "These practices will never be put an end to, till Rhode Island is reduced to the subjection of the British Empire!"

Rhode Island's maritime commerce got started almost as soon as the first Europeans arrived from Massachusetts in 1636. These people were not the inexperienced bumpkins they had been when they first stumbled off the boat from England.

The harsh wilderness of the Plymouth and Massachusetts Bay colonies already had taught them to be resourceful. At the same time, they were no more willing to settle for a life of barebones subsistence than we would be. But they realized that, to trade for civilization's amenities, they had to have something to trade in return. Early leaders, especially rich ones like William Coddington and William and Anne Hutchinson, who settled Aquidneck Island in 1638, were very much aware of the business potential of Narragansett Bay and the bountiful lands around it. The climate, they realized, was the best in New England. With heavy investing, know-how, hard work and luck, they transfigured the lower Bay wilderness into a burgeoning agricultural society in less than a decade.

While Providence and the northern towns divided land equally among farmers, Aquidneck Island families like the Coddingtons, Hutchinsons, Coggeshalls and Brentons set up huge landed estates, with tenant farmers doing most of the clearing, crop planting and cattle raising. They quickly realized that many of the Bay islands were excellent for grazing these cattle because they easily could be cleared of predators, and they didn't have to be fenced in. While growing numbers of sheep, oxen, cows, horses and hogs grazed and rooted away on little islands, farmers on estates great and small raised corn, apples and grains. Smaller farmers in Providence, Pawtuxet and Warwick did the same.

Within a few more decades, huge, southern-style plantations, complete with slaves, had sprung up across the Bay from Newport, in the Narragansett Country. Rhode Islanders soon were exporting their grain-fed livestock to neighboring colonies as food, and as the basis for new herds and flocks that arose in the Plymouth and New Haven colonies, in Dutch New Netherland in what is now New York State, and on Long Island.

After awhile, trade even picked up with Rhode Island's arch-enemy, Massachusetts, which usually was willing to let bygones be bygones when it came to making a buck. By 1650, trade with the West Indian colonies had become commonplace. But there still was no direct commerce with England;

business with the mother country had to be carried on through Boston.

Newport's outstanding harbor was Rhode Island's center of maritime activity. As yet, Newport was little more than a village with one street (Thames), where pigs rummaged freely and wolves were a problem. Nonetheless, Newport had begun its climb toward becoming the financial and political capital of the whole colony — and one of America's most important commercial centers.

Two ominous events in 1649 signaled the arrival of a darker side to Rhode Island's colonial economy. One was on June 11, when William Withington of Newport chartered half of the ship *Beginning* to take fifteen cows and sheep to the West Indies, and then go to "Guinney" (West Africa), which almost certainly means that Withington had inaugurated what would become a lucrative Rhode Island slave trade.

In November that year, a Dutch privateer captain named Blaufeld decided to give Newport the dubious honor of being his homeport for selling off captured vessels and their contents. Privateers weren't much more than legalized pirates. Governments would authorize them to capture vessels belonging to countries they were at war with or otherwise didn't like. Then the government and the captain, or the captain and the crew, would "split the take." Not only did Newport welcome Blaufeld with open arms but, when some of his crew wanted to set up on their own, Captain Jeremy Clarke of Newport sold them a ship!

Certainly the most important year for Rhode Island's early economy was 1657, for that's when the Quakers arrived. Though a persecuted minority, they were pretty evenly spread throughout the English domains. A large number of them were successful merchants. Welcome nowhere but in Rhode Island, New England's Quakers set about not only converting large segments of the populace but also in establishing themselves as merchants here. Because they had associates all over the English world, this opened up whole new markets to Rhode Island. This was one time the colony's religious toleration paid some especially big dividends. The Quakers succeeded in converting nearly half the population, including William Coddington, and business boomed.

The Crown, however, made a pig's breakfast out of all this (albeit temporarily) in 1686, when Rhode Island was effectively reduced to the status of a county within the Dominion of New England, an entity designed to bring all the colonies from New Jersey to Maine under more control. As usual, Rhode Island wouldn't cooperate, refusing to carry out orders, and ignoring proclamations. In 1689, a mob overthrew New England Governor Sir Edmund Andros, and that was the end of the Dominion. Rhode Island soon got back to normal, politically and economically.

Newport's walk toward wealth became a run during the wars of the late 17th and early 18th centuries between Britain and France. King William's War (1689-1697) brought in all sorts of loot from privateering activities. The Wanton family, in particular, started amassing a fortune in this way, beginning in 1694. During Queen Anne's War (1703-1713), King George's War (1739-1748), and the main French and Indian War (1756-1763), privateering reached all-time highs, with as many as fifty such vessels operating out of Newport.

At the same time, Rhode Islanders worked out all kinds of amazing arrangements to trade with the very enemy they were bludgeoning on the high seas. Local magnates found they could send ships to neutral ports in the West Indies, then trade with the French, and anyone else, to their hearts' content. One popular come-on was to sail with some prisoners of war right into an enemy port under a flag of truce. There, they would trade their captives for British prisoners and, just happening to have a full cargo of goods on board, trade them, too. A cute variation on this was to take captives during privateering, then cruise directly to an enemy port to do some deals.

Rhode Island would issue privateering commissions to just about anybody. Honest-to-goodness pirates flocked to Newport to vacation and refit their ships, with many actually being commissioned as privateers by the colonial government. Captain Thomas Paine, renowned soldier, pirate and privateer, actually settled in Newport in 1683, but moved across the East Passage to Jamestown a few years later. Paine's friend, none other than Captain William Kidd, also found himself welcome in Newport. A sort of human squirrel, Kidd is even rumored to have buried some of his famed treasure on one or another of the islands in Narragansett Bay.

By the end of the French and Indian Wars, Newport merchants owned some 200 ships, with Providence and Bristol building up fleets of their own. Taking the lead in commercial life along with the Quakers were the growing number of Jews in Newport, who brought Rhode Island into yet another worldwide trade network.

It was in the early decades of the 18th century that Rhode Island's economy started becoming rooted in commerce instead of agriculture. Trade shifted from cattle, dairy products, fish and lumber to items that could be imported from somewhere else, then exported at a profit. This was a tricky way to do business, but there really wasn't much choice: The colony's markets were expanding quickly, but resources at home were limited. This shift allowed prosperity to continue, but only on the shakiest of foundations.

Under these new circumstances, the most important, and questionable, commodities were rum and slaves. Merchants would import molasses, mostly from illegal sources, then have it distilled into rum at one of over fifty distilleries in Newport and Providence. Much of this rum went to Barbados, where it was traded for slaves. By the 1760s, it's believed, half of Newport's merchant fleet was involved in this traffic. Providence and Bristol were deeply involved, too.

Between the end of the French and Indian Wars and the start of the American Revolution, Rhode Island's economic road got bumpier because of unprecedented British control under King George III. Even as the rise of Providence over Newport was beginning, the clouds of rebellion began gathering on the horizon. Nothing in Rhode Island would ever be quite the same.

-PFE

During Rhode Island's earliest decades, the General
Assembly met in different parts of the colony. The Old
State House in Providence, which got that name after
the current State House opened in 1901, is one of five
historic General Assembly meeting places that still exist.
It was completed, more or less, in 1762. It saw service
as a court house at a time when Newport still was
Rhode Island's de facto capital. The tower was a 19th
century addition.

-Photo by Paul F. Eno

John Greene,
Friend of the Pirates

Rhode Island was really hopping in 1690. The short-lived Dominion of New England and its governor, Sir Edmund Andros, had been toppled, leaving a great deal of confusion. People in the English Colony of Rhode Island and Providence Plantations were bumbling about, trying to reorganize under the 1663 Charter. The courts were in chaos. Taxes went uncollected.

Everybody in New England was nervous because they weren't sure how England's new monarchs, William III and Mary II, would react to the overthrow of Andros. Rhode Islanders were so jumpy that practically nobody could be found to be governor, deputy governor, or a member of the General Assembly. Nobody wanted to be left holding the bag if William and Mary turned around and restored the Dominion government.

As if that weren't enough, it also was a year of one of those innumerable wars with France and its allied native tribes in America. In July, a fleet of French privateers descended on Block Island, terrorizing the inhabitants and robbing them blind. They even tried to attack Newport a few days later.

While the Quakers had been great for Rhode Island's economy, they were useless in a fight because of their total pacifism. Since they controlled Rhode Island politically, the colony seemed to be at the mercy of the enemy. The Quaker governor, Walter Clarke, resigned so he wouldn't have to make war plans.

Into this mess hobbled seventy year-old John Greene Jr. of Warwick, a non-Quaker, who accepted the post of deputy governor mainly because nobody else would. Since his new boss, Governor Henry Bull, was even older than Greene and not good for much, Greene took the "bull" by the horns and set out to get some privateers for Rhode Island. Greene and a hastily assembled council of war confiscated two Newport ships and, within three days, turned them into makeshift war vessels.

Whoever coined the term "motley crew" must have been thinking of the crews of these two Rhode Island privateers. The retired pirate, Thomas Paine of Jamestown, was brought out of mothballs to captain one of the ships. The crews consisted of a few seamen, some leading Newport citizens, a couple of merchants, a shipbuilder, some Native Americans, and a doctor.

These brave Rhode Islanders sailed out to meet the French as they returned from a raid on New London, Connecticut. There followed a brief battle off Block Island, and the French high-tailed it off to the south.

Greene soon became the privateers' hero. He issued a commission to practically anybody who wanted one, without requiring any particular proof that the captain actually intended to attack the enemy and not just become another Captain Kidd. After awhile, Greene started grinding out general commissions that didn't even apply to a particular ship or captain. He didn't even bother to keep records! Of course, this did wonders for the colony's economy as loot, whose origin may or may not have been the enemy, flooded into Newport.

By and by, authorities in England started hearing complaints that somebody in Rhode Island was single-handedly swelling the pirate population of the North Atlantic and Caribbean. A special committee, headed by the Earl of Bellemont, was set up to investigate, and the panel quickly found that the culprit was John Greene. They estimated that, in 1691 alone, the feisty deputy governor had commissioned over thirty privateers. Some of these had been well known pirates. The committee also discovered that Newport was outfitting and arming private vessels right and left, whether or not they had privateering commissions.

The good earl, convinced that Greene was three sheep short of a flock, dubbed him "a brutish man of very corrupt or no principles of religion." Actually, Greene just had the same sympathy for privateering and piracy that most Rhode Islanders had.

John Greene retired in 1701 at the age of eighty one at the request of Governor Samuel Cranston. The governor felt that he had to give in to pressure from the Crown to get rid of Greene, rather than risk losing the colony's liberal charter rights. Greene, a venerable character to the end, died in his old home port of Warwick on November 27, 1708, at the age of eighty eight.

-PFE

Chapter Four

Keeping Our
⚓ Independence? ⚓

At no time did Rhode Island show its independent spirit more fiercely than before, during and even after the American Revolution. The big irony is that the colony really didn't have to fight for independence in the same way the others did: It was practically an independent republic already because of the ultra-liberal Royal Charter of 1663. The Revolution, at least for Rhode Island, actually was a fight to *keep* this independence in the face of increasing British encroachment.

Before the French and Indian Wars, British rule in America was pretty *nonchalant*, except on rare occasions. London generally had a "hands-off" approach to the colonies, and taxes, if there were any, usually weren't too bad. There were customs laws and tariffs, but royal officials, and even their bosses in London, could be bought off pretty easily by the wealthy merchants, who thought nothing of skirting the law when possible. Most people realized that this actually was good for the Empire: The Americans were free to produce what they wanted and make all the money they could, spending much of it by buying British goods, which directly benefited the mother country.

This "laid back" attitude on the part of the British was especially vital to Rhode Island in general and Newport in particular because they depended on trade in things that would be heavily regulated and taxed if British laws were enforced. Without free trade in items like sugar, molasses and slaves, the local economy would be largely demolished. This unofficial free trade went hand-in-hand with the political freedom granted by the 1663 Charter to give Rhode Island the independence its people cherished so much.

But wars are expensive, and Britain had been at war with France, and sometimes Spain, off and on since 1689. The French and Indian War of 1756-1763 alone was a massive undertaking. Except for two islands off the coast of Newfoundland, which are part of France to this day, the war pushed that nation out of North America once and for all. Naturally, the colonies had helped with these wars and, by 1763, most of them had massive war debts. To make matters worse, Britain, after reimbursing the colonies to some degree, practically was broke itself.

In Rhode Island, debate over the war debt and the economic depression it caused resulted, as usual, in everybody splitting into bitter political factions. The so-called "Ward-Hopkins controversy," over who should pay the most taxes to clear up the war debt, was monumental even by Rhode Island standards. Interestingly, this battle helped solidify the first two political parties in America, one gathered around Samuel Ward of Westerly, and the other headed by Stephen Hopkins of Scituate. Each battled for the governorship and seats in the General Assembly so they could make the other party's members pay more taxes. Simply put, this was a battle between north and south — Providence and Newport — for domination of the whole colony. Hopkins and Providence steadily advanced, but the battle for ascendancy would not be complete until Newport's population and economy were decimated by the American Revolution.

Meanwhile, Britain, desperate for money, made the fateful decision to start getting some serious, direct income from its colonies. In America, they justified this by the quite reasonable idea that the colonies ought to help pay for their own defense, past, present and future. It's not a dissimilar argument from the one the U.S. Government uses to impose the federal income tax today.

All the colonies were surprised when the French and Indian Wars wound down and things didn't return to normal. They were alarmed when the wartime naval patrol along the Atlantic seaboard became a permanent fixture, with the job of enforcing British customs regulations. Much like the U.S. Coast Guard today, the Royal Navy was authorized to board all domestic vessels to inspect their documents and cargoes for compliance with the law. And to encourage customs agents, many of whom were Americans, to enforce the law, Britain let them keep half of all ships and cargo impounded. This unwise practice led to all sorts of injustice and corruption. Even before the end of 1763, the HMS *Squirrel* and the revenue cutter *St. John* sailed into Newport Harbor to make sure no shippers got out of line.

Barely had this begun to sink in when, in 1764, Parliament passed the Sugar Act. Since this law actually cut in half the tariffs on imported molasses, one would think Rhode Islanders would have been overjoyed. Molasses was used to make rum, a staple of Rhode Island trade. But the Sugar Act actually was a disaster for the colony: Rhode Islanders always had smuggled in most of their rum, and paid no tariff at all! Now, with strict law enforcement, they could rarely get out of paying, and even half the original rate cost them big money. Parliament knew this perfectly well when it passed the law.

In 1765 came the hated Stamp Act, which required the purchase and use of revenue stamps on everything from legal documents to playing cards. This sent all the colonies into a furor and nudged them none too gently onto the path that eventually led to rebellion. In fairness, it should be pointed out that people in Britain were going through the same, if not worse, taxation and tough times as their brethren in America. Particularly hard hit were the Scots, whose country had been forced by the English in 1701 to join Great Britain, which previously had consisted of England, Wales and a few islands. When Americans began to chant "no taxation without representation," many Britons could say the same thing because some areas of the realm were without elected representatives in Parliament.

At any rate, Rhode Island didn't take these measures lying down. There were violent clashes between some Newport residents and the Royal Navy, especially after 1765, when the Navy started drafting or "impressing" seamen both from vessels entering and leaving the harbor and from the city itself. After the Stamp Act riots in Newport in the summer of 1765, the General Assembly adopted a measure saying that Rhode Islanders were "not bound to yield obedience to any law designed to impose any internal taxation whatsoever upon them."

Rhode Island simply ignored the Stamp Act. Samuel Ward, who had succeeded Hopkins, was the only colonial governor who refused to take the required oath to support the hated law. The general storm caused by the Stamp Act forced Parliament to repeal it in 1766.

The so-called Townshend Duties, which mandated that tariffs be paid on British goods as well as foreign ones, were passed in 1767, but didn't cause much of a flutter in Rhode Island. As a matter of fact, the colony clouded the issue by refusing to join other colonies in boycotting British goods. So frustrated were New York, Pennsylvania and Massachusetts that they started boycotting Rhode Island goods! When the movement against British products broke down in 1770 after the repeal of all the duties except the one on tea, most people blamed Rhode Island.

Throughout these years, trouble continued between the Navy and many Newporters, and they continually harassed each other. The British pushed tensions a notch higher in 1772, when the revenue cutter *Gaspee* arrived, and accosted every vessel in the vicinity of Aquidneck Island, from merchant ships to boats carrying firewood. The king's sailors, who by no means came from the highest classes of society, roughed up civilians, stole cattle from farms, and caused much property damage.

On the night of June 9, *Gaspee* made the mistake of running aground on Namquid (now Gaspee) Point in Warwick while chasing a merchant vessel. Late that night, a party of men led by John Brown and Abraham Whipple of Providence attacked and burned the ship. Though a royal commission investigated the affair, they couldn't get any local who was sober or reliable enough to testify. As with previous incidents, none of the perpetrators was caught.

In the following year, 1773, tensions escalated. In response to the "Boston Tea Party," Parliament whipped up the Coercive Acts, which included closing the port of Boston, and some tampering with colonial charters. It took a threat to their beloved Charter to get Rhode Islanders to realize that they had to start getting along with the other colonies. Before long, Rhode Island took the lead in helping the people of now impoverished Massachusetts, and in calling for a congress of all the colonies.

The First Continental Congress met in Philadelphia in 1774 with, oddly enough, Stephen Hopkins and Samuel Ward as Rhode Island's delegates. With this act of both anger and unity by all the colonies, and even though outright independence was in the minds of only a few as yet, it can safely be said that the American Revolution had begun.

Most of us are used to thinking of the revolution as a time of ever-present gallantry, with larger-than-life American heroes galloping across battlefields with rag-tag but victorious armies. Throughout the colonies, everybody prayed for the revolutionaries, put up "liberty trees," and plotted against the British, who never had any right to be here in the first place. The truth, however, is that the American Revolution was a brutal war fought by opposing armies that were ill-trained and ill equipped. Terrible atrocities were committed by both sides, often against unarmed civilians. Desertions from both armies were epidemic, and mutinies among the American troops were not uncommon.

Moreover, the colonists always had considered themselves transplanted British, and most had a very difficult time, at least at first, in thinking of their trans-Atlantic cousins as "the enemy." As a matter of fact, most historians believe that as much as three quarters of the colonial population either was indifferent to the outcome of the Revolution or opposed to it outright. Canada's Atlantic provinces are filled with people whose ancestors, known as "loyalists," left the American colonies, including Rhode Island, to escape the Revolution. Some people in Calais, Maine, and other border towns actually took their houses apart and floated or otherwise transported them into Canada so they wouldn't have to live outside British territory. Some of the worst atrocities of the war were committed by revolutionaries against these loyalists, who believed that their fellow colonists were traitors for rebelling against their lawful king and empire.

The British themselves were divided in their opinions, especially since many of them had family or friends here. Several prominent British politicians argued eloquently for the American position, at least before the Americans took the course of rebellion. In general, the official British reaction, arrogant as it may have been, was much the same as ours might be if Alaska declared its independence from the United States. (Don't look now, but when this was written, the governor of that state belonged to the Alaska Independence Party!)

Few 18th century Americans had any sense whatever of an American nation; it was colony — later state — first, America second. British abuses were many and real, but one can argue that the revolutionary feeling of the time, fanned by the press, was rash. One also could argue that the situation would have resolved itself in a few years, and that the colonies would have gained a peaceful independence in due course anyway, as did Canada in 1867.

Given what they were up against, it's amazing that men like George Washington and Rhode Island's own Nathanael Greene, brilliant generals though they were, accomplished anything. Were it not for the French, who joined the war on the American side to spite Britain for past defeats, it's unlikely that revolutionary leaders would have made it anywhere but to the gallows.

In any case, the situation went from bad to worse in 1774 and 1775. Rhode Island's General Assembly chartered new militia units, including the Kentish Guards, the Newport Light Infantry, the Providence Grenadiers, the Pawtuxet Rangers, and the Glocester Light Infantry.

At the same time, loyalists in Rhode Island and elsewhere

formed units of their own to aid the British, or "the regulars" as they were known. Among their leaders were some prominent citizens from Aquidneck Island and the Narragansett Country. As the Revolution went on, though, most of these loyalists and their families, including nearly half the population of Aquidneck Island, were driven away, their property seized by mobs and given to people who agreed with the revolutionaries. Some were arrested, murdered, or otherwise abused. Governor Joseph Wanton, overthrown in 1775, was himself a revolutionary turned loyalist.

Despite its size, Rhode Island contributed a great deal to the revolutionary cause. Men from the state served in regiments that saw action in practically every theater of the war. The unusually well-trained First and Second Rhode Island Regiments served from the beginning of the war to the end, and proved to be among George Washington's most reliable units.

General Nathanael Greene, an amazing man with no prior military experience, ended up in command of the American army in the South. Serving at the side of Washington and the French military advisor, the Marquis de Lafayette, Greene was a real hero of the American Revolution.

Significant naval contributions came from Rhode Island, too. In 1775, after revolutionaries had closed the customs house at Newport, the *HMS Rose* and other British ships appeared. They harassed everything that sailed on Narragansett Bay, occasionally bombarding Newport, Bristol and Warren. The General Assembly then put together a small navy under the command of Abraham Whipple, of *Gaspee* fame. Rhode Island's little navy scored America's first sea victory on June 15, when it captured a British vessel.

A quaint incident illustrating that people are people, no matter what their period in history, has come down to us from 1775.

A Newport man named Coggeshall, "being somewhat drunk or crazy" blundered out onto Long Wharf one day, lowered his pants, and flashed his posterior at a nearby British revenue cutter. The annoyed Brits at once "fired two four-pound shot at him," blowing up part of the wharf. Coggeshall himself scampered away just in time, apparently unharmed.

But Rhode Island that year took more serious action than simply "mooning" the British. A sloop owned by John Brown was sent to Philadelphia, where it was renamed *Providence*, to become the first vessel in the Continental Navy. Its first commander was none other than the legendary naval hero John Paul Jones. In addition, Stephen Hopkins's brother, Esek, became the first commander-in-chief of the navy. *Providence's* replica and modern namesake, owned by the City of Providence, is a common sight today at tall ships visits, shore-community events, and other festivities held on or around Narragansett Bay.

Rhode Islanders like to believe that their colony was the first to formally declare its independence, on May 4, 1776. But this isn't entirely accurate. What actually happened that day was that the General Assembly repealed a rule that had government officers swear allegiance to the monarch. This was, to be sure, a *de facto* revolution in itself. But until it ratified the Declaration of Independence on July 20, Rhode Island officially remained the "English Colony of Rhode Island and Providence Plantations."

On that day, American independence was proclaimed from the State House in Newport, and jubilation reigned in the town among those of the revolutionary persuasion. The party didn't last long, though, since the British occupied Newport in December, effectively closing Narragansett Bay. As a matter of fact, nothing much happened during the early years of the American Revolution in Rhode Island, at least as far as actual battles were concerned, because more than a third of the state was occupied by the British until 1779. This occupation often was brutal. Troops raided farms and villages along the Bay, burned crops and buildings, and killed or stole livestock. They destroyed every house but one on Prudence Island, and most of those in Jamestown.

The revolution finished the Narragansett planters in South County (called King's County before the war and Washington County later). Still smarting from a decade of British law enforcement that had disrupted the West Indies trade, area plantations were devastated first by the closing of

From this balcony at the Old State House in Newport, the Declaration of Independence was proclaimed on July 20, 1776.

-Photo by Paul F. Eno

Narragansett Bay and then by British foraging raids. South County would never be the same. Newport itself was prostrate. Its population plunged from 9,209 at the war's outset to 5,530 by its end. Its best merchants and thriving shipping gone, its wharves and warehouses rotting, the economic and political leadership of Rhode Island passed to Providence. There was plenty of hardship there, too, but the colony's oldest town remained unoccupied by the British, and was relatively unscathed throughout the war. Providence even played host to American troops and, later, the French.

Rhode Island's revolutionary government kept badgering the Continental Congress to mount a drive to get the British out of the state, but it took until August 1778 for this to happen. The effort, supported by a French fleet, was to include a grab for Newport, but it all ended in failure for a number of reasons. For one thing, the British had just reinforced Newport. In addition, Admiral Lord Howe and a British fleet ar-

rived just after the French fleet did. After General John
Sullivan and his Continental troops broke camp at Tiverton
and crossed to Portsmouth on the first leg of their invasion
of Aquidneck Island, the French suddenly decided to set sail
in hopes of tangling with the British fleet somewhere off Newport.

Then, of all things, a hurricane hit, disabling both fleets! It
was a tough situation for Newport, already heavily damaged
by French naval bombardments, and now by the fierce
weather. Food was scarce as the Americans crept closer. But
the French never returned, and American officers, including
Nathanael Greene and the Marquis de Lafayette, agreed with
Sullivan that, without French support, retreat was the only
option.

The so-called Battle of Rhode Island actually was a
rearguard action fought toward the end of August so the
Continental Army could retreat from Aquidneck Island.
Nonetheless, it was the largest land battle ever fought in New
England, with 6,000 to 8,000 men on each side. It also saw
heroic action by America's first African-American/Native
American fighting unit, the First Rhode Island Battalion.

During the next few months, the British gradually filtered
away to fight elsewhere, and they finally left Newport on their
own in October 1779. Basically, they decided that the town
wasn't worth holding, and left to help their comrades with
the war in the South. In July 1780, 6,000 French troops and a
small fleet under Jean Baptiste Donatien de Vimeur, Comte
de Rochambeau, better known to us simply as Rochambeau,
arrived in Newport in hopes of linking up with Washington.
Before beginning their famous march across southern New
England in June 1781, the French brought a certain amount
of economic relief to Newport, since soldiers, then as now,
love to spend money.

After this, the war in Rhode Island effectively petered out.
The American Revolution officially ended with the Treaty of
Paris, on February 3, 1783. Far from bringing relief in Rhode
Island, the revolution's end opened a new era for the ornery
inhabitants of the contrary colony that had become the inde-
pendent state, and they had every intention of keeping it that

way.

When Congress passed the Articles of Confederation in 1778, Rhode Island hurried to ratify them because they created just the kind of decentralized national government it wanted so that state independence could be preserved. Rhode Islanders had no intention of exchanging submission to Parliament for submission to Congress. It was just this persnickety attitude, however, that sowed dissension among the colonies and led to the move for a stronger central government.

One of the first things the Confederation Congress had to do was find a way to pay for the war. At its wits' end for money, Congress twice tried to establish a national import tax, but You-Know-Who blocked both the 1781 and 1783 attempts to do this, sending several states into a rage. Adding insult to injury, Rhode Island turned around and established its own import tax to help pay its own war debt. After this, one congressional delegate fumed that this "cursed state ought to be erased out of the Confederation!"

There actually were several attempts to get Rhode Island kicked out of the United States, especially after it tried to pay its debts with a massive issue of worthless paper money, doing more damage to the American economy. As time passed, Rhode Island grew more and more aloof. By the time the other states called for a constitutional convention in 1787, Rhode Island essentially was an independent nation.

James Madison himself carped: "Nothing can exceed the wickedness and folly which continue to rule there. All sense of character as well as of right has been obliterated."

Rhode Island never sent delegates to the Constitutional Convention, held in Philadelphia. When delegates there finally hammered out the Constitution as we know it, presenting it to the states for ratification in 1788, Rhode Island refused even to call a ratifying convention of its own. Instead, it put the Constitution before the people in the form of a referendum. Newport and Providence both boycotted the referendum because they thought there should have been a convention. Consequently, the proposed Constitution got plastered here 2,708 to 237.

But the other twelve states ratified it and, by late 1789, only

Rhode Island remained outside the Union. George Washington, now president of the reorganized United States of America, and Congress started to think about economic sanctions against the little state that wouldn't fall into line. At last, fearing threats from Providence merchants over the looming sanctions, the General Assembly called a ratification convention and, in May 1790, Rhode Island reluctantly joined the Union, barely ratifying the Constitution, by a two-vote margin. Even then, the measure included an "out" clause in case Rhode Island didn't like what it had gotten into!

Along with the sanction threat, what probably helped tip the scales were a public-relations visit by President Washington, as popular here as anywhere else, and the new Bill of Rights, which helped ease the minds of Rhode Islanders about federal power. Had they looked ahead to the 1990s and 2000s, and a federal bureaucracy with its heavy hand over every American home, they might have thought again.

Even though Rhode Island was finally in the Union, the state convention suggested twenty one amendments to the Constitution, most of which would have weakened the federal government! Of course, none of these ever got anywhere. Despite all this, Rhode Island was to become the most loyal of states and be one of the quickest to industrialize, therefore doing its part to boost, rather than undermine, the American economy.

-PFE

The Capture
of General Prescott

During the twenty months the British occupied Newport during the American Revolution, several events occurred that changed the course of the war, but none had more of an impact that the capture of British General Richard Prescott.

THE PLAN

It seemed like a dangerous and exciting operation. It would involve rowing from Tiverton to Warwick Neck to Portsmouth and back in the dead of night, probably with musket balls flying past their heads. They would go by whaleboat, with muffled oars, to Aquidneck Island, where some of their revolutionary compatriots were being held by the British, and where these Rhode Island militiamen would execute a daring plan.

Their second in command was Lieutenant Colonel William Barton, and the 450-man militia regiment was camped along the Sakonnet River in Tiverton. Their task had been to keep watch for British troops across Narragansett Bay in occupied Newport. In their spare time, the Rhode Islanders held whaleboat races, a sport in which they excelled. On July 4, 1777, Barton supervised a five-whaleboat race, watching for the best and most powerful crews for more than just awarding a prize: He wanted the best boatmen for his daring raid on the island.

The idea had come about some two weeks before, when a Newport man named Coffin had made his way through enemy lines to Tiverton to report on the movements and operations of British troops. One part of Coffin's story was of great

Colonel, later General, William Barton of Warren, who led the swashbuckling 1777 raid to capture British General George Prescott on Aquidneck Island.

-Courtesy of the Providence Journal Co.

interest to Barton and his commander, Colonel Joseph Stanton. It seemed that British General Prescott had taken over the house and grounds of an affluent loyalist named Henry John Overing. Although a troop of British dragoons was camped next to the house, only one sentry was on duty, making it an easy target for anyone who was after Prescott. Not only was the British commander not admired by his men, he was hated by most of them for his harsh command style.

Several of the Rhode Island soldiers had been raised in the area and knew the terrain. Tak Sisson, a giant African-American, was a slave sent to fight as a revolutionary by his master, Thomas Sisson, in place of a friend of his who had been drafted and didn't want to go. Thomas Sisson aided the Revolution more than he could imagine when he gave Tak to Barton. Others in the regiment — Samuel Weaver, John Hunt and Samuel Cory – also were from the area and were familiar with the surroundings.

Colonel Stanton had complete faith in his subordinate. Barton was a big, awkward-looking man who had risen to high rank in just two years since his enlistment. Stanton, after hearing Barton's plan to capture Prescott, gave the order.

Headquarters Camp at Tiverton: Lieu. Col Barton
You will proceed to the Island of Newport and attack the enemy and where you think proper and report to me your findings.

It was up to Barton to call the troops together and explain as much of the plan as possible without being specific, thereby guarding against any "leaks" that might get back to the British.

"You need not be ashamed to refuse," Barton said as he outlined scant details of what promised to be a dangerous undertaking. "Those who wish to go with me, take two steps forward."

The entire regiment of 450 men advanced two paces, and forty were selected, based on their knowledge of the area and their ability to row quickly and quietly. Except for Barton and Stanton, no one knew the plan's details.

As Barton readied his expedition, General George Washington was at a low ebb in his quest to beat the British. Losing as many men to desertion as he was gaining by enlistment, Washington had seen New York and Long Island fall into enemy hands. The British were laying Newport barren.

Once beautiful forests, with farms and streams, were turning into wasteland. Trees had been cut down for firewood, and many buildings and homes had been burned or turned into troop quarters. The war seemed to be going nowhere.

THE CAPTURE

Prisoner exchanges were common during the Revolutionary War.

Barton thought highly of General Charles Lee, the flamboyant former British soldier of fortune who had served in the Polish army after falling into disfavor with his British superiors. Having returned to America to join the revolutionaries, Lee had been captured by his former compatriots while his guard was down after a night of wine, women and song. He had been held in New York City for more than a year.

What neither Barton nor Washington knew was that, while in custody, Lee did not suffer the indignities of a cold, wet cell, giving only name and rank. He in fact tutored British troops about the Continental Army's procedures, and he was free with what he knew about Washington's war plans. Lee's actions would result in a court martial and resignation from the army, but not until shortly before his death. But in 1777, Washington wanted Lee back. Barton knew that if Prescott could be captured and exchanged for Lee, it would work favorably for the new United States.

No moon was shining on the night of July 5, 1777, as Barton and his men boarded five whaleboats, oars muffled with sheepskin. They began to row toward Bristol through Mount Hope Bay, the first stop on their mission to Portsmouth and Prescott. Within minutes, a severe thunderstorm, accompanied by high winds, struck the Bay, separating the five boats. Throughout the night and for much of the following day, the men struggled to keep the boats afloat and themselves alive. It was only ten miles from Tiverton to Bristol, but it took an exhausted crew twenty six hours to get there. Finally, Barton was able to feed his men and tell them, in detail, of his plan to go to the Overing house, capture Prescott, and take him to Providence. He reiterated that no one had to continue, nor would anyone be poorly thought of if he turned back. Once again, no one backed out.

Barton's wife and children were living in the family home-
stead, where Barton himself had been born and raised. It was
still standing in 2000 as a private home in the Town of Warren. The house was only a few miles from Bristol, where Barton
camped on the night of the storm. Under cover of darkness,
he made his way to see his family. His wife was told nothing
of the adventure. He had married Rhoda Carver after meeting her on a trip to Bridgewater, Massachusetts, shortly after
his twenty-first birthday.

William Barton had been born on May 26, 1748. His father,
Benjamin, was a hat maker, and kept a shop in Warren. One
of five children, William soon became an apprentice, and
eventually opened his own hat-making business in town. He
and Rhoda would have nine children and, after the war, would
move to a larger house on South Main Street in Providence.

On July 9, at 9 p.m., Barton gathered his crew of forty men
and ordered them not to plunder or take "spirituous liquor,"
and to observe the utmost silence. The operation was about
to begin.

Barton's boat led the flotilla, with a ten-foot pole and a white
handkerchief tied to it as a guide through the darkness. Care-
fully, the militiamen made their way between Prudence and
Patience Islands, avoiding Hope Island, where much of the
British Fleet was stationed. Pulling to within a mile of the
Overing house on the Portsmouth shore, they began moving
toward the spot where the sleeping British general would be.
Luckily, Prescott had been drinking heavily that night after a
fresh supply of wine and Santa Cruz had been delivered from
Newport.

The five boats made their way around Prudence Island, then
headed east. Less than a mile from the shore where they
planned to disembark, the sound of voices and galloping
horses could be heard, bringing the mission to a heart-stop-
ping halt. For a terrifying minute it looked as though word of
Barton's daring operation had reached Prescott — and that
it might be a capture in reverse.

As Barton and his men waited to see what would happen,
the British dragoons continued into the night. John Hunt, fa-

miliar with the area, advised Barton to put ashore on a beach opposite the Overing house. Within minutes, all five whaleboats were out of the water. It was July 9, five days after the men had set out from Tiverton. Today, that journey would take only about an hour.

One man was left behind to guard each boat. Straight ahead, through a field of rye and blackberry thickets, lay the Overing house. As they approached the house, they came upon a small creek with high banks that led to the front of the structure. Making their way along these banks, they could see the outline of the house, surrounded by a fence. It also was surrounded by camps, dragoons on one side and infantry on the other.

Barton may have been outnumbered, but these camps each were about 300 feet away from the house, allowing Barton and his men to carefully creep near without being detected. Stationing men at each window and door, Barton, Hunt and Tak walked boldly through the front gate, and approached a lone sentry standing in front of the main entrance.

They met the challenge.

"Who comes there?"

"Friends," answered Barton.

"Advance, friends, and give the countersign," the guard ordered.

"We have none," responded Barton, "but have you seen any deserters?" Before the sentry could answer, his arms were pinned to his side, and he was warned that he was a dead man if he made a sound.

The Overing house was owned by a Quaker named Henry John Overing, who purchased it and a large tract of land in 1771, living comfortably with his wife and young son. Prescott found the house during an excursion around Aquidnick Island. He also found Mrs. Overing, to whom he took an instant liking. Mrs. Overing returned the attention showered on her by the arrogant and powerful British general, but only to preserve her family's safety. Tonight, she would get her revenge.

Barton, Hunt, Tak and several others quickly entered the house and went upstairs in search of Prescott. The first bedchamber they entered was Overing's, and they found him cowering in his bed. When asked where Prescott was, he pointed downward, to the main bedroom on the first floor. Silently Barton made his way down the stairs to the bedroom, and upon entering saw a short, gray-haired man sitting up in bed.

"Are you General Prescott?" Barton demanded?

"I am," answered Prescott.

"You are my prisoner."

"I acknowledge it, sir!"

Barton put his hands on Prescott's shoulders, forcing the naked general out of bed. Servants employed by Overing were now awake, and lights were on. Major Barrington, Prescott's aide, had jumped out of his bedroom window into the waiting arms of Barton's men. Prescott tried to pull on a pair of trousers and grab a shirt before being pushed out of the house and toward the escape boats, but Barton was impatient. Wrapped only in a blanket, the pompous general was unceremoniously taken captive.

Although surrounded by forty captors, Prescott complained about not having any shoes or trousers, and demanded that Barton send someone back for his sword. Barton had given orders that Prescott not be harmed, and that he be treated with respect because of his rank. But even Barton was becoming agitated by the cranky old general's constant griping. Finally, Barton told Tak to go back to the Overing house quickly, and grab the general's sword and trousers. While Tak was carrying out this dangerous assignment, two of Barton's men made a "basket" with their arms, and carried Prescott. Tak returned safely with the sword and trousers just as the party reached the escape boats.

"You have made a damn bold push tonight," Prescott told Barton. Not receiving a reply, Presott ventured to ask if he would be harmed.

"Not while you are in my hands," Barton reassured him.

Perhaps Prescott was recalling his own treatment of people who were helpless under his charge. A farmer who had refused to haul cannon with his ox team had been whipped under Prescott's orders. The farmer was Thomas Austin, and when he recovered, he had joined Barton's regiment and was one of Prescott's captors that night.

Barton, Prescott and the others reached the beach where the boats were waiting, and quickly piled in. Barton warned his three prisoners not to make a sound, or it would be their last. Quietly the padded oars carried five whaleboats and forty four men past British ships anchored in Narragansett Bay.

Suddenly, rockets were sent up by troops at the Overing house. Worse, cannon fire was heard in the direction of the fleeing boats. Inexplicably, no activity came from the fleet only 100 yards from the whaleboats.

With a shivering, complaining British general and forty three other men frantically rowing through the calm waters, daylight began to break as Barton's party put ashore at Warwick Neck. They immediately brought Prescott to Arnold's Tavern near the landing.

Prescott, whose feet were swollen from wearing shoes that were too small, pleaded for a larger pair. Samuel Cory, one of Barton's closest friends in the party, retrieved a pair from an officer of the Warwick garrison, and thrust them onto Prescott's aching feet. Cory and his family and friends had suffered at the hands of troops under Prescott's command.

Barton ordered the best breakfast he could find for his prisoners, then put them on a stagecoach bound for Providence and the next leg of their journey, which he hoped would result in the release of General Charles Lee. A heavy guard accompanied Prescott and the two others. When they arrived in Providence, they were held for several weeks until arrangements could be made to take them to New York and General Washington's headquarters.

General Richard Prescott's capture was the best news Washington had received all month. Word quickly spread across the Atlantic about how Prescott had been captured without his pants on, and on September 27, 1777, the *London Chronicle* printed a poem about its native son's debacle.

What various lures there are to ruin man:
Woman the first and foremost all be witches,

> *A nymph thus spoiled a General's mighty plan,*
> *And gave him to the foe without his britches.*

The "nymph" was Mrs. Overing, who, while putting up with Prescott's advances, was glad to hand him over to Barton without his breeches.

Prescott was exchanged for Lee in time for Lee to join Washington at Valley Forge, Pennsylvania, in 1778.

THE REST IS HISTORY

On May 28, 1778, British troops attacked Bristol, setting fire to nearly every structure, including the Episcopal Church and Congregational Meeting House. There was widespread looting, and large amounts of brass were carried off. Men were taken prisoner, and women had their jewels and anything else of value stolen from them, and from their homes. The raiders then set their sights on the next town, Warren, as they made their way toward Providence.

Word of the attack on Bristol reached General Sullivan, in command of revolutionary troops in Providence. He immediately contacted Barton and ordered him take a unit of horsemen to Warren to warn the people of the impending assault. Joined by troops who were stationed in nearby Barrington, which would have been the British target after Warren, Barton soon had a large force of armed men.

The British troops already were in Warren, and had begun their burning of buildings, including the Town House, where Barton had spent many hours with his friends and associates planning the town's future. Galloping into town, Barton spotted a British soldier putting a torch to a building, and chased him away, shouting, "You damned coward, I'll hack you to pieces in less time than takes me to get you!"

The surprised British retreated to Popasquash Point, where they boarded boats and fled to safety. Barton raised his sword and was about to encourage pursuit when a bullet ripped into his thigh and lodged in his groin. He had succeeded in driving the British out of Warren, but he also had engaged in his last fight of the Revolutionary War.

Barton was taken to a nearby house, where a doctor named

Winslow removed the slug, which the Barton family saved for years. He was able to return to duty on a limited basis, but he suffered from the effects of the groin injury for years. Barton was laid up for three months and, as late as 1785, after the war was over, he went to New York City to seek more advanced medical treatment. It was there that he received the stunning news that he explained in a letter to Rhoda on September 6, 1785.

It is the opinion that nothing would do but extarpation of one of my testicles. Oh horrid, m.d., I leave you to judge how horrid I must feel to go into the Hotest Battels ever fought would not be half so dreadful.

Barton elected not to have the surgery.

Although his active participation in the war was over, Barton was promoted to general and placed in charge of the Rhode Island State Militia, a job similar to that of present day National Guard adjutant general. He also was elected to the General Assembly, and appointed by the federal government as a customs inspector.

During this time, the French had become involved in the war against the British, driving them out of Newport by 1783 as hostilities drew to a close. While the French were in Rhode Island, Barton enjoyed frequent visits from the young Marquis de Lafayette and his fellow officer, the Comte de Rochambeau. Barton and Lafayette were to remain lifelong friends, with the Frenchman playing a bizarre role in Barton's later life.

Barton's accomplishments were not confined to the capture of General Prescott and saving the Town of Warren. Following Prescott's capture, Barton devised another plan for a dangerous mission, this time into Newport. British deserters had begun trickling into his Tiverton camp, and one of them gave him an answer to the riddle of how the British were supporting themselves financially. Locked in the loosely guarded Malbone building in downtown Newport was the British treasure, piled high from constant looting of Aquidneck Island.

Gathering the same forty men who had helped him capture

Prescott, Barton told them his plan to land on the outermost tip of Newport, then spread out to avoid capture, and meet in the rear of the Malbone house. One day before they were to set out, the British treasure suddenly was moved to a well fortified encampment near their headquarters. Someone had apparently tipped off the British that Barton was about to raid the booty, and further damage British efforts in Newport.

On July 27, 1777, Congress honored Barton by voting to give him a coveted sword denoting his bravery on the battlefield, and to thank him for capturing General Prescott. The Rhode Island General Assembly awarded Barton $1,120, which he split with the forty men who had helped him. In 1778, Barton was sent to Newport under a flag of truce in an attempt to alleviate deplorable conditions on prisoner-of-war ships in the harbor. Bringing supplies helped, but Barton failed to negotiate better conditions for the captured Americans. The British took a hard line on captives, unlike Barton, and in at least one recorded incident killed two Continental Army officers with their own swords.

Barton's final command was over a light infantry corps consisting of fifty-four men in each of four companies.

BAD LUCK IN VERMONT

Barton, Vermont, was organized on March 28, 1798. The mystery of how it got its name began shortly before the Revolutionary War officially ended. A group of veterans had petitioned the independent Republic of Vermont for a sizeable tract of land on which they planned to develop a town called Providence, after the town in Rhode Island. On October 20, 1781, the petition was granted, although the name was not Providence but Barton.

General William Barton, whose fighting days had ended with his wound in Warren, was the leader of the veterans who had sought the petition. While no one spoke of it for years, Abner Allyn of Charleston, Vermont, eventually explained how Barton had taken his knife and scratched the name "Providence" off the petition, putting his own in its place. Nothing was done about it then, and the name Barton,

Vermont, remains today.

The first settlers began arriving in 1795, and they found Barton already living in his town, in a cabin he had built on fourteen acres he had cleared to raise wheat. During the summer of 1796, Barton built the town's first sawmill, and later constructed a large log cabin that housed a school and a church. He lived alone, having left his wife and nine children in Providence.

Barton began selling timber and lots and, in 1797, those transactions were beginning to get him into more trouble than he had ever faced during the Revolutionary War. Barton, whose fame had not followed him to Vermont, sold a piece of property to Jonathan Allyn, a relative of the man who would tell the story of how the town got its name. Allyn took possession of the property, only to discover that Barton had also sold it to someone else!

Allyn sued, as did several others who felt they had been cheated by Barton. The lawsuits totaled $3,000, a sum that was whittled down to $300 as the years passed. After eleven years of litigation, a judge ruled that Barton would have to pay a fine or go to prison. He chose the latter, maintaining his ignorance of the land deals, and claiming he was a victim of political games. Barton would be held, the judge said, until he paid, little realizing that the stubborn old soldier would never pay. He was taken to a log cabin that was used as the Caledonia County jail, in Danville, Vermont, sixty miles south of Barton. It was 1811, and William Barton was sixty-three years old.

The prison at Danville was anything but a maximum-security facility. Located on the town common and next to the Danville Inn, the jail was surrounded by trees to which were tied chains, creating a prison from which anyone could escape when the guards were not looking.

Other prisoners, realizing they were better off incarcerated, with regular meals, than free, gladly worked on local farms during the day and returned to an honor camp at night. Barton did no work and kept to himself at first, but eventually he was allowed to stay at the Danville Inn, where he began telling the story of his capture of General Richard Prescott, and other war tales. He was rarely without a rapt audience. He also was without the money that he had been sending to his family in Providence.

When the War of 1812 broke out, Barton petitioned Congress for $75, citing his age, and infirmities from wounds suffered in the Revolutionary War. The petition was granted, and the money sent to his family. Barton petitioned the Vermont legislature for his own release from prison, but that was denied until he paid the $300. As the years passed, Barton's only family member to make the 300-mile journey from Providence to Danville was one of his sons. Barton would not see his entire family for fourteen years.

In 1824, the aged Marquis de Lafayette was invited by President James Buchanan to visit the colonies he had helped free from British rule. One of the stops he made during his one-year tour was Rhode Island, where he inquired about his old friend General Barton. Lafayette was shocked to learn of Barton's whereabouts, and when his tour took him to Lyndon, Vermont, the French hero asked details of Barton's fate. Without hesitation, Lafayette drew a draft for the amount Barton owed, and dispatched an aide to pay it. Quietly, Lafayette left Vermont, and returned to his ship *Brandywine,* stopping next in New York City for more acclaim.

Within days, Barton was released from Danville and told he could go home. Proclaiming his innocence, the seventy seven year-old general, infirm with years, boarded a stagecoach for Providence and the family he had not seen in so long. It was later written that Barton sat with tears in his eyes, singing Revolutionary War songs during the long trip. Upon arrival in Providence, he was greeted as a returning hero by family, friends and supporters.

TAPS

General William Barton died at his home at 28 South Main Street, Providence, on Saturday, October 22, 1831, several days after he had suffered an attack of apoplexy. The *Pawtucket Gazette* eulogized him as

...a venerable old soldier of the American Revolution. For true

*patriotism and unwavering courage few men were more distin-
guished. Full of years and full of glory the old soldier has been
gathered to his fathers. His last march is finished and he sleeps in
that tent which sooner or later is pitched for all mankind.*

The *Providence Daily* remembered the capture of Prescott.

*One of the most hazardous achievements of those times of daring,
it was conduct not surpassed by any deed of heroism on the page of
history.*

The article also mentioned Barton's misfortune in Vermont,
and his land dealings, "in the transfer of which, however, he
unfortunately became entangled in the toils of law, was sub-
jected to numerous and heavy expenses, which eventuated
in his imprisonment there most unjustly."

The newspaper reported that Barton was ill for several
months, closing with, "Now sleep the brave, who sink to rest,
with all their country's honors blest."

Barton's funeral was held at his home, and flags were lowered to half staff throughout the state. The procession moved
from Barton's house to North Burial Ground on North Main
Street under the escort of the Independent Company of Ca-
dets, the Artillery, Volunteers and Light Infantry. On his coffin was placed the sword given to him by Congress for his
capture of Prescott more than fifty years before. Minute guns
were fired from the moment the coffin left South Main Street
until it was lowered into the ground. When Barton's obituary
appeared in the *Providence Daily*, it included a reprint of the
story that had run in the *Providence Gazette* on July 12, 1777,
chronicling the Prescott episode.

Behind Barton's grave is a small black stone with one inscription. "Jenny" is printed there, along with "born and died
in the family of General Barton, aged 70. Honor to honor is
due."

-GVL

George Washington's Right-Hand Man

The memories of few Rhode Islanders are as honored as that of Nathanael Greene, the son of a Warwick anchor maker, who went on to become one of the most extraordinary people in the American Revolution. Most Rhode Islanders today probably don't realize just how extraordinary he was, or how sad an end he met.

Ironically, the future general was born into a wealthy but strict Quaker family on August 7, 1742. Greene became an avid reader at an early age and, much to the chagrin of his family and their Quaker friends, his taste in books ran to the military accomplishments of history's great generals. In 1773, his less than pacifist views got his Quaker congregation upset, and he was pressured into leaving it.

A year later, Greene helped organize the Kentish Guards militia unit in Warwick, Coventry and East Greenwich, newly chartered by the Rhode Island government as the American Revolution approached. Oddly enough, he himself was only a private! That same year, Greene married Catharine Littlefield, and they lived in Coventry, where he managed his late father's forge and mill.

On the night of April 19, 1775, news of the skirmishes at Lexington and Concord reached Greene, and he was completely inflamed. By the end of May, the Kentish Guards and several other Rhode Island units were on the march, headed for Boston to offer their services to revolutionary forces in Massachusetts. When they reached the Massachusetts border, however, they were overtaken by a messenger from Rhode Island's governor, Joseph Wanton, a loyalist who had refused to sign their military orders. In effect, this was an unspoken order to go home. Within a month, however, Wanton had been sacked by the revolutionaries, and Private Greene, in a career leap far beyond the term "upwardly mobile," was General Greene. Soon he and his troops were on their way to Boston at the behest of the General Assembly.

Why lawmakers suddenly made Greene a general isn't clear, but history would show that they couldn't have made a wiser choice. When General George Washington, new commander-in-chief of the Continental Army, got to Boston, he immediately took Greene under his wing, and the two rapidly became friends. Though he had no military experience other than parading around and target shooting with the Kentish Guards, Greene soon found himself, at thirty three, the youngest general in the Continental Army. Washington had a keen eye for ability, and Greene's intelligence and practical business knowledge weren't lost on him.

Both Greene and his wife, Catharine, shared the terrible winter of 1777-1778 at Valley Forge, Pennsylvania, with the Continental Army. In 1778, Greene became quartermaster general of the army, and found his wits tested to their utmost with the impossible job of finding enough food and supplies for the troops, especially during the just as horrible winter of 1779-1780 at Morristown, New Jersey.

In August 1778 came the unsuccessful attempt to throw the British out of Rhode Island by attacking Aquidneck Island and Newport. In the Battle of Rhode Island that month, Greene commanded the right flank of the Continental forces, while none other than the Marquis de Lafayette commanded the left. After this, the Greenes were able to return to Coventry for about two weeks. But the following winter saw them both back with the army, this time at Middlebrook, New Jersey.

After General Benedict Arnold exchanged his blue uniform for a red one, Greene applied for and got command of the fortifications at West Point, New York, in October 1780. But only a short time later, Washington asked him to relieve the less-than-outstanding General Horatio Gates, and take command of the Continental Army in the South.

On his way to North Carolina, Greene stopped at

The statue of General Nathanael Greene in Statuary Hall at the U.S. Capitol. Each state is entitled to place two statues there. Rhode Island's other statue commemorates Roger Williams.

-Photo by Paul F. Eno

Washington's headquarters at Preakness, New Jersey, to get final instructions. He found out that things in the South were so bad that even Washington didn't know what was going on. The commander-in-chief gave Greene *carte blanche* to do whatever he had to to straighten things out. Probably no-one was more surprised than Greene when this turned out to be the start of the most brilliant period of his career.

His job was about as tough as anyone could imagine. Lord Cornwallis, the British commander in the South, was in control of South Carolina and Georgia, and had a great deal of support because much of the population was loyalist. And with the Continental Army there a shambles, the British were virtually unopposed, reinforcing all the time. All their major defeats had been in the North.

Greene appeared at the headquarters of General Gates, near Charlotte, North Carolina, on December 2. He found his new command in such horrendous condition that he later wrote that it had only "an imaginary existence." The "army" had few men, no organization, and no discipline. The troops had little or no clothing, few supplies, and no money to buy any. There was no medical care, only a little ammunition, and abysmal morale. The "soldiers" had gotten into the habit of going home whenever they felt like it, and returning when they pleased.

Nathanael Greene had to create an army almost from scratch. To the consternation of everyone, especially the British, Greene, within nine months, had hammered his army into a first-rate fighting force, recruiting new men, restoring discipline, and building up high morale with a "can do" attitude. In that same brief period, Greene and the southern army managed to maneuver Cornwallis into Virginia, virtually conquering Georgia and the Carolinas (with the exception of Charleston and Savannah).

In Virginia, the French, George Washington, and what was left of his army pounced on Cornwallis, laying siege to the British at Yorktown. While even Washington didn't realize it, Cornwallis's defeat there in October 1781 was the last real action of the war. It wouldn't have happened had it not been for Nathanael Greene.

After the war, Greene was something of a national hero. He and Catharine, who was in Charleston during the final months of fighting, finally got to return home to Coventry in November 1783. Since they had long since disposed of business interests there, they decided to make a temporary move to Newport. After that, Greene planned to head for one of the southern plantations he had been given for his wartime service, hoping to use it to earn back money he had lost because of the war.

It seems that Greene often had used his own credit to buy desperately needed supplies for his troops. Now, national hero or not, the merchants wanted their money. Greene expected Congress to reimburse him for these wartime expenses, but it never did. His only choice was to sell an estate in South Carolina. By the time his affairs were settled, he didn't have much left except his Georgia plantation, not far from Savannah. In 1785, the Greenes went to live on this plantation, located on the banks of the Savannah River. At last, things seemed to be looking up. But even this was not to be. On June 19, 1786, less than two months before his forty-fourth birthday, Nathanael Greene died, a victim of sunstroke.

Thus passed the greatest military hero in Rhode Island history.

-PFE

Scituate's
Most Famous Son

When you look at the chaotic conditions in Rhode Island at the beginning of the 18th century, and its united, well-oiled administration 100 years later, you may wonder what happened. Prominent among the reasons was an adopted son of Scituate.

Stephen Hopkins was something of a "renaissance man" in the realm of public service. He was adept at government, fiscal planning, business, and even military affairs. He was a local man with a national vision, something very unusual in the Rhode Island of his day. Hopkins probably did more than anyone else to get Rhode Island's act together. To do it, he evidently had to be something other than Mr. Personality, for many accounts indicate that he got quite steamed up over political arguments, and he sometimes got involved in dealings that led to accusations of corruption. But while he may have had the joviality of a cactus, there is little question that everyone, including some of America's most distinguished men, admired him.

Hopkins was born in South Providence in 1797, the son of Quaker parents. When he was a small boy, the family moved to Chopmiscook, or Chopmist, in northwestern Scituate. In those early years, the settlement had no roads, no store, no school, and not even a church. Throughout his early life, Hopkins was close to his two grandfathers, intelligent men who instructed him in mathematics and surveying. His public life began in Scituate when he became town moderator at the age of twenty one. From that time on, Stephen Hopkins was a very busy man. Soon he was elected town clerk, and stayed in that job for nineteen years, even while serving as Town Council president from 1736 until 1742. He also was a judge of the Court of Common Pleas for Providence County, and Scituate's representative in the General Assembly.

In 1742, Hopkins decided to move to Providence and have a try at commerce and law. Though hardly a refined gentleman, he did rather well at it. He had a brilliant, well-trained mind, honed by years of reading. The attributes that would distinguish him soon became apparent. Hopkins had a real knack for organization. On the commercial side, he got involved with the four Brown brothers, Moses, Joseph, John and Nicholas. Between them, they had new wharves and warehouses built, along with a system of insurance policies for shippers.

Hopkins found himself chief justice of the Superior Court in 1751, moving up to the governorship in 1755 for what was to be the first of ten terms. This was especially significant since it marked the beginning of the bid by Providence and the northern towns for ascendancy over Newport, the colony's political and economic capital.

With the end of the French and Indian Wars in 1763, Rhode Island faced a huge war debt. The questions of tax apportionment and political patronage, along with just plain regional rivalry, fired what became known as the "Ward-Hopkins Controversy." Throughout the 1760s, Stephen Hopkins and Samuel Ward of Westerly sparred and maneuvered for political advantage in the colony. If one wasn't governor in a given year, the other one was. Their respective followers constituted what can be considered the first two political parties in America.

In 1765, after Parliament had dreamed up the Stamp Act, Hopkins wrote a pamphlet called "The Rights of Colonies Examined," widely acclaimed for its eloquent argument for "no taxation without representation."

Appropriately, Ward and Hopkins were selected as Rhode Island's representatives to the First Continental Congress in 1774. By that time, Hopkins was an energetic sixty-seven years old. Two years later, he became a signer of the Declaration of Independence. John Adams had some warm words about

Hopkins during those years before and during the American Revolution.

> *The pleasantest part of my labors in...Congress...was in the Committee on Naval Affairs.... Governor Hopkins of Rhode Island, above seventy years of age, kept us all alive.... When the business of the evening was over, he kept us in conversation until eleven and sometimes twelve o'clock. His custom was to drink nothing until eight in the evening....it gave him wit, humor, anecdotes and learning. He had read Greek, Roman and British history, and was familiar with English poetry...and the flow of his soul made all of his reading our own.*

Surely the cactus of yore had blossomed strikingly.

George Washington liked Hopkins too, and visited him at his Providence home in 1781, when the general was in Rhode Island to plan campaigns with Count Rochambeau and the French, newly arrived in the area.

Stephen Hopkins died in 1785 at the age of seventy eight. A friend said after his death, paraphrasing the ancient Greek statesman Themistocles, that Hopkins "did not understand the art of music, and could not play upon the flute, but he understood the art of raising a small village into a great city."

-PFE

Mary Gould Almy:
Loyal to King and Empire

In war, who the enemy is depends on your point of view. During the Revolutionary War, American loyalists sincerely saw the revolutionaries as a radical minority of, at best, misguided citizens who sought to wrench America from its lawful king and empire. If the loyalists could hear us refer to the revolutionaries as patriots rather than traitors, they would do cartwheels in their graves.

These people, who considered *themselves* patriots, weren't necessarily blind to British abuses, they just thought there were more sensible ways of working out the problems. Just as in the Civil War less than a century later, many families found their loyalties split, often with tragic results.

Rhode Island was full of Quakers who were opposed to all war, no matter what the cause. Because of their intense pacifism, many of these Quakers had an additional reason to remain loyal to the British Crown. One of these was a courageous woman named Mary Gould Almy, who was born in Newport in 1735 and lived there until her death in 1808. Her story has a special poignancy because she was married to a Continental Army officer. Many of her letters provide an intensely personal account of the horror of finding one's home and family in the middle of a brutal war.

Mary hadn't seen her husband, Benjamin, in nearly three years. Before the Battle of Rhode Island, in August 1778, he got word to her that he himself was serving with General John Sullivan, General Nathanael Greene and the Marquis de Lafayette in the revolutionaries' attempt to drive the British from Aquidneck Island. Almy asked his wife to keep a written record of what was expected to be the battle for Newport. She began her story with both loving and harsh words, penned after the engagement, on September 2.

Once more, my dear...I am permitted to write to you. Great has been your disappointment, and great has been my sorrow...but I beg not to dispute at so great a distance. By your desire...I am to give you an account...of the siege; but first let me tell you, it will be done with spirit, for my dislike to the nation that you call your friends is the same as when you knew me, knowing there is no confidence to be placed in them, and I foresee that the whole will end, as this maneuver did...to the discredit of the Americans.

Mary opened with July 29, when a French fleet, intending to help the Continental Army in the coming battle, was sighted off Newport. At first, she said, everybody thought it was Lord Howe and the British fleet. Finding that it was the French, everyone scrambled to defend the town.

....At 11 o'clock, they (the French) all drop anchor off Brenton's Neck...there to wait until the people of your side of the water were ready to attack the lower part of the (Aquidneck) island.

Mary told of the anxiety in the town over the next few days, and of word that Lord Howe was on his way to their defense. She wrote of her terrified children.

Cursed ought, and will be, the man who brought all this woe and desolation on a good people...but judge you, what preparation could I make...six children hanging around me, the little girls crying out, 'Mamma, will they kill us?' The boys endeavor to put on an air of manliness, and strive to assist, but step up to the girls, in a whisper, 'Who do you think will hurt you? Aren't your pappa coming with them?' Indeed, this cut me to the soul.

With "every shot whistling over our own heads," Mary recorded how she and the children fled their home as the French ships began to bombard the town. Each carrying a heavy bundle of belongings, they pushed their way through the panic-filled streets to Brenton's Neck, where she left the little ones on a cousin's farm for safety. The next day, Saturday, August 8, she felt compelled to return to her own house, where she had boarders, and did so in the greatest danger.

To attempt to describe the horrors of that night would pronounce me a fool, for no language could put it in its proper colours. Fire and sword had come amongst us, and famine was not afar off, for want of bread was great.

The next day, Lord Howe finally turned up and, after some maneuvering by both fleets, Howe left and the French followed, both hoping to do battle at sea. But a hurricane suddenly arrived and scattered both fleets. Meanwhile, the revolutionary army edged closer to Newport, hoping that the French fleet would return at any moment.

The food situation was grave for Newport. On August 12, Mary wrote:

The storm still continues....No business going forward; all the shops still kept shut; nothing is to be seen in the streets but carts and horses and some old, worn-out drivers, who care not who was king, or who rebelled against him. It was enough for them to know, if someone did not conquer soon, they and their horses must soon die....I am not like the driver....I am for English government, and an English fleet.

Mary reported on August 13 that people were frightened because of the earthworks the Continental Army was building within sight of Newport, in preparation for battle. Artillery shots were exchanged, but the battle never came. By the end of the month, unable to wait longer for French support, General Sullivan's army was in retreat. The only real battle fought was a rearguard action to cover the withdrawal.

News that the danger was passing came to Mary on August 31, when she also told the first news of her husband.

At 10 o'clock Thomas Hill came in and told me he saw you on Friday and that you...should be at home at breakfast (today) with a

number of gentlemen. Oh! Mr. Almy, what a shocking disappoint-
ment to you. Can you keep up your spirits? Heaven, I hope, will
support you, so positive, so assured of success. Remember, in all
your difficulties and trials of life, that when the All-wise disposer
of human events thinks we have been sufficiently tried, then our
patience in waiting will be amply repaid by a joyful meeting.

Indeed, Benjamin and Mary Almy were reunited at some
point, for our next word of them is that they were again running the Newport boarding house together after the war's
end. Mary, obviously willing to let bygones be bygones, joined
Benjamin in hosting President George Washington when he
visited Rhode Island shortly after the state ratified the U.S.
Constitution in 1790, the last of the thirteen original states
to do so.

Though she took the losing side in the revolution, Mary
Gould Almy certainly deserves to be ranked among Rhode
Island's heroes because of her immense courage, dedication,
and a healthy touch of that contrariness that made — and
still makes — Rhode Island "the independent state."

-PFE

You decide!

THE AMERICAN REVOLUTION

Any American schoolchild will tell you that, in 1776 at least, the Americans were right and the British were wrong. Well, that's not the only point of view. What do you think?

America did the right thing in declaring independence

• King George III and the British government ignored American needs, refusing or neglecting to assent to necessary laws.

• Americans were barred from representation in Parliament, yet were taxed and legislated to death by London.

• The king dissolved colonial legislatures whenever he felt like it, and often made them meet in unusual or far-off places, as Thomas Jefferson put it, "for the sole Purpose of fatiguing them into Compliance with his Measures."

• Britain balked at naturalizing non-British immigrants to the colonies, discouraging settlement of new lands to the west.

• The king's legal whims hampered the courts.

• Britain kept inundating the colonies with new civil servants, "and sent hither Swarms of Officers to harrass our People, and eat out their Substance."

• Britain kept armies in America without the consent of the local legislatures, and independent of their authority.

• Private citizens were obliged to give these troops room and board if told to do so.

• Britain kept too tight a control on America's trade with other nations. This was hard on Rhode Island.

• Rights to trial by jury were suspended at royal caprice.

• With even the hint of revolution in the air, the British plundered some American villages, farms and homes, sometimes using foreign mercenaries. There were atrocities of this kind along the shores of Narragansett Bay.

• The British sometimes forced Americans into their military service, and stirred up the natives against the colonists in some places.

• After all this, London turned a deaf ear to American petitions for redress.

• We as a people were more than mature enough to become a nation, and had gone as far as we could go with the British. It was time.

America made a mistake in declaring independence

• Only about a third of the American population favored the revolution. The rest either didn't care or were against it entirely, wanting to remain British. So much for democracy.

• After defending the colonies in the French and Indian Wars for over seventy years, Britain was broke. The heavy taxes imposed in the 1770s were simply a desperate attempt to recoup from the ones who had been defended.

• The Americans' complaints didn't apply just to America. People in many areas of Britain had it just as bad or worse – taxation without representation, arbitrary laws, having to house and feed troops – the works.

• Many in Britain, even some members of Parliament, believed many of our complaints were valid. Had we worked harder with them, the revolution might have been avoided.

• America would have gained a peaceful independence in the normal course, just as Canada did in 1867.

• The revolution established a culture of "violence is the answer" in America that plagues us to this day.

• Some of Thomas Jefferson's grievances, especially about taxes, could just as easily apply to the government in Washington today!

-PFE

Chapter Five

Rhode Island's Last
⟵ Identity Crisis ⟶

To many of us, the War of 1812 is one of the most mysterious events in American history. There are quite a few people who couldn't tell you with whom it was fought, let alone why. But for Rhode Island, the factors that led to the war, and the circumstances the war created, made for the state's last real identity crisis before it finally found itself.

As usual, Rhode Island's position dripped with irony. The war was so unpopular here that the state joined the rest of New England, and possibly New York, in thinking seriously about seceding from the Union and forming what Massachusetts firebrand Timothy Pickering called a "Northern Confederacy." Such a move could well have led New England back into the waiting arms of the British Empire, and there would have been little that Washington, D.C., could have done about it.

At the same time, however, Rhode Island produced America's greatest naval hero of the war, who led Rhode Islanders in winning the most important naval battle. Nevertheless, events connected with the war virtually finished Rhode Island as a major force in maritime commerce. But this made the state turn to textiles and manufacturing, which opened a whole new world, and eventually led to an industrial golden age.

All this was the result of a long and confusing series of happenings following the American Revolution. Even after Rhode
Island formally joined the Union by ratifying the Constitution in 1790, it was far from smooth sailing when it came to
relations between the cantankerous state and the rest of the
U.S.A. Rhode Islanders, always jealous of their long-held independence, still generally mistrusted the other states and
the new federal government.

This was especially true in economic matters, since Rhode
Island's economy always was precarious. As was true
throughout much of New England, Rhode Island's merchants
just weren't used to obeying the law. Before long, they were
dodging United States revenue cutters and trade regulations
just as they had those of the British before the revolution. To
make matters worse, all American shipping suffered from
the crazy international situation at the very end of the 18th
century and the beginning of the 19th.

Basically, nobody was getting along. Britain and France were
at each other's throats, as usual. American merchant sailors
of British birth were being "shanghaied" on the high seas
and pressed into British naval service. The British rationale
was that many of them had deserted from the British forces
during the revolution.

The French, meanwhile, having overthrown the monarchy
that had helped win the American Revolution, were harassing American shipping because the United States refused to
come to terms with France's new, radical government. This
resulted in a naval war with France. Even the Spanish, who
owned Florida and much of the far West, were hostile because
they were afraid of America's expansionist ideas.

Rhode Island's economy suffered from this all-around mess
because it was hard to carry on the normal oceanic trade on
which the state still depended. In June 1807, the *HMS Leopard*
fired on the *USS Chesapeake* off Virginia, when the American
vessel refused to hand over some British defectors. Three
American sailors were killed, and the whole country rose in
a furor. Rhode Islanders were among the loudest in demand-
ing war, and in pledging their lives to fight it. But New En-

gland contrariness being what it is, it was a different story when President Thomas Jefferson asked for their money instead — in the form of economic sanctions against Britain, Rhode Island's biggest foreign trading partner.

When Jefferson got Congress to pass the Embargo Act that December, it would have been an economic disaster for New England in general and Rhode Island in particular had not merchants and shippers here been so expert at getting around the law. This amazing piece of legislation virtually forbade trade with anybody. Nothing could be legally exported from the United States, and imports from Britain were drastically cut. Drastic as well were federal enforcement methods.

Officially, Rhode Island's foreign exports fell from $1.6 million in 1807 (very big money in those days) to only $240,000 in 1808. Using words like "unjust, tyrannical and unconstitutional," the Rhode Island General Assembly sent an official protest to Washington early in 1809, stating clearly that the state's secession from the Union was not out of the question.

As was the case in the South before the Civil War some fifty years later, this growing secession fever in New England was largely the result of a fundamental disagreement about what kind of society and economy America should have, and, more specifically, about who had the right to call the shots in what areas: Washington or the states. Fanned by politicians of the Federalist Party and the many newspapers that agreed with them, the idea of New England as an independent nation went back to a feud between the liberal theories of Thomas Jefferson, whose disciples were the Republicans, and Alexander Hamilton, represented by the conservative Federalists. The Federalists ran Rhode Island and much of the rest of New England during this period, while Republicans were in the White House.

The Embargo Act and the War of 1812 were just the "straws that broke the camel's back," as far as the Federalists were concerned.

Prompted in part by New England's threat of secession, Congress repealed the Embargo Act in March 1809, and Jefferson signed the measure, resigning himself to the idea that "...we must fight it out (with the British), or break the Union."

Three days afterward, President James Madison, another Republican, took office. There followed a series of blunders and misunderstandings by everyone involved in the international trade crisis. These were compounded by Britain's war against Napolean, and America's inability as a neutral power to carry on trade with one side without getting into trouble with the other.

Mostly because of the almost unbelievable lack of communication with the other countries involved, Congress declared war on Britain (and almost included France) on June 18, 1812.

Often called the "Second American Revolution," this war was supposed to be for the high-minded purpose of defending American honor, free trade, and the rights of sailors on the high seas against the first war's sore losers. But American leaders actually saw it as a chance to conquer British-ruled Canada, and otherwise engage in empire building while Britain was busy trying to hold off Napolean.

"Mr. Madison's War" was unpopular everywhere, but in New England the state governments and most of the people were furious, especially after early American military efforts proved inept. While Rhode Island grudgingly sent its quota of 500 recruits to fight in the regular army, the pro-British Federalist governor, William Jones, refused to allow the state militia to fight for the federal government.

While must Rhode Islanders were huffing and puffing against the war, the war was actually helping the state's economy. The old tradition of privateering reawakened with gusto, and vessels operating out of Narragansett Bay preyed cheerfully on British shipping. The 160-ton brig *Yankee*, owned by James DeWolf of Bristol, alone captured or destroyed $5 million to $6 million worth of British property. Of course, the motivation was not patriotism but profit.

Merchants continued trading with the British on the sly, especially by overland routes through northern New England to Canada.

Probably because they hoped Rhode Island and the rest of New England would secede, the British never attacked

Narragansett Bay, though they blockaded the Atlantic Coast as far north as Connecticut.

Despite their feelings about the war, Rhode Islanders worried about British attack because towns along the Bay were sitting ducks. Ships of any size could sail up and down the Bay in a matter of hours, and Warren, Bristol, East Greenwich, Warwick and Providence had practically no fortifications. Throughout most of the war, there was little or no United States naval presence here. Also vulnerable were Westerly and other towns along the coast.

Rhode Islanders soon took matters into their own hands. Residents donated money to support such home-grown militia units as the Providence Marine Corps of Artillery. Foundries in Pawtucket and other northern towns manufactured muskets and cannon that were stashed at strategic points in case of an emergency. As the war dragged through 1812 and 1813, citizens of all ages pitched in to help raise earthworks to defend Bay towns.

As soon as war was declared, the federal government had made some effort to set up a squadron of gunboats to defend the Bay. Oliver Hazard Perry of South Kingstown, then a twenty-six year-old naval officer, was assigned to the project. From the Newport base where he and his sailors had tried to enforce the Embargo Act, he organized a force of twelve vessels and 350 men. But almost as soon as he did it, Washington ordered the force cut by two thirds, telling Perry that volunteers from the populace would have to help man the boats in case of attack.

Perry was fighting mad, but soon had bigger fish to fry. Early in 1813, he was given one of the most vital assignments of the war: To supervise the building of a squadron of ships on the southern shore of Lake Erie, then to take the ships into battle against the British.

While trying to throw the British off the Great Lakes may not sound very important, it was. American attacks on Canada had been a flop. Unless the United States controlled the Great Lakes, the entire Mississippi Valley and what was then the western frontier would be wide open for invasion. As it was, the British virtually owned lakes Erie and Ontario.

So, in February 1813, Master Commandant Oliver Hazard Perry left his wife, Elizabeth, and their baby son in Newport and headed west to join 150 of his men. Many of these volunteers were Rhode Islanders who insisted on being where the action was with their friend and commander. Among them was Perry's twelve year-old brother Matthew.

In the words of one American statesman, this amazing group of men, "the Rhode Island stock," built from scratch "six vessels, the *Lawrence* of twenty guns...the *Niagara*...the *Ariel* of four guns...the *Porcupine*...the *Tigress*...." It's arguable that Perry's greatest achievement, even more than winning the coming battle, was the successful construction of these ships in only a few months, virtually in the middle of nowhere.

With his six new vessels and four older ones, Perry battled the British on the morning of September 10. It was then that he hoisted his flag with the famous motto, "Don't give up the ship." While he lost his flagship, the *Lawrence*, he moved to the *Niagara,* and from there finished off the British fleet.

In his simple victory message to Washington, Perry coined another sentence for which he is famous: "We have met the enemy and they are ours."

One quarter of Perry's men were Rhode Islanders. Rhode Island officers captained five of the vessels, and men from our state commanded fifty-one of the fifty-four guns. Perry and the other Rhode Islanders returned home to a heroes' welcome, hometown boys regardless of what people thought of the war. There is little question that they brought about the turning point of the war by effectively destroying British power on the Great Lakes. While the war wasn't officially over until February 1815, news of Perry's victory was what spurred the British government to start negotiating for peace because, unless New England seceded, there was nothing to be gained without control of the Great Lakes.

Despite the naval victory and the opening of secret negotiations in Belgium, the war crawled on. In September 1814, the frustrated British seized 100 miles of Maine seacoast, and had a fleet poised to descend on Boston. But even this didn't drive New England closer to the Union.

So, proud as Rhode Island was of Perry and his men, the

state sent four delegates to a convention of the New England states at Hartford, which met in secret session from December 15, 1814, to January 5, 1815. There were observers from New York, too. While extremists wanted secession and a separate peace with Britain at once, the prime purpose of the convention was to mull New England's proposal to defend itself with its own forces using federal tax money collected within its borders.

Most delegates agreed that if Congress didn't accept this and other demands, secession would probably result. But as New England's ambassadors headed for Washington to deliver the demands, news arrived of the signing of a peace treaty at Ghent, Belgium, and of Andrew Jackson's unexpected victory over the British at New Orleans. These timely happenings defused the threat to the Union. Secession would never again be a serious threat in New England.

For Rhode Island, the crowning irony of all came after the war, when everybody suddenly realized that the state's economy was being transformed. Largely because of the war, the age of maritime commerce was ending, and the era of textile manufacturing was beginning. It was to be Rhode Island's heyday.

By 1815, there were no less than 149 factories within thirty miles of Providence, with a total of 130,000 spindles that produced 27,840,000 yards of cloth. Amazingly, Rhode Islanders now found themselves supporting the very trade measures they had once opposed: Their new manufacturing interests now needed strong federal tariff protection.

Along with the rest of the country, Rhode Island finally seemed to know where it was going. Unity and prosperity — industrial prosperity — were on America's horizon, at least for the North, and Rhode Island would be the leader. Instead of being the schemers and secessionists, Rhode Islanders only a few decades later would be the first to respond to Abraham Lincoln's call for troops to preserve the Union in its worst crisis of all: the Civil War.

-PFE

The Rhode Islander
Who Captured Lake Erie

In the Rotunda of the U.S. Capitol is a magnificent painting that every Rhode Islander should see. Its subject is Oliver Hazard Perry of South Kingstown, Rhode Island's most celebrated naval hero, and certainly one of America's greatest. With his knack for getting things done, and his brilliant leadership ability, Perry was able to help turn the War of 1812 around in favor of the United States through his victory over the British on Lake Erie.

Perryville, just south of Wakefield, bears his name because this is where he was born on August 23, 1785. It's interesting that Rhode Island's two greatest war heroes, Oliver Hazard Perry and Nathanael Greene, had a common ancestor who was, ironically, a Quaker.

Both the sea and service to their country evidently were in the Perry family's blood. Oliver's father, Christopher, was a naval officer during the American Revolution, and his younger brother, Matthew, was the one whose 1853 naval expedition opened Japan to trade with the West. Oliver was educated in the best private schools of Newport, and began his naval career in 1799 as a midshipman, or officer cadet, on his father's ship. He was only fourteen. He saw service in the West Indies and, in 1801, against pirates in the Mediterranean Sea. In 1805, he was promoted to lieutenant.

When Congress passed the hated Embargo Act in 1807, Perry found himself back in Newport with the unenviable job of having to enforce that law with a few gunboats. He wasn't popular and, for that matter, the U.S. Navy wasn't either. Many times, Perry was on the verge of resigning from

*William H. Powell's 1873 painting of Oliver Hazard Perry's victory on Lake Erie is in the Rotunda of the U.S. Capitol. It shows him leading a boat crew through heavy British fire to the **USS Niagara**, where Perry took command, leading the Americans to victory.*

-Photo by Paul F. Eno

the Navy, but something always prevented him. The biggest "something" of all happened in and after 1812, when the United States went to war with Britain. At first asked to defend Narragansett Bay against a possible British attack, Perry later requested, and got, the job that would make him famous.

"You are just the man I have been looking for!" crowed Commodore Isaac Chauncey when he made the assignment.

So, in March 1813, the twenty-eight year-old Master Commandant Perry arrived on the Ohio shore of Lake Erie to oversee the building of a fleet to help get rid of the British on the Great Lakes. With him were 150 volunteers, many of whom were Rhode Islanders from his old command. This was practically an impossible job because these men were in the wilderness with few resources for building, let alone arming, the vessels. To make matters worse, there was a British base right across the lake, on the Canadian side, where ships were being readied for battle.

Perry was frantic for manpower. By mid-July, he had only

300 men, and had just received a message from the War Department to get out onto the lake and start fighting. Beside himself, he wrote to Chauncey: "For God's sake, and yours and mine, send me men!"

In response, Perry got sixty old and sickly sailors. Furious, he went out into the countryside and started recruiting every farmer, woodsman and traveler he could find, dangling $10 before each one for one month's service. This was a princely sum for the times.

By some miracle, Oliver Hazard Perry pulled it off, and in only a few months. By scaring up not only sailors but carpenters, blacksmiths and scrap iron, and setting up a supply line from Pittsburgh, he had six new ships armed and ready to sail by early August. By using special floats, he got his vessels over the sandbar that protected his base and, on September 10, defeated the British, making the apparent United States failure on the Great Lakes a victory. It was the turning point of the war because, without control of the lakes, the British lost their big chance to capture the Ohio and Mississippi Valleys, and they knew it.

After the war, Captain Oliver Hazard Perry took command of the *USS John Adams*. In 1819, he was sent on a diplomatic mission to Venezuela. While there, he caught yellow fever and died. Buried at Port Spain, his remains were returned to Newport in 1826, where they were reburied with great honor. The jacket that Perry wore during the Battle of Lake Erie is on display at the Museum of Rhode Island History at Aldrich House in Providence.

-PFE

The Ironic Governor
Willian Jones

Rhode Island's history is filled with irony. One of the most ironic situations was that of Governor William Jones, a hero of the American Revolution who, during the War of 1812, ended up a British sympathizer and a thorn in the side of the young United States Government. Today, many of us would be tempted to write Jones off as a traitor. But, as with most things in life, it isn't as simple as that: There were indeed two sides to the story.

Jones was a Newporter, born there on October 8, 1753. He became a carpenter, and was working at this when, in January 1776, he got a commission as a lieutenant in one of the two regiments raised by the Rhode Island General Assembly, and which would go on to do great things in the American Revolution. Building a terrific battle record in New York and New Jersey, and as commander of marines aboard the frigate *Providence*, Jones was captured by the British on May 10, 1780.

After the war, Jones went to Providence and ran a hardware business with his brothers. He represented the city in the General Assembly, beginning in 1807, and, in 1811, at the age of fifty seven, was elected governor of Rhode Island. Jones belonged to the Federalist Party, and understanding what that meant is the key to knowing William Jones, and Rhode Island, at this crucial time.

The Republican Party of today got its start in the Federalist Party of Jones's day. Basically, the Federalists believed in the ideas of Alexander Hamilton: that people were unequal in both intelligence and social standing, and that only the "best" people should govern the country for the good of all. They wanted an economy based on commerce and industry, and a strong central government based on a rigid interpretation of the Constitution.

Strangely enough, the Republican Party of Jones's period became the Democratic Party of today. This party followed Thomas Jefferson in believing in a "natural aristocracy" of the common folk.

"Those who labor in the earth are the chosen people of God," Jefferson had said. They stressed an economy based on agriculture and other non-industrial pursuits. They also liked what would come to be called "states' rights," and a loose interpretation of the Constitution. Both points of view had deep roots in different social philosophies that went all the way back to ancient Greece, and both would cause plenty of trouble for the United States. As a matter of fact, the battle between these very different ideas about what America was supposed to be would lead to the Civil War. It sometimes creates tension between the states and the federal government even today.

So, while William Jones and his Federalist colleagues ran Rhode Island and New England, the Republicans held power in most other parts of the country and, in the person of Jefferson himself, in the White House.

The French Revolution, which overthrew the monarchy that had helped America win its independence, began in 1789. Jefferson and the Republicans thought all this was great because here was a radical people's uprising that seemed to stand for everything the Republicans believed in. Later, they got upset with the new French government, especially when Napolean took over, but they still admired the basic revolutionary ideas. Meanwhile, the Federalists looked at the Republicans with the same fear and mistrust they had for the French revolutionaries, who had massacred the "best" people in their own society, and thrown their country into chaos. The Federalists looked to the solid, conservative principles of British society to save America from what the French – and the Republicans — represented.

This, along with the many economic reasons, was why William Jones and most other Rhode Islanders opposed the War of 1812 against Britain, which was declared and directed by the Republicans. With all this in mind, perhaps it's easier to see that Jones and those like him were, in their own view, actually being patriotic by opposing the federal government and siding, at least in spirit, with the British.

After the war started, President James Madison ordered that the state militias be transferred to the jurisdiction of the federal government. Along with the Federalist governors of Connecticut and Massachusetts, William Jones refused, saying that Washington had no right to take militias from their own states. This was in 1813.

The following year, Jones warned Washington that "notwithstanding our respect for the law and our strong attachment to the union of the states, there may be evils greater than can be apprehended from a refusal to submit to unconstitutional laws."

It isn't surprising that Jones sent four delegates to represent Rhode Island at the Hartford Convention at the end 1814. Today we might be carrying New England passports and saluting the Pine Tree Flag if the hated war hadn't ended just a short time later.

In spite of these sorry times, Rhode Island at the end of the war found itself on the road to industrial greatness. William Jones, who was governor until 1817, was a leader in helping Rhode Island conquer the peace that followed. Despite views that to modern Americans might seem odd, he well deserves his place among Rhode Island's great leaders. He died in Providence on April 22, 1822, respected as a man of courtesy, honesty and dedication.

-PFE

Chapter Six

Rhode Island's
⚓ People Arise! ⚓

As this book was being readied for publication in 2004, Rhode Island lawmakers were talking about a constitutional convention. So it was one of those rare times when people outside the court system were paying attention to the Rhode Island Constitution: a document that wasn't easy to come by.

Few people realize that it took an armed uprising against the state government to dislodge the Royal Charter of 1663, and finally get a constitution into place in 1843. Named for its shining star, Thomas Wilson Dorr of Providence, the "Dorr Rebellion" or "Dorr War" was the main event of a long battle for a state constitution that would give every Rhode Islander a fair shake. Don't let its comic-opera aspects fool you: Some historians consider the Dorr War the most important happening in Rhode Island history. It was a battle between old and new, native and immigrant, country and city. Before its echoes died away, it had involved the president of the United States, Congress, the U.S. Supreme Court, and several other states. It sent shock waves to every corner of the nation, prompted debate among America's finest lawyers and scholars, and had affects that still are felt today. Of course, Rhode Island was never the same again.

Ever since 1663, when it arrived in the form of a huge parchment in a great big box, Rhode Islanders had loved their Royal Charter. This was because the Charter was one of the most liberal documents of its time, making Rhode Island practically an independent republic, and throwing in human-rights guarantees that were way ahead of their time.

When the American Revolution came, Rhode Islanders fought just as hard to maintain their own independence as to gain it for the whole country. Compared with most of the others, the state was out in front when it came to democratic principles and civil liberties. But throughout America, it was still rich aristocrats who made most of the decisions. Unless a man owned land, he usually couldn't even vote. Women, "people of color," and other minorities, of course, had little to say about anything, let alone government. In some states, many freedoms, particularly religious ones, still weren't guaranteed. In Rhode Island, religious freedom and free speech were old traditions already. A majority of men could vote because a majority of men either were farmers who owned rural land or town dwellers who owned at least a house, thanks to the prosperity brought by maritime commerce.

After the revolution, Rhode Island and Connecticut were the only states that kept their colonial charters as instruments of government. Connecticut adopted a constitution in 1818, but Rhode Island continued rumbling along with its Royal Charter.

Following the War of 1812, when Andrew Jackson pranced onto the scene with the age of man-on-the-street democracy, and other states were liberalizing, Rhode Island suddenly found itself one of the least democratic. This was largely because, almost under Rhode Islanders' noses, the state's economy had shifted away from the farm and the wharf, and had turned to the mill and the factory. As the populations of Warwick and other northern towns started to grow, fewer and fewer people there owned land. Two big problems — both caused by the Charter — started to show that it was out of whack when it came to this new economic reality. The heart of the problem was the way the Charter set up the General Assembly. Representation was fixed, regardless of how or where the population grew. Newport had six representatives,

Providence, Portsmouth and Warwick four each, and all other towns two each. There was no legal way to amend the Charter, so the problem couldn't be fixed. Because of this, the now numerous rural towns that had stopped growing could easily outvote in the General Assembly the towns that were growing. The old Newport elite, and the farmers and landowners in the countryside, refused to change the rule that a man had to own at least $134 worth of property (respectable for the times) in order to vote. Hence, the new generation of urban workers, and other city dwellers who didn't own land, found themselves second-class citizens with virtually no chance to change things.

As the 1810s turned into the '20s and '30s, the problem got worse as thousands of foreign immigrants, primarily Irish at first, poured into northern Rhode Island's swelling urban areas. Eventually, most of these became American citizens. The rural Yankees weren't about to give the vote to the foreign-born, naturalized or not, especially if they were Roman Catholics, whom they were afraid had primary loyalty to "a foreign potentate" – the pope.

The seeds of the mess that turned into the Dorr War actually started to sprout as early as 1782, when South County towns called for reform because they had been told to pay an unequal share of the state's Revolutionary War debt. Ten years later, Smithfield, a growing town whose people felt they had been gypped by the Charter, called for a constitutional convention to help fix the apportionment situation. After the General Assembly quadrupled its taxes, Providence and six other towns joined this call, with a convention of their own in 1796, which got nowhere. Significantly, the idea that the people could bypass the state government, and get together on their own to draft a constitution, was voiced as early as this.

From 1811 to 1821, several reformers tried to get things moving toward an equitable state constitution, largely without success. In 1824, a statewide constitutional convention finally got off the ground. The document that resulted was progressive in some ways — it included a formal bill of rights and would have made General Assembly representation more equal — but it did practically nothing to resolve the right-to-vote dilemma. No matter. The proposed constitution sank at the polls two-to-one, again because those who could vote wanted to keep things the way they were.

Thomas W. Dorr and a home builder named Seth Luther entered the picture in the mid-1830s with their founding of the Constitutional Party as a reaction to the constitutional convention of 1834, which also failed to produce anything. Dorr managed to get elected to the General Assembly from Providence, and he worked hard for reform. Nonetheless, the Constitutional Party petered out after a few years, and Dorr and his followers realized they were dead in the water.

During the 1830s, Rhode Island was controlled by the Democrats (the party that would become today's Republicans), who favored the Charter. The opposing party was the Whigs, who wanted better apportionment but, out of fear that the immigrants weren't loyal to America, didn't want to extend voting rights.

The frustration of Dorr, Luther, and other voting-rights activists started coming to a head in 1840, when they founded the Rhode Island Suffrage Association. They organized mass demonstrations in Providence, complete with bands, parades and torchlight processions. Naturally this raised eyebrows among those in power, and created fear in many a heart at the State House. These 1840 rumblings from the people were partially the result of agitation in Rhode Island by New York's Equal Rights Democrats. Their pamphlet on how the people could get reform by establishing their own government was popular reading among those who were denied the vote. It especially impressed Dorr.

Fearing trouble, the General Assembly authorized yet another constitutional convention, this one set for November 1841. But the activists, with Dorr now their acclaimed leader, knew there wasn't an ounce of sincerity in that move. Fed up, they called a "People's Convention" in October, and drafted a constitution of their own — with plenty of voting rights and liberal reapportionment. The "Dorrites," as they came to be known, even organized a popular referendum (boycotted by the Charter people, naturally) in which they invited all white men to participate. Their would-be constitution was approved by nearly all of the 14,000 men who showed up. Because there were only some 23,000 adult white males in the state, Dorr proclaimed that the people had spoken, and that the Charter government was history.

Needless to say, this resulted in months of chaos to which Samuel Gorton himself could hardly have taken exception. The state government was alarmed, and it outlawed the "People's Constitution" on April 2, 1842. Ignoring this, the "People's Government" elected Dorr governor of Rhode Island on April 18. Two days after Dorr's election, the regular state elections took place, and Governor Samuel Ward King of Johnston was re-elected.

A few weeks later, on May 3, the People's Government inaugurated Dorr in a Providence foundry. The next day, the Charter government inaugurated King in Newport. In this tense situation, Rhode Island found itself with two governments, one legal but unpopular, the other popular but illegal. Yet, even as Dorr's "administration" got under way, the Charter government started making shrewd moves to cut the support from under him. After outlawing Dorr's government, Governor King appealed to President John Tyler for federal support in case of an armed uprising. Washington gave him the assurances he wanted. Tyler even ordered an increase in the number of federal troops stationed at Fort Adams in Newport. The Charter government, now calling itself the "Law and Order Party" also inflamed the sectional, religious and ethnic fears of the population by spreading all sorts of drivel about the Dorrites' sinister intentions. The Charter people even buttered up the African-Americans.

Most importantly, the Charter government in February had approved its own "Freemen's Constitution," which extended suffrage to all native-born white males. This stole much of the thunder from Dorr's cause, and spurred many defections from his side when push came to shove that spring. Dorr went to Washington to appeal to President Tyler, but to no avail. On the way home, Dorr's dejection turned to enthusiasm once again when political bosses in New York City, where immigrant power was considerably stronger than in Rhode Island, received him like a hero, and promised to send their state militia to support him in the effort to dislodge the Charter government once and for all.

Dorr was greeted by cheering crowds on his return to Providence, where he set up a command post on Federal Hill. Governor King, with genuine fear, issued a general call to arms for those loyal to the Charter government.

On the night of May 18, 1842, Dorr and a band of 234 armed supporters tried to attack the Cranston Street Armory. They dragged two ancient cannon from the Mall, but the night was wet, and the things refused to work. Not a shot was fired during this farce, but the Dorrites managed to yell insults at the armory's 200-odd defenders before breaking up in disarray. This attempt at violence only managed to horrify all but Dorr's most extreme supporters. The next day, Dorr fled to Woonsocket, a hotbed of Dorrism because of its large number of landless workers, and vainly tried to reorganize his forces.

Then, his movement temporarily in shambles, Dorr secretly left for New York. The Rhode Island militia was at his heels until he crossed into Connecticut. The "People's Governor" continued his agitation from afar. By June, rumors were circulating that pro-Dorr troops and equipment were massing along Connecticut's border with northwestern Rhode Island. Then, in mid-June, small Dorrite demonstrations started in Woonsocket, and Dorrites seized and fortified Acote Hill in Chepachet, seventeen miles from Providence.

Governor King sent a frantic plea to Washington for help. The president sent the secretary of war to Rhode Island, telling him to muster the militias of Connecticut and Massachusetts, and even federal troops in Newport, to help defend the Charter government from the expected invasion, which never came. Dorr had plenty of sympathizers in Massachusetts, so King sent the Kentish Guards of Warwick and East Greenwich to Pawtucket to help guard the bridge over the Blackstone River, which at the time was still the border between Rhode Island and the Bay State.

Dorr himself arrived in Chepachet on June 25, with a small band of volunteers from New York, and was greeted by about

1,000 of his stalwarts. Dorr's actual intention was simply to get the People's Government going again. In his own mind, the military preparations were for defense only. Meanwhile, King found out that Dorr was back, and sent out another frenzied call for troops. Virtually creating a special army overnight, King sent 3,500 impromptu soldiers marching toward Chepachet on June 27. Then King had the General Assembly declare martial law throughout the state.

When the Dorrites heard about the enormous force that was after them, Dorr sent his followers home, and himself beat a hasty path to New York's friendlier shores. When the Charter army arrived on the 28th, they stormed Acote Hill, only to find its "fortifications" occupied by a cow. But they took a number of "prisoners," mostly curious bystanders or dejected Dorrites who were on their way home.

Martial law lasted for forty days. In the state of galloping paranoia that prevailed, nearly 300 people were taken into custody in often indiscriminate arrests. Many homes were ransacked in search of evidence against the owners. The search of one Warren home caused a massive civil lawsuit that reached the U.S. Supreme Court.

After all this bumbling, to say that Dorr actually won the "war" would seem ridiculous. But, in a way, he did. Late in 1842, the state government summoned another constitutional convention, which came up with the Constitution we have today. This document in many ways met the demands the Dorrites had cried for all along. Although it kept the $134 property qualification for naturalized citizens who wanted to vote, it gave the vote to native African-American males as a reward for supporting the Law and Order Party. The Constitution was overwhelmingly ratified in a referendum, and it took effect in May 1843.

Dorr himself later came home, and spent time in jail for "treason against Rhode Island." Efforts to get vindication for Dorr and the People's Constitution from the U.S. Supreme Court and Congress proved fruitless. While he was later pardoned, Dorr was a broken man, and died in 1854, convinced that he had been a failure.

Dorr and those who fought beside him were certain that

they were upholding the principles exalted in the Declaration of Independence by seeking to overthrow an oppressive regime. After all, Thomas Jefferson had said clearly that a little revolution now and then was good for America!

Probably the most important legal and philosophical point of the whole business was that those principles didn't really hold true in the eyes of the very governments established upon them. When President Tyler and Congress refused to recognize Dorr, and the Supreme Court refused to challenge that lack of recognition, it can be argued that the principles of the American Revolution were dealt a fatal blow, or at least radically altered.

As for Rhode Island, the conservative state had become more democratic, but the independent state had finally become a comfortable home for the *status quo.*

It's fascinating – and very ironic – to consider the fact that one of the reasons for the proposed constitutional convention in the early years of the 21st century was to reduce the power of the General Assembly and increase the power of the governor! This would do away with the dominance of the legislature — one of the last remnants of the Charter of 1663 — and, some might say, reduce the voice of the people as expressed through their representatives, all so that we could be like every other state.

Thomas W. Dorr would do somersaults in his grave!

-PFE

The Man
Who Meant Well

Whoever said "The road to hell is paved with good intentions" must have been intimately acquainted with Thomas Wilson Dorr, one of the most praiseworthy yet tragic figures Rhode Island has ever produced. Dorr was an unlikely revolutionary. A brilliant soul, his high-minded principles and lofty intentions were no match for the practical know-how of his enemies. He died a relatively young man, beaten, broken, bitter, and unjustly maligned by many historians.

Descended from a Revolutionary War hero on his father's side and from a companion of Roger Williams on his mother's, Dorr was born in 1805 to Sullivan and Lydia (Allen) Dorr. His father was a rich Providence merchant and industrialist, and he was liberal with his money as far as his son's education was concerned.

After graduating from Harvard at an age when most of us would just be finishing high school, Dorr went on to become a lawyer in Providence and New York. It was in the latter city that he ran into leading voices of the equal-rights movements spawned during the era of Andrew Jackson. These men were a profound influence on Dorr. Back in Rhode Island, Dorr became a leader of the Constitutional Party in 1834. As a state representative from Providence, he raised eyebrows by constantly lobbying for equal rights in Rhode Island, primarily in the form of the vote for all adult white males, not just those who owned $134 worth of real estate.

Dorr comes across as a headstrong, but often naive, man who ended up with what could be described as the wrong execution of the right idea. As his popularity grew among those who couldn't vote, his suffrage movement became more and more militant. This may have been because it all went to his head somewhat. In many ways, Dorr was his own worst enemy, despite his intelligence. Had Dorr not put so much trust in the promises of military support he got from corrupt New York politicians, he probably would have been more careful in his dealings with Rhode Island's government. Had he been more moderate, he might even have convinced federal authorities to at least stay neutral on his claim to authority in Rhode Island under the People's Constitution. And if he hadn't chosen the military alternative at the Cranston Street Armory in May 1842, he wouldn't have lost most of his following. And so on.

It's important to remember, though, that Dorr never meant to be an insurrectionist. He fully believed in the legality of the People's Constitution, and he really thought the Charter government would step aside peacefully once the upwelling of grassroots support for the document became clear.

When Dorr fled Chepachet on June 27, 1842, just before the Acote Hill fiasco, he spent the night in Thompson, Connecticut, then headed for his second exile, this time in New Hampshire. From there, he wrote letters urging Rhode Islanders to boycott the referendum for Rhode Island's proposed constitution, late in 1842, because he felt that the People's Constitution was still in force.

Failing in every attempt to save his cause, Dorr decided to return home and face the music. In his sixty-page *Address to the People of Rhode Island,* written just before he left New Hampshire, he tried to explain all his feelings, and his whole course of action.

When Dorr reappeared in Providence, on October 31, 1843, he was arrested immediately, and hurled into jail. On April 26, 1844, his trial for "high treason against the state" opened before the Rhode Island Supreme Court, with a judge and jury who were just itching to crucify him. Dorr conducted much of his own defense, which was another blunder, even though he was a lawyer. By May 6, it was all over. Dorr was sentenced to life imprisonment at hard labor. His supporters were outraged, and the issue soon came to national attention. It wasn't long before Dorr's imprisonment became a political liability for the "Law and Order Party" rulers. Dorr was freed on June 27, 1845, after political victories by the Dorr Liberation Society.

Attempts to legally vindicate Dorr and the People's Constitution went on for years. Finally, in 1851, the General Assembly restored Dorr's political rights and, in 1854, reversed the judgment of the Supreme Court that had convicted him of treason. But Dorr refused to take heart from these things.

"All is lost save honor," he wrote.

He died in Providence on December 27, 1854, at the age of forty nine. Even though he believed he was a failure, Dorr still refused to give up his tenacious beliefs. His bad judgment and worse luck do nothing to overshadow the enormous influence he had on the history of Rhode Island.

He is buried in Swan Point Cemetery, Providence, under a simple stone. A marker proclaiming the "People's Constitution" is there, along with the U.S. and, ironically, the Rhode Island Governor flags.

-PFE

The grave of the "People's Governor," Thomas Wilson Dorr, at Swan Point Cemetery, Providence.

-Photo by Paul F. Eno

Rhode Island's
First Working Class Hero

Seth Luther was a home builder who joined hands with Thomas W. Dorr in the early 1830s to fight for voting rights for the "average Joe" in Rhode Island. While Dorr was born a part of the state's well-to-do "in crowd," Luther was a man who got his hands dirty every day by doing hefty manual labor.

A self-educated chap who read every book he could get his labor-calloused hands on, Luther had that rare quality of being both a fiery writer/speaker and a man who knew what he was talking about. In the early 1830s, while he was a journeyman carpenter, he was known as a labor agitator as far away as New York City and Boston, where he helped form the Boston Trades' Union. Along with barber William I. Tillinghast, Luther led the Providence Workingmen's Association.

"Men of property," Luther remarked in an 1832 address, "find no fault with combinations (*meaning conspiracies, PFE*) to extinguish fires and to protect their precious persons from danger. But if poor men ask justice, it is a most horrible combination."

He never hesitated to call on the principles of the American Revolution, in which his father had fought. And in his flowery prose, he constantly thumbed his nose at Rhode Island's political and social establishment: those "mushroom lordlings, sprigs of nobility . . . small potato aristocrats."

He even argued for the equal treatment of women in the workplace as early as 1819.

Luther sometimes went a little overboard with sarcasm and

swagger in his speeches to workers, threatening violent rebellion, but he quite rightly cried that Rhode Island's denial of the vote to men who didn't own $134 worth of real estate was "contrary to the Declaration of Independence, the Constitution of the United States, the Bill of Rights of the State of Rhode Island and the dictates of common sense."

It isn't hard to see his influence in Dorr's later militant actions when we read Luther's words "resist tyranny, if need be, sword in hand!"

"The people" have, he added, "a right to...form a Constitution, and submit it" for adoption "as the law of the land."

It can be argued, especially by labor historians, that Seth Luther was a more important factor in the Dorr War than Dorr. It also can be argued that he was Rhode's Island's answer to Vladimir Lenin. Certainly, Luther was one of America's first workers' activists, and he is a true hero to today's labor movement, where his name is still known and honored.

Seth Luther shares with Dorr a place among the nation's most memorable reformers, and among Rhode Island's most courageous figures.

-PFE

The 'Battle'
of Acote Hill

Few motorists know the name of the little hill they skirt as they drive into Chepachet from the east on Route 44. Fewer still know its significance in Rhode Island's history.

It's Acote or Acote's Hill, at 505 feet above sea level, tied with North Scituate's Bald Hill as the state's 52nd-highest named summit. And it was there that a nearly bloodless and seemingly comical "battle" was fought at the end of the Dorr Rebellion. On a deeper level, however, what happened on and around Acote Hill during the summer of 1842 marked the end of an era both for Rhode Island and America.

The mill towns of northern Rhode Island were the places where support for Thomas W. Dorr and the People's Constitution were strongest. As a matter of fact, it was Dorrite militia that controlled much of the state's northern areas during the spring of 1842. Impromptu units with names like Dorr's Invincibles, the Johnston Savages, the Pascoag Ripguts, the Pawtucket Invincibles, and the Harmonious Reptiles lived up to their names, patrolling conspicuously, and acting as vigilantes in the area.

It was Chepachet, then, that Dorr chose when he decided to return to Rhode Island after his New York exile. Looking at that busy but still lovely village today, it's not hard to imagine the scene on June 25, 1842, when Dorr arrived with "Big Mike" Walsh, a hack of Dorr's allies, the corrupt New York City Democratic administration. With them were about a dozen goons from a New York immigrant ghetto. These New Yorkers supported Dorr for a number of complex political reasons, and the otherwise honorable Dorr accepted the sup-

Site of the last "battle" of the Dorr Rebellion, this is Chepachet's Acote Hill today.

-Photo by Paul F. Eno

port for a number of equally complex reasons.

Rumors of Dorr's return had sparked considerable alarm in Providence, which expected a massive invasion by forces of the "People's Governor" at any moment. A defending army numbering some 3,500 men, and led by West Point graduate William Gibbs McNeill, was organized with a frenzy. Governor Samuel Ward King and other Charter potentates obviously had it in their heads to smash the Constitution forces once and for all, at their "fort" on Acote Hill. They also planned to occupy Woonsocket, a hotbed of Dorrism, and cut off any rebel escape to Massachusetts or Connecticut. The Charter army marched from Providence on June 27. Little did they know that Dorr's supporters in Chepachet already had dwindled from about 1,000 to only 225 diehards. Dorr's idea had been to convene his "People's Legislature" at Sprague's Tavern (today's Stagecoach Tavern) in Chepachet on the Fourth of July. But none of its members showed up.

When Dorr heard of the formidable army the Charter forces were sending, he wisely decided to call off the showdown and send all his followers home. Some, however, got no farther than the tavern. Dorr himself fled to New Hampshire, where the sympathetic Democratic governor took him in.

Meanwhile, the Charter army marched on. They captured a Dorrite messenger near Greenville, and found out about the disbanding of Dorr's army. But McNeill and other leaders thought they still should attack Acote Hill, capturing as many "rebels" as possible for their propaganda value. The report that appeared in the June 28 issue of the pro-Charter *Providence Journal* told that the state militia "has taken the insurgent fortification. Dorr has fled but large numbers of his men have been captured."

The truth was that state troops had made fools of themselves by charging up Acote Hill, only to find the makeshift "fortifications" occupied by a startled cow. As for the capture of "large numbers of his men," this was mainly the indiscriminate rounding up of practically anyone who was handy. In one of the most shameful incidents of the whole affair, according to local sources, Charter forces surrounded Sprague's Tavern, found the door locked, and faced off through the windows with a few Dorrites inside. State troops backed down, but not before one of them blasted a hole in the door, wounding a man inside, and creating the only casualty of the whole operation.

Glocester town historian Edna Kent reports that, literally adding insult to injury, some of the state troops virtually commandeered Sprague's Tavern for much of the rest of the summer, while they terrorized the country 'round. They reportedly guzzled thirty-seven gallons of brandy, twenty-nine gallons of West India rum, thirty-four flasks of liquor, dozens of bottles of old Madeira wine and sherry, twelve dozen bottles of champagne, and two dozen bottles of cider. Between them, the troops and their horses supposedly chowed down 820 bushels of oats, seventeen tons of hay, fifty bushels of corn, sixteen bushels of meal, and a quarter ton of straw. In all, the militiamen are said to have sucked up 2,400 dinners and smoked 11,500 cigars.

The unfortunate Mr. Sprague, who apparently was the source of most of this bounty, never collected a penny from the state government.

This whole affair was a fiasco, with innocent people being confined in filthy cells without due process, searches and seizures without warrants, and the gross abuse of civil liberties for the people of Chepachet and the surrounding country.

The "Battle of Acote Hill" was, of course, the swansong of Thomas W. Dorr, one of America's greatest, albeit unorthodox, reformers. The effective end of the People's Constitution movement, the "battle" also might be called the symbolic end of the spirit of the Declaration of Independence.

-PFE

The Murder
of Amasa Sprague

Did Rhode Island hang the wrong man when Irish immigrant John Gordon swung from the gallows in front of what is now the State House in Providence? Gordon's life came to an end on Valentine's Day 1845, and no one has been executed in Rhode Island since, despite many capital offenses deemed far worse that the one for which Gordon was arrested, convicted and hanged.

In those years, there was a prison at the site of today's State House, and this is where Gordon met his fate amid controversy rarely seen even in today's headlines.

THE CRIME

New Year's Eve 1843 fell on a Sunday, and being a man of routine, wealthy industrialist Amasa Sprague finished his dinner, bid his wife, Fanny, and his four children goodbye, and left his Cranston Street mansion for his weekly walk to check Carpenter Place, property he owned on Plainfield Pike in Johnston. Sprague had built his sumptuous home across from the Cranston Print Works, which he and his brother, U.S. Senator William Sprague, operated as their family business.

It was a cold, windy December 31 when Sprague bundled his five-foot, nine-inch, 190-pound frame into heavy clothing and set out on foot to view his holdings. It was 3:20 in the afternoon when he walked slowly along a well-worn path on land now making up St. Ann's Cemetery. There was a small building called Dyer's Schoolhouse and, being a Sunday, a church service conducted by Rev. Solomon Risley was ending. One of the congregation was Elsie Baxter, who would later recall seeing Sprague walk by.

As Sprague crossed a small bridge over Pocasset Brook, and began walking up an incline toward Carpenter Place, the silence of the snow-covered scene was shattered by the crack of a gunshot. A musket ball struck Sprague in the right wrist, knocking him off his feet, and causing him to brace himself with his left hand as he hit the snow. Although wounded and bleeding, Sprague struggled to his feet and, instead of heading to Carpenter Place, just over a mound, he started to run back toward the bridge, a mistake that would prove fatal.

Dripping a trail of blood, Sprague ran across the bridge, only to be met by the butt of a gun against his skull. He and his attacker fell from the bridge and, while the injured Sprague fought back, he was no match for his assailant. Within seconds, the mill owner lay mortally wounded in the snow, which was rapidly turning red with his blood.

Michael Costello had worked around the Sprague mansion as a handyman for three years and, since his work week included Sundays, he was finishing a long day, and was anxious to get home to his family. At 4:30 p.m., Costello left the Sprague house and started toward his own home nearby. Taking the same path as Sprague, Costello noticed some blood on the bridge where the struggle had occurred. Although it was getting dark, Costello saw a man lying beneath the small span. The body seemed to be resting on its hands and knees, and he did not recognize it as his boss. Instead of checking the body, Costello made his way to Carpenter Place and told the occupants what he had just seen.

He then hurried to the home of Dr. Israel M. Bowen, who was not there but was expected to arrive shortly. Several neighbors who had gathered to welcome the new year accompanied Costello to the scene to view the body and await Dr. Bowen. Once there, Bowen turned the body, discovering that it was the well known Amasa Sprague. He immediately sent one of the men to fetch the state coroner, Robert Wilson, who ordered the body taken to the Sprague mansion.

A pistol was found at the scene, and police impounded the weapon as evidence. Sprague had died of massive head wounds, including one so severe that it had penetrated his brain. Most of the bones in his face were broken. Word of his murder sent shock waves through the Cranston community, and started a long, bitter battle between two factions in Rhode Island: those for and those against capital punishment.

THE GORDONS

Nicholas Gordon came to America from Ireland in the 1810s. He settled in Cranston, opening a grocery store near the A&W Sprague Company, another of that family's enterprises.

The Gordon store was popular with folks in and around the town, especially since Gordon sold liquor. Eventually, Gordon was required to obtain a liquor license, but because Amasa Sprague paid his employees monthly, production would drop significantly for the first two days after payday. Determined to put a stop to this, Sprague lobbied the Cranston Town Council to deny Gordon a liquor license. A meeting was called to take up the issue, and the council sided with the influential Sprague.

Naturally this strained Gordon's business, and the storekeeper remained livid. Sprague may have had another reason for wanting Gordon to fail. On one occasion, he was seen to have met Gordon on a path. Grabbing the immigrant, Sprague pushed him aside, saying, "Get out of my way, you damned Irishman!"

Gordon managed to make a living without selling liquor. He eventually sent for his mother, Ellen; sister, Margaret; and brothers, William, Robert and John; and William's ten year-old daughter, to come from Ireland and live with him in Cranston.

Amasa Sprague was laid to rest in a small plot behind his home. His family posted a $1,000 reward for the arrest and conviction of his killer. When names of those with a possible motive were considered, Nicholas Gordon topped the list. On the occasion of the liquor-license debacle, Gordon had been heard to tell Sprague that he would see him again before the year was out. A woman, Susan Field, told reporters she heard Gordon say, "Goddamn the man" who ever took his liquor license from him; he would "be the death of him."

The only people in Cranston who did not pay their respects at the Sprague funeral were the Gordons.

On Monday night, January 1, 1844, police went to Nicholas Gordon's home on Cranston Road, and arrested both him and his brother John on suspicion of murder. They were held as a large party searched the area where Sprague had been found. A coat with blood on the sleeve, and a box of gunpowder, were found. Also recovered was the broken stock from a musket, also containing blood and hair. Footprints in the snow were traced to the back door of Nicholas Gordon's house, although by this time there were hundreds of such prints from the throng of people playing amateur detective.

Police broke down the door of the Gordon's house, and searched for more clues. They did the same at the adjoining grocery store, where they found still-wet boots and more clothing that contained what looked like bloodstains. Police arrested Gordon's elderly mother, his three brothers, and even the family dog, which they believed had accompanied the Gordons when they killed Sprague! Spared arrest was William Gordon's ten year-old daughter.

THE TRIAL

On January 15, it was announced that Nicholas, John and William Gordon would be held for the murder of Amasa Sprague. Their eighty year-old mother, who had been incarcerated at the grim, cold state prison on Smith Hill, and the dog, were released.

The next day, William Sprague, Amasa's brother, resigned from the U.S. Senate to return home and run the family business.

On March 27, all three Gordon brothers were indicted for the murder of Amasa Sprague, and the trial was set for April 8. Rhode Island Attorney General Joseph M. Blake and Attorney William M. Potter represented the state. The Irish community had raised enough money to hire four lawyers for the Gordon brothers. They were Samuel Currey, John P. Knowles, Samuel Y. Atwell and Thomas F. Carpenter.

Reporters were allowed to cover the trial, held in Providence, but not to write about it until proceedings were over. Carpenter and his team put on an excellent defense.

Blood stains on the jacket found when police entered Nicholas's store were discovered to be dye picked up when John had worked at a small print shop in Johnston. It was shown that both William and John has attended Mass in Providence on the morning of the murder, and had spent much of the rest of that Sunday with their mother. A bruise on John's face was due, his mother testified, to drinking too much and falling.

A court reporter put on the stand by the prosecution read from notes taken at a preliminary examination of Mrs. Gordon, indicating that John had left the house at 2 p.m. on the afternoon of the murder, and returned at 4 p.m. He then, the notes indicated, went back out until 7 p.m.

Another witness testified that there were no bruises on John's face the day before the murder. Slowly, William was being cleared, but his younger brother John was not. No one could explain where John was when Sprague was slain.

RHODE ISLAND'S LAST EXECUTION

The jury received the case at 6:30 p.m. on Wednesday, April 17, 1843. Within two hours, they returned with their verdicts. William was not guilty. John was. Nicholas was to be tried later. The following day, John was sentenced to be hanged; the execution was set for February 14, 1845.

In October, Nicholas was tried and acquitted because of a hung jury.

On January 10, 1845, the Rhode Island General Assembly was petitioned for a reprieve for John, but lawmakers voted 36-2 against it. A jury of twelve men had been convinced that John, out of love for his brother Nicholas, had settled the family's account by killing Amasa Sprague. Governor James Fenner refused to intervene.

Until he died, John Gordon proclaimed, "I did not shed any of Amasa Sprague's blood!"

On the morning of the execution, John Gordon carried with him two handkerchiefs, one from his mother, which he kept, and the other from the prison warden, which he dropped. A gallows had been constructed in the courtyard of the state prison under the direction of the high sheriff of Providence County, Roger Williams Potter. As he was brought from his cell to the gallows, accompanied by a priest, Father Brady of Sts. Peter and Paul Church (not yet a cathedral), Gordon told him, "I forgive them. I forgive all my persecutors, because they did not know what they were doing. I hope all good Christians will pray for me."

Gordon shook hands with Father Brady, and a black sack was placed over the head of the condemned. The trap door was sprung, and soon John Gordon was dead. His body was immediately cut down and taken by wagon to his mother's house, where it lay for two days. On Sunday afternoon, more than 1,400 people accompanied the wagon from Broad Street in Providence up Benefit Street to North Main Street and North Burial Ground, where John Gordon's remains were put in the tomb of an undertaker named Swarts (a common practice in those days, when graves could not be dug in frozen ground).

Some of those who marched in the long procession had come from Massachusetts and Connecticut, but Sprague employees were forbidden to take part.

Six months after John Gordon was buried, his body was removed from the Swarts tomb and taken to St. Mary's Cemetery in Pawtucket, where it was buried in a permanent, unmarked grave, near the George Street entrance and on the right side of the steps. A cobblestone marked it, but researchers have been unable to locate it.

AFTERMATH

When John Gordon was hanged, many people believed he was convicted on insufficient evidence. Opponents of the death penalty began to grow and, in 1852, the General Assembly voted to abolish it for all crimes.

There is a footnote to the story of Amasa Sprague and John Gordon that has become as much legend as fact. An Irishman known widely as "Big Peter" also worked for Sprague at the print works when the murder occurred. Like the Gordons, he loathed Sprague. During the Gordon trial, mention was made of a "person or persons unknown" being involved in the crime. Soon after Sprague was killed, Big Peter disappeared. Many years later, as he lay on his deathbed in his native Ireland, he reportedly confessed to murdering Amasa Sprague.

The Sprague family remained in the news for the rest of the 19th century. One of Sprague's children, Almira, married Thomas A. Doyle, mayor of Providence for a total of eighteen years. Sprague's youngest son, William, became governor of Rhode Island, and personally led Rhode Island troops early in the Civil War.

-GVL

Chapter Seven

Rhode Island
⚓Wows the World⚓

Rhode Islanders have always been among the world's greatest survivors. With a tiny land area, few resources and almost always surrounded by enemies of one sort or another, our forbears here learned early to live by their wits. During much of the 19th century, Rhode Islanders not only survived, but found ourselves at the very top of the heap. And the magic words were: instinct, innovation and industry!

Rhode Island started out in the 17th century with a farming economy. The outstanding cattle bred here and sent elsewhere were the beginnings of the booming maritime trade of the 18th. But in the early 19th century, things like the 1807 Embargo Act, hostility to American products in big markets like Britain and France, depressions, high tariffs, pirates and other menaces were sinking the state's maritime commerce. Into the economic vacuum poured industry. It was funded, ironically, by Rhode Island families who had made their money in the sea trade.

Actually, industry had been no stranger to Rhode Island. As far back as the 1790s, rich families had been investing locally in enterprises that were needed to keep the sea trade strong. These included lumbering in western Rhode Island; tanneries, forges and iron shops in places like Pawtucket and

Scituate; and, of course, shipbuilding in towns like Bristol and Warren. By 1800, Rhode Island's tremendous wealth of water power had prompted grist mills and other such enterprises to spring up all over the place, especially along the many rivers and streams of the northern towns. But it took the business instinct and innovative talent of a man like Moses Brown of Providence to really get the show on the road.

Brown was frustrated by America's economic dependence on Great Britain, which had persisted after the Revolutionary War. As he saw it, the touchstone of this dependence was something ridiculously simple: yarn. American weavers had to get their yarn from Britain because they didn't have the technology to mass produce it themselves. Brown was determined to build a strong textile industry in Rhode Island. The only problem was, he didn't know anything about textiles or how to get hold of Britain's jealously guarded textile-making technology. His first attempt, a small spinning operation in Providence in 1789, was a bust.

Things changed when Brown and his son-in-law, William Almy, teamed up with Samuel Slater, an English immigrant who had worked in Britain's textile industry. Slater not only was a mechanic who knew textile machinery but also an innovative organizer. History records what happened next: The mechanized and water-powered Brown-Almy-Slater mill in Pawtucket became the first successful cotton-spinning establishment in America, and is popularly known as the birthplace of the American Industrial Revolution.

Warwick wasn't far behind. Excited by Slater's success and the Pawtuxet River's water-power possibilities, Job Greene built a cotton mill at Centreville in 1794. Mills appeared in Apponaug and Pawtuxet about 1800, Crompton and Natick in 1807, Lippitt in 1809, Phenix and Pontiac about 1810, Riverpoint in 1812, Clyde in 1828, and Arctic in 1834. Most of this growth took place in what is now West Warwick, which was part of Warwick until its incorporation in 1913.

Slater's operation impressed others, and Rhode Island's textile industry ballooned over the early decades of the century, despite temporary setbacks caused by stiff British competition after the War of 1812, and a depression following an economic crash in 1829. The industry was helped by connections the Browns and other Quaker families had with their merchant brethren in other cities.

The Rhode Islanders pioneered modern methods of marketing and distribution, aided by the growing transportation system they helped build with their money: turnpikes, canals and, later, railroads. Rhode Islanders now hailed the high import tariffs that had once driven them crazy, because they helped protect this growing economic empire from foreign competition. Textile companies proliferated, new mill villages and company towns appeared practically overnight, and immigrants were welcomed, for once, because they provided a bottomless barrel of cheap labor. By 1860, one out of three Rhode Islanders in the work force was employed in some aspect of textile manufacturing, either with cotton or woolen products.

Processing cotton and wool was by no means the whole story of Rhode Island's industrial success. The best power looms, spinning frames and braiding machines that were the core of the textile industry were designed and made here, too. The manufacture and export of these machines – high-tech stuff in their day — joined hands with other sorts of metal-products manufacturing to make Rhode Island a heavyweight competitor in this arena as well.

All sorts of metalworking firms appeared in the 1830s, mostly in Providence. Among these were Brown & Sharpe, Eagle Screw Company, Barstow Stove Company, New England Butt Company, and Builders Iron Foundry. Under the leadership of George H. Corliss of Providence, Rhode Island was producing the best steam engines in America, beginning in the 1850s. This was especially important because as soon as coal-fired steam engines became practical, they started to replace water as the source of power for factories. This freedom from water power was a real boost for Warwick's textile industry, which immediately began to expand in the 1850s with such corporate giants as B.B. and R. Knight, and the Orient Print Works.

While jewelry production in Rhode Island developed more slowly, the precious-metals industry had started to become a big factor in the state's economy in the second half of the 19th century. By this time, four Rhode Island metals firms and one jewelry company had become known as the "Five Industrial Wonders of the World."

When the Civil War started, Rhode Island was the most industrialized state in the Union. Providence was home to the world's largest tool factory (Brown & Sharpe), file factory (Nicholson File), steam-engine factory (Corliss), screw factory (American Screw), and silverware factory (Gorham Silver). Rhode Island's achievements drew gasps at industrial expositions all over the world, and they were a center of attraction at the American Centennial Exposition of 1876, in Philadelphia.

In this hyperactive economy, it didn't take long for the rich Providence-area families to start banks, insurance companies and other service institutions. In 1809, the Farmers Exchange Bank of Glocester gained the dubious distinction of being the first bank in America ever to fail. But this lit a fire under the General Assembly, and got lawmakers to enact the first comprehensive banking statute in America.

Providence had long since displaced Newport as the state's focal point. Throughout the century, the city at the head of the Bay became more and more powerful. Besides being the state capital, it had most of the banks and industries, and it was the undisputed transportation center of southern New England. Money generated by these boom times built more and more roads, bridges and railroads, as well as dreams of even more glory in the minds of leading mid-century families like the Browns, Spragues, Knights, Perrys and Aldrichs. These people wanted to see Providence become the hub of southern New England and a major port. Most of their transportation projects were bent in this direction.

But below the level of smoke-filled board rooms, big-time planning, and vast wealth there was another world, inhabited by the people who made it all happen – the workers.

When Moses Brown and Samuel Slater were getting their act together at Pawtucket in the 1790s, all such operations relied on what amounted to "piece work" by women and children at home, while the men farmed or whatever. A fact that romantic historians never dwelt on was that Slater introduced industrial child labor and the factory sweatshop to America. Under his "Rhode Island System," whole families were recruited to work in the mills, and most of the early workers were women and children who could be spared from farm work. By 1820, the Rhode Island textile industry employed more children than women, and twice as many women as men.

Rigid schedules and factory discipline were a bizarre experience for most early workers, and it took them a long time to get used to it. This was, of course, long before the days of effective labor unions. But an attempt by Slater and other Pawtucket mill owners to cut wages in 1823 led to the first textile-workers' strike the following year. It lasted a week.

Still, in the beginning, most mill owners felt paternal when it came to their workers, and most workers saw their top bosses as benefactors. Rhode Island's mill villages were the best examples of this. Workers usually got to live in what we would call a duplex, most of which were simple but decent, for low rents. They shopped in company stores, where prices usually were low, and attended company social events and even company churches. On the other hand, the company owned just about everything in their lives.

Things had started to change for the worse by the 1840s, when mechanization was under way in the mills. The textile industry in Massachusetts had pulled ahead, and Rhode Island moguls were determined to regain the upper hand. New machines were installed, and workers found themselves in dirty, noisy factories where industrial safety standards were virtually unknown. Things simply got worse for workers because the mill owners suddenly felt paternal only toward their new machines.

Change for the better was a long time coming for Rhode Island workers in general. Labor organizing took place in fits and starts, and it wasn't very effective until the 20th century. In the 1830s, a crusade to curtail child labor and introduce the ten-hour day fell flat. Another stab at the ten-hour day flopped again as late as 1876. Life wouldn't get much better for workers until the years just before World War I.

At the dawn of the 20th century, Rhode Island's industrial diversity was breathtaking. This proved a very lucky thing, since the state's textile industry was starting to pull out and head for the South. Jewelry, rubber products and the metal industries quickly filled the widening gap. This new century brought many other changes. Two world wars and the Great Depression forever changed the face of Rhode Island industry. The dwindling of power and wealth for the old families, and the growing power of labor, simply hastened the changes that resulted in what we see today.

While jewelry and, to some degree, metalworking remained prominent in the state's economy as the 21st century dawned, most of the old giants were gone. Rhode Island was building its 21st century "post-industrial economy" using the best of the old and the best of the new, service-oriented industries.

-PFE

Rhode Island
Renaissance Man

Zachariah Allen was amazing even in a state that specializes in remarkable people. Inventor, industrialist, conservationist, philosopher, military strategist and scientist, Allen can easily be called a renaissance man of the most public sort.

Allen was born into a creative and all-around illustrious Providence family on September 15, 1795. His father, a cotton importer, was the one who introduced calico printing in the United States. Zachariah's whole life was steeped in public service, even though his favorite interests were things scientific and mechanical. He certainly lived at the right time: Rhode Island's industrial coming-of-age was tailor-made for a man like him.

In 1822, after he became owner of the mills at Georgiaville in Smithfield, Allen found out what pains-in-the-neck droughts could be for mills that depended on water power. Nearly 1,000 spindles had to shut down for eight weeks that year because of a drought. At his wits' end over this, Allen sat down and invented the modern reservoir. He cooked up a brilliant plan for a system of northern Rhode Island reservoirs and smaller mill ponds to keep water for mills in constant supply. Because of this, some 15,000 spindles kept going during the horrible drought of 1876.

Allen also invented a hot-air furnace for home heating, an automatic cut-off valve for steam engines, and he even wrote about the possibilities of solar energy. He pioneered industrial insurance as one of the founders of the Manufacturers' Mutual Fire Insurance Company. A founder of the Providence

Institution for Savings (later to become Old Stone Bank), Allen also formed the company that built Smith Street in Providence.

Even though there was no labor union to make him do it, Allen tried to take care of his workers. He kept them on the payroll during dry seasons (before his reservoirs made the weather academic) and built the model mill village of Allendale in North Providence. At his death on March 17, 1882, Zachariah Allen was president of the Rhode Island Historical Society, and is still one of the most highly regarded people in the state's history.

-PFE

The Railroad that Sank
With the *Titanic*

When the British luxury liner *RMS Titanic* slipped beneath the frigid waters of the North Atlantic in the wee hours of April 15, 1912, she took more than the 1,500 souls who perished with her. Into dark oblivion also went, by bizarre coincidence, plans to make Rhode Island the commercial hub of New England and a center for global trade.

This dream rested with a man named Charles M. Hays of Montreal, president of Canada's Grand Trunk Railway. The Grand Trunk was locked in fierce competition with its American counterparts for the best piece of the pie in the thriving transcontinental freight business. But Hays was president of another, lesser known Grand Trunk company, the Southern New England Railway, which had big plans for Rhode Island.

Hays's brainstorm began early in 1910, when he was casting around for a southern terminus for a huge, new Grand Trunk line down through New England. Providence was his obvious choice. His vision called for an eighty five-mile rail extension from the end of his Central Vermont Railway tracks at Palmer, Massachusetts, southeast through nearby Massachusetts, through the mill towns of northwestern Rhode Island to Woonsocket, and thence to Providence. The planned Woonsocket-to-Providence connection alone would have cost $5 million and taken two years to build.

When legal notices about the proposed charter of the Southern New England Railway appeared on February 10, 1910, everybody in northern Rhode Island got excited. An Italian consular official in Providence even stated that at least one

major trans-Atlantic shipping company was planning to locate in Providence because of its pending new rail connections to the rest of North America.

Initial plans called for the main line to run from Woonsocket,
through Lincoln, Cumberland and Pawtucket to the Providence port facilities. But there would have been branch lines
into other mill towns, notably Burrillville and Scituate. The
main tracks were to skirt Providence proper, through North
Providence and Johnston, and end up at Field's Point, where
a huge terminal was planned. Leaders in other towns dreamed
that a last-minute route change would bring the main line
through their own communities.

Hays said early in 1911 that the Southern New England
Railway was "out to get Rhode Island's freight business." This
greatly excited Charles A. Mellen, president of the growing
New York, New Haven and Hartford Railroad, but not for
the same reason it excited Rhode Islanders. "The New Haven" already had a virtual monopoly on the state's freight
and passenger service, and even owned most of the electric
trolley-car lines. Mellen blustered that Hays had launched
"an unprovoked attack" on his railroad. Hays harrumphed
in return that "the territory is not sacred to the New Haven,"
vowing to put his railroad through, no matter what.

Meanwhile, the state was buzzing about a future filled with
trains chugging in from the north and west, loaded with Canadian wheat and other goodies, then leaving stuffed with
Rhode Island machinery, textiles and rubber products. When
Governor Aram Pothier signed the Southern New England's
charter in April 1910, he said it was "one of the crowning
achievements of my administration."

For two years, officials worked out little necessaries like land
condemnations, and dickered with a none-too-happy New Haven Railroad about Grand Trunk tracks crossing its right of
way.

But Hays and Rhode Island would never see his dream even
approach fulfillment. In March 1912, Hays went to London
for a meeting with the Grand Trunk's Board of Directors. He
chose to return the following month in the most luxurious
manner possible. Of course, he had to pick the *Titanic*. Re-

portedly, Hays stood on the ship's A deck as she began to list, and proclaimed with the haughty arrogance of his day, "You cannot sink this boat!"

With news of the disaster's full extent – the collision with the iceberg in the last hour of April 14, the vain attempts to save lives, and the loss of 1,500 – Rhode Island leaders flew into a panic about the loss of Charles M. Hays, in whom all their hopes lay. Nonetheless, work on the railroad began the following month. Construction crews, made up mostly of Italian immigrants, set up camp at Harris Pond in Woonsocket. On May 10, Governor Pothier pulled the lever on the first steam shovel, amidst a happy crowd of 500. Horns honked and bells bonged throughout the city.

Work was soon well under way. Basic construction on grades and bridges between Woonsocket and Providence was complete, especially at Albion, Ashton and Lonsdale. Lots of work had been done at the North Providence and Johnston end too. Suddenly, on November 9, orders came from Hays's successor, Edson J. Chamberlin of New Hampshire, to hold everything. He blamed an unsettled national economy, and promised that the work stoppage was only temporary.

Rhode Islanders were furious. The Providence Board of Trade called the action "the most dastardly plot against the commercial progress of this city." In fact, the Board of Trade was right: The railroad's derailing really was the outcome of a dastardly plot! On December 24, 1912, a federal grand jury in New York gave angry Rhode Islanders a Christmas present in the form of indictments against Mellen, Chamberlin and Grand Trunk Board Chairman Alfred W. Smithers for conspiring in restraint of trade. The three had secretly agreed to keep the Grand Trunk out of Rhode Island and to preserve the New Haven's reign.

Under the holiday wrappings, however, the package was empty. Despite revelations about the scheme, and continuing enthusiasm for the project in Rhode Island, the Southern New England Railway had run out of steam for good. The company limped along until 1926, doing virtually nothing, and finally went into receivership. The last of its right of way land went up for sale in 1932, and demolition of the bridge abutments began the following year, though remnants of them may still be seen.

Thus did the world's worst maritime disaster sink Rhode Island's best chance up until that time to become the major port its leaders were still trying to make it in 2000.

-PFE

Chapter Eight

Rhode Island
 # for the Union

When Ken Burns's blockbuster documentary *The Civil War* first aired in 1990, it quickly became the most watched program in the history of the Public Broadcasting System (PBS). In one of the production's most sublime moments, the narrator quotes an eloquent, passionate, and deeply spiritual love letter from Major Sullivan Ballou of the Second Rhode Island Regiment to his wife, Sarah, back in Smithfield (the part that today is Central Falls). Ballou, only thirty-two years old, died from wounds suffered a week later, at the First Battle of Bull Run, July 21, 1861.

Twenty million television viewers had tears in their eyes. After the broadcast, the telephones rang for weeks at the Rhode Island Historical Society, with people from all over the nation wanting to know where they could get copies of the letter.

Any Civil War buff has heard many such stories of patriotism, love and courage on both sides of this terrible and complex conflict. And the Ballou letter in particular renders an inspiring picture of Rhode Island as a patriotic state whose sons, and even daughters, gladly gave their lives for home, hearth and Union.

Well, that's not quite how it began.

The Civil War was by far the most complicated debacle in American history, and, as the war began, many Rhode Islanders were confused and undecided about which side was right. This should come as no surprise: Despite the fact that many historians, most history texts, and certainly most history teachers today like to boil it all down to a conflict over slavery, the war's causes were many and complicated.

Looking at the big picture as objectively as possible, one can argue that the Civil War (or the "War of Northern Aggression," as many Southerners still call it) was what historians call a "nationalist revolution," an attempt by the Southern states to establish their own country, the Confederate States of America, by seceding from the United States, just as all the states had done in 1776 by seceding from the British Empire. As American colonial leaders believed in 1776, Southern leaders in 1860 believed that the central government was overbearing, overtaxing, and was getting more powerful than the founders of the nation had intended. In short, they wanted local control rather than control from Washington.

But how can we forget slavery?

While no civilized person today would deny that slavery is the most hideous institution ever inflicted on humankind, feelings about it on both sides before and even during the Civil War weren't always clear, especially for the average citizen. There were some pro-slavery forces in the North and some anti-slavery forces in the South. When the war began, only about seven percent of people in the South – the economic upper crust — owned slaves. The number of slaves had been steadily decreasing for years, and many an economist would have told you that the whole institution was dying anyway.

The top Southern general, Robert E. Lee, who hated slavery and never owned a slave on his own, freed all the slaves he inherited through his wife's rich family. He and a few other Southern leaders thought rightly that enshrining slavery in the Confederate Constitution was a terrible blunder. On the other hand, some Northern generals, including the eventual top commander, Ulysses S. Grant, owned slaves at one time or another. There even were some African-Americans who themselves owned slaves.

Abraham Lincoln clearly was revolted by slavery. But in his famous letter to journalist Horace Greeley, Lincoln said that the war was being fought not to end slavery, but to preserve the Union. "My paramount object is to save the Union, and not either to save or destroy slavery.... If I could save the Union without freeing any slave, I would do it—if I could save it by freeing all the slaves, I would do it—and if I could do it by freeing some and leaving others alone, I would also do that."

Lincoln was as good as his word. When he issued his Emancipation Proclamation in 1863, it didn't include slaves in states and regions loyal to the United States. The last slaves were officially freed in Delaware, a northern state, in 1866, a year after the war ended. There is evidence that some even remained in bondage in "loyal" states until the Fourteenth Amendment to the Constitution passed in 1868. Rhode Island, by the way, had been the first American colony to ban the importation of slaves, on June 13, 1774.

Nevertheless, it seems clear that slavery as a reason for the North to keep fighting grew as the Civil War progressed. At the war's outbreak, the rank-and-file on both sides would have told you they weren't fighting about slavery one way or the other. But as the Northern armies advanced and stories of the pitiable condition of many liberated slaves filtered back, the government used them to help build the abolition of slavery into a moral crusade, without which Northerners would very likely have given up and let the South go.

After the war and for the rest of the 19th century, Northern writers would glorify the North's crusade against slavery, deify the "martyred" Lincoln, and extol the Union's preservation as a divine mandate to expand the nation even to the point of overseas empire.

All things considered, it's perhaps most accurate to say that, while the North didn't start fighting because of slavery, the South almost certainly was defeated because of it. In any case, the South lost the war, so the North got to write the history.

Despite many Rhode Islanders' doubts, the attack on Fort

Sumter by Southern forces on April 12, 1861, crystallized our thinking, and the state did fall into line behind the Union. Led by its dashing young war governor, William Sprague, Rhode Island responded to Lincoln's eight wartime calls for a total of 18,898 Rhode Island troops by mustering 25,236. Some 1,878 of these joined the Navy or Marine Corps, and almost as many, 1,837, were African-Americans joining the "U.S. Colored Troops" or the one heavy artillery battery that was of "African Descent."

On April 18, 1861, only three days after Lincoln's first call, the volunteer regiment known as the "Flying Artillery" left Providence for Washington, D.C. Its descendant unit, the 103rd Field Artillery, still exists as part of the Rhode Island Army National Guard. Two days later, Colonel (later General) Ambrose Burnside and Governor Sprague himself led 530 men of the First Rhode Island Regiment in a huge parade from Providence's Exchange Place.

Rhode Island units were to fight at the First Battle of Bull Run (where Sullivan Ballou was fatally wounded). The Second Rhode Island Regiment fought well at this first major battle of the war. But elements of the First Rhode Island Regiment, depending on whose story you believe, either broke under fire and ran off into the blue, or retreated in an orderly manner. It was common enough for any troops who had never seen combat to break and run, and many Northern units did that day, which saw a Confederate victory. The First Rhode Island Regiment lost eleven men during the engagement, and the Second lost twenty eight.

Burnside commanded a brigade of the First at Bull Run, and later went on to lead Rhode Island troops in the attack – one of the first amphibious operations in U.S. Army history — on Roanoke Island, New Berne and Beaufort, North Carolina, in January 1862; and the battle of Kelly's Ford, Virginia, in March 1863. Even though his record of victory wasn't exactly sterling (many military historians consider him an idiot), Burnside ended up one of the most famous Northern generals, having had major commands at the terrible battle of Antietam (the bloodiest of the war), and the battle of South Mountain, both in Maryland in 1862, and even at

This artillery piece at the Rhode Island State House was used by state troops at the Battle of Gettysburg in 1863.

-*Photo by Paul F. Eno*

Fredericksburg, Virginia, in December 1862.

As if to illustrate the persistently divided loyalties of at least some Rhode Islanders, there is the odd story of Lt. J.C. Beveridge, as reported in the *Worcester National Aegis and Transcript* of February 21, 1863.

Lt. Beveridge, on furlough from the Second Rhode Island Regiment, apparently was enjoying a shave in a Worcester, Massachusetts, barber shop a few days before the report appeared. When a group of locals entered, noticed his uniform, and asked him about the war, Beveridge received them with open arms and mouth. The group later alleged that the officer had, in so many words, said that Lincoln was a blockhead, and that Confederate President Jefferson Davis should have been in the White House. Beveridge reportedly went on to say that he had two brothers in the Confederate Army and, that if he had known then what he knew now, he would be there himself.

Beveridge was promptly arrested on suspicion of treason, but pleaded that he had been misquoted and misunderstood.

Other Rhode Island officers vouched for his loyalty, but to no avail. Beveridge was discharged from the regiment, clean shaven but disgraced.

His claim that he had two brothers in the Confederate Army might well have been true. A number of northern men, many with Southern family connections, went south to join the Confederates, and a fewer number of Southerners headed in the other direction. In another strange twist, Lt. Col. Frank Wheaton of the Second Rhode Island had a father-in-law, Samuel Cooper, who left his native New York to go south, ending up a Confederate general.

Nevertheless, Rhode Island troops fought honorably for the Union throughout the war, notably at Chancellorsville (April-May 1863), Gettysburg (July 1863), the Appomattox Campaign of April 1865, and just about everywhere in between. The Second Regiment in particular served from the war's first major battle to what was nearly the last. Altogether, 1,685 Rhode Islanders died of wounds or disease, and sixteen earned the Congressional Medal of Honor for deeds on the battlefield.

Rhode Island served the Union in other ways. For fear of

A monument to Rhode Island troops at the Gettysburg battlefield.

-*Photo by Paul F. Eno*

southern sympathies in Maryland and its proximity to the front, the U.S. Naval Academy moved from Annapolis to Newport for the duration, occupying the Atlantic House hotel, at the corner of Bellevue Avenue and Pelham Street, with training facilities and vessels at Goat Island.

The North's industrial might was a prime factor that tipped the scales in the Union's favor, and Rhode Island, as an industrial giant, did more than its share in that department as well. The state's factories, such as Providence Tool Company and the Burnside Rifle Company, turned out everything from belt buckles to swords and musket parts, to iron hoops and horseshoes. The textile mills pumped out thousands of blankets, tents, uniforms, caps and coats, all made on sewing machines provided by Brown & Sharpe. Builders Iron Foundry, in what is today West Warwick, produced artillery pieces.

Regardless of causes, loyalties, or the constitutionality of secession, one thing is absolutely certain about Rhode Island's role in the Civil War: The state that had made so much profit from the grisly trade of slavery in the 17th and 18th centuries had done, by accident or design, more than its share to eradicate that evil from the face of America.

-PFE

The Govenor
Goes to War

In the months leading up to the Civil War, Rhode Island's rich, dashing young governor, William Sprague, of Providence, embodied all the doubts and much of the Southern sympathies that characterized many in the state. An unabashed racist, he was a scion of the powerful, A&W Sprague mill-owning family that competed with the Browns for economic and political dominance in the state.

Born in Cranston in 1830, Sprague started out in the family's company store, moving on to the bookkeeping department. The death of his uncle, William Sprague III, in 1856, catapulted the twenty-six year-old William into a company partnership. He loved to flaunt his wealth, and he lived an extravagant lifestyle.

Then he got interested in politics. After spending $125,000 on campaign deals, and strongly suggesting that his family's 12,000 employees vote for him if they were eligible, Sprague was elected governor in 1860 as a Democrat, at the tender age of twenty nine, over anti-slavery activist Seth Padelford. Don't confuse young William with his Uncle William, who sat in the governor's chair in 1838-1839.

Southern states had threatened to secede if Abraham Lincoln was elected in 1860. At the authorization of the General Assembly, Sprague appointed five delegates to the little-remembered Virginia Peace Convention, an effort at compromise among the states, which took place before Lincoln's inauguration in March 1861. Sprague and other state leaders told the delegates to lean toward whatever the South might demand to stay in the Union. As if that weren't enough,

Sprague supported the legislature in its repeal of the state law intended to frustrate slave catchers if they pursued fugitive slaves into Rhode Island.

All this Southern sympathy had dollar signs behind it. Sprague and other Rhode Island textile magnates wanted to maintain their good relations with Southern cotton growers, on whom their industries depended.

When the war broke out in 1861, however, Sprague was first in line to express his patriotism. He even did what many rich leaders did at the war's outset. In response to Lincoln's call to arms, Sprague and his family spent $100,000 of their own money to raise and outfit troops. He even donned the uniform himself, went to Washington, and personally led state troops at the First Battle of Bull Run, July 21, 1861.

"The boy governor" literally rode into battle on a white horse, which was promptly shot out from under him. Unhorsed, Sprague then ran to the artillery his family had paid for, helping the gun crews in this first major battle of the war, at Manassas, Virginia, not far from Washington. The press and Washington society may have been shocked that the war didn't end at Bull Run, as had been expected, but they loved Governor William Sprague.

> Around their campfires, Rhode Island troops were singing:
> "Of all the hosts that New England can boast.
> From down by the sea unto highland
> No state is more true or willing to do
> Than dear little Yankee Rhode Island
> Loyal and true. Little Rhody
> Bully for you, Little Rhody
> Governor Sprague was not very vague
> When he said, "Shoulder arms, Little Rhody."

But there was definitely financial method to Sprague's madness. If he had lost the Southern cotton growers, he had attained the federal trough at the earliest beginnings of what we today call "the military-industrial complex." Government contracts for anything and everything made of cloth poured into Rhode Island mills, especially Sprague's. Not long after

Bull Run, Sprague headed back to Providence, where he was re-elected governor in 1861. Offered a commission as a brigadier general that August, he turned it down. In March 1863, Sprague resigned as governor to become U.S. senator, a post he held until 1875.

Meanwhile, his flamboyance, among other things, bankrupted the Sprague industrial empire. Sprague, in self-imposed exile, died in Paris on September 11, 1915. He is buried in Swan Point Cemetery, Providence.

-PFE

The Sprague family tomb at Swan Point Cemetery, Providence

-Photo by Paul F. Eno

He Almost Went Down
with the *Monitor*

John W. Butts was a well known and successful hat finisher in Providence. He was able to retire early and build a farm in East Providence, where he and his wife raised a large family.

Two of their sons, Edwin and Francis, joined the Union Army at the outbreak of the Civil War, Edwin going into the Navy and Francis into the Army. Edwin was twenty-seven years old at the start of the war, but Francis was only seventeen and still attending high school in Providence.

Like most young men of the time, Francis Bannister Butts was eager to see action in defense of his country. On September 30, 1861, he enlisted in the Rhode Island Volunteers, Battery E, Light Artillery. He soon took part in the siege of Yorktown, Williamsburg and Fair Oaks, Virginia, and was promoted to corporal. While on duty, he and many of his Battery E comrades fell ill from malaria. On August 2, 1862, Butts was sent to a Pennsylvania hospital for recuperation. While there, he was offered the chance to join the Navy, as his brother Edwin had done. Butts agreed, was transferred as a seaman on October 5, and became a clerk in a paymaster's office.

THE CALL GOES OUT

November 2, 1862, was a day Francis Butts would remember for the rest of his life. A call went out for volunteers to join the crew of the then-futuristic "ironclad" ship *USS Monitor*, which had gained fame that April in a landmark battle with the *CSS Virginia*, the one-time wooden ship *USS Merrimac* the Confederates had captured and turned into their first ironclad. It was the world's first battle between iron warships.

It was considered the chance of a lifetime for any young sailor, and believing he would share in that glory, Butts volunteered, along with 200 other men who had the same idea. That number was pared to sixteen, then to seven, of whom Butts was one. He was now part of the *Monitor's* crew, but his joy at being selected soon turned to loathing when he discovered it was the "worst craft for a man to live aboard that ever floated upon water."

Butts described the ship in a story he would write twenty years later and preserve in his family's archives. He described a brush with death in the story of the *Monitor's* last hours afloat.

The first night we anchored at the mouth of the river and the following day after a pleasant sail down the Chesapeake, we arrived amidst a salute at Hampton Roads (Virginia) and anchored at Newport News.

Within days, he was to find on board "the most laborious of any in the service." The quarters were small, with fourteen inches allowed for each man's hammock.

Separate engines were working over our heads to keep extra attachments atop the vessel going and a man rarely allowed to sit a moment on the berth deck, even if he had the leisure.

The deck of the *Monitor* was about a foot above the waterline, and even a small wave would sweep over its surface.

"I venture to say my feet were not dry once in the whole time I was on board the *Monitor*," Butts wrote.

Christmas was bitterly cold and lonely for the crew. Confederate forces had blown up the *Virginia* when the *Monitor* returned to Hampton Roads, but also had begun to build more ironclads. On the Union side, there eventually would be some sixty *Monitor*-class vessels constructed.

"We soon noticed that preparations were going on which we expected to become prominent," Butts recalled in his memoir, "and we anchored off Fortress Monroe." The *Monitor* had taken on a full supply of coal, along with several tons of shot and shell, and it looked like the action most sailors craved, after weeks of boredom, was about to occur.

I was quite cheerful over the prospect of being called into action. More so because I knew the eleven inches of iron plates were there to keep off the sharpshooter's bullets.

Frances Bannister Butts

The *Monitor* had proven itself impregnable against any artillery then in use, but Mother Nature had other ideas for the ship that nothing could beat.

The commander of the *Monitor* was Captain John P. Bankhead. He had received orders to proceed to Charleston, South Carolina, when the rough seas and rains subsided. A storm had been holding the *Monitor* in place for several days, and did not break until December 29.

Captain Bankhead ordered the *Monitor's* anchor hauled in at dawn on the 29th, and by noon the ship and crew were heading south under the escort of the powerful, side-wheeled steamer *USS Rhode Island*. The weather was dark and stormy, and winds were picking up from the west. The *Monitor* left Hampton Roads and rounded Cape Henry but, by early afternoon, conditions had worsened. Early in the morning on the 30th, the winds had shifted to the south-southwest, and increased to gale force.

"It was my trip at the wheel at twelve o'clock," wrote Butts. By nightfall, the *Monitor* was seventy miles out to sea, where the waters were dangerous and the waves high. They were crashing over the lower deck of the ship, and Butts described the scene of "men on the *Rhode Island* who thought several times that we would have gone down. It seemed like we were

out of sight several minutes as the heavy seas entirely submerged the *Monitor*."

Butts had been stationed at the wheel, which was rigged on
top of the turret, where the officers were standing. He heard
them talking about the terrible winds and driving rain, which
caused them much concern on such a craft.

*I began to think this would be the last time I would volunteer for
anything and I remembered what I had been taught in the service,
that a man always got into a mess if he volunteered.... All officers
were on the turret except those on duty in the engine room as the
Monitor rode huge waves that threw them about the ship. The water was splashing down with a shock that would sometimes take us
off our feet, while the next would sweep over us and break far above
the turret and if we had not been so protected by rifle armor we
would have been washed away.*

The water was running down through the coal bunkers,
causing further grief for Bankhead and his crew. By 8 a.m.,
the coal was too wet to use, and the water was submerging
the pumps. Bankhead ordered the chief engineer to start the
powerful main pump.

"A stream of water eight inches in diameter spouted from
beneath the waves when the big pump was activated," Butts
recalled.

It was time to send distress signals to the *Rhode Island*, which
was now in front of the *Monitor* instead of at its side, to avoid
drifting into it, and to prevent tow lines from getting caught
in the wheels of the wooden vessel. As the *Rhode Island* drifted
closer to the *Monitor*, one of the ironclad's officers shouted
through a trumpet horn that the *Monitor* was sinking, and
that the lifeboats should be deployed to rescue the men.

*I was ordered to leave the wheel and was kept employed as mes-
senger by the captain who ordered the tow lines to the Rhode Island
cut. I saw a man attempting to obey the order swept from the deck
and carried by a heavy sea leeward and out of sight for a moment. I
saw him swept by a heavy sea far away into the darkness, only to
hear his voice once say, 'farewell.'*

THE WRECK OF THE IRON-CLAD "MONITOR."

USS Monitor *fights for life in a storm off Cape Hatteras in December 1862.* **USS Rhode Island** *is in the background. Francis Bannister Butts of East Providence is one of the men on the* **Monitor's** *deck.*

-*Courtesy of Casemate Museum, Fort Monroe, Va.*

Francis Butts had seen death for the first time. The *Monitor's* anchor was let go, and hit bottom in sixty fathoms (about 360 feet) of water. The boiler fires that powered the engines were nearly out, and the pumps virtually useless under the volume of seawater that continued to leak into the ship.

Suddenly, the rain stopped and the skies cleared, but the winds picked up, causing the sea to roll even more. The tow lines cut by the *Monitor* crew when it dropped anchor had become entangled in the wheel of the *Rhode Island,* and they were forcing the bigger ship dangerously close to the already battered ironclad. A small rescue boat that the *Rhode Island* had lowered to take on the *Monitor's* crew was crushed between the two vessels. The heavy winds had pushed the *Rhode Island* to the side of the *Monitor,* and the two vessels bumped several times.

Some of the seamen bravely leaped down on deck to guard our sides and lines were thrown to them from the deck of the Rhode Island which now lay the whole length against us floating off astern but not a man would be the first to leave the ship although the captain ordered them to do so.

Butts's remarkable memory also brought back the haunting image of a young engineer's last moments of life.

I think I was the last to look at him as he lay seasick in his bunk, apparently watching the water as it grew deeper and deeper, conscious of what his fate must be. He called me as I passed his door and asked if the pumps were working. I replied that they were. 'Is there any hope?' he asked me and feeling a little moved at the scene and knowing what must be his end, I replied, 'There is always hope.'

As Butts climbed down the turret ladder, the sea broke over the *Monitor* and came pouring through the hatchway with such force that it knocked him off his feet. At the same time, the steam broke from the boiler room as the water hit the last of the fires. The first of two rescue boats from the *Rhode Island* was only inches from the *Monitor* when the captain gave the order to abandon ship. Fifteen men crowded into the boat in their desperate jump to safety, shocking Butts.

I was disgusted at witnessing the scramble. And not feeling in the least alarmed about myself, resolved that I, an old haymaker as landsmen are called would stick with the ship as long as any officer. I saw three of these men swept from the deck and carried leeward to find their graves beneath the angry sea.

Despite many of the officers and enlisted men abandoning the foundering *Monitor*, Butts remained on guard, passing buckets from the lower hatchway to a man on top of the turret.

I took off my coat, one that I had received a few days previous and rolling it up with my boots, drew the tompion (barrel plug) from one of the guns, placed them inside and returned the tompion. We had a black cat on board which sat on the breech of one of the guns howling one of those hoarse and solemn tunes which one can appreciate, unless filled with superstitions which I have been taught by sailors who were afraid to kill a cat. I would almost as soon touched a ghost. But I caught her and placing her in another gun, replaced the wad and tompion. But I could still hear that distressing yowl. As I raised my last bucket to the upper hatchway no one was there to take it. I scrambled up the ladder and found that below had been deserted. I shouted to those on the berth deck to come up because the officers had left the ship and the boat was alongside.

When Butts climbed to the top of the turret, he saw the second rescue boat, filled with men, and three other sailors standing on the *Monitor's* deck, trying to get to it. They had to climb to the rescue boat by hanging onto a rope and making their way to safety. Suddenly, one of them was swept from the *Monitor* by a breaking wave, and sent to his death in the raging sea. A second man was trying to leap onto the boat, but he too disappeared. The third man looked as though he had made it by jumping from the *Monitor*, grabbing the rope and swinging to safety.

Then it was Butts's turn. Carefully he climbed from the top of the turret to the deck below, and the moment his foot touched the surface, "The sea broke over the deck and swept me as it had the others. I grabbed one of the smokestacks and hand over hand ascended to keep my head above water, and it required all my strength to keep the seas from tearing me away."

Butts found himself dangling in the air at the top of the smokestack. Facing almost certain death, he let himself fall, hoping to again grasp the ropes from the rescue boat. There was no rope and no boat, and Butts found himself below the water.

As I rose above the water, I spouted up, it seemed, more than a gallon of water that had found its way into my lungs. I was as then twenty feet from the other men whom I found to be the captain and one seaman. The others having been washed overboard or rescued.

Those survivors on the boat were struggling at their oars to keep from being washed onto the *Monitor's* deck. Already aboard the rescue boat were the first lieutenant and other officers. Captain Bankhead remained on his dying ship, shouting for Butts and the others to jump to safety. The others yelled to Bankhead to go first, which he did. It nearly turned out to be the last words they ever spoke, because as soon as the *Monitor's* captain was safe, the lieutenant ordered, "Cut the painter! Cut the painter!" (The painter was the rope that tied the rescue boat to the sinking ship.)

Butts and his mates were about to be abandoned to die.

Butts suddenly grabbed the painter, "….in less time that I can explain it, exerting my strength beyond imagination I hauled in the boat, sprang, caught on the gunwalk, was pulled into the boat with a boathook in the hands of one of the men and took my seat with one of the oarsmen."

As the rescue boat pulled away from the doomed ironclad, Butts saw several men standing on top of the turret, afraid to venture down to the deck. Soon they were swept to eternity. During the gale, the *Rhode Island* had drifted nearly two miles from the rescue boats. When Butts and the others finally reached the ship, the first rescue boat had just managed to discharge its ragged occupants. Getting from his boat to the *Rhode Island* would prove to be just as hazardous to Butts as getting off the stricken *Monitor*.

We were carried by the sea from stem to stern. But to make fast would have been fatal. And the boat bounded against the ship's sides. Sometimes it was below on the wheel and then, on the summit of a huge wave, far above the decks. Then the two boats would crash together, and once while our surgeon was holding on to the rail he lost his fingers by a collision which swamped the other boat. Lines were thrown to us from the deck of the Rhode Island, *which were of no assistance for not one of us could climb a small rope. And besides the men would immediately let go their holds in their excitement to throw another.*

With heavy seas and howling winds, the rescue boat and the *Rhode Island* moved alternately, one rising at the same time the other fell. During one of these passes, when the boat was at the bow of the steamer, Butts managed to grab a rope. When the smaller boat rose again, he came within a foot of the rail. If there had been a man there he could easily have hauled Butts aboard.

But they all followed after the boat, which at that instant was washed astern. And I hung dangling in the air over the bow of the Rhode Island, *with our acting master hanging to the cat head* (a beam projecting from the bow, GVL) *three or four feet from me. And like myself, both hands clenching a rope and bawling for someone to save us.*

Butts and his mates were beginning to lose hope. Their hands were growing painful and weaker, until the acting master lost what remaining strength he had.

"He slipped a foot, and with his last prayer, 'O, God!' I saw him fall and sink to rise no more," Butts wrote.

The *Rhode Island* rose and fell too, sometimes with part of her keel out of the water, when Butts found himself thirty feet above the salty foam, clinging to a rope with aching hands, and calling in vain for help. The wind drowned out his cries, and he was later to admit he had given up hope. He thought about his family and friends at home, and then about nothing. The sea rolled over him again, bringing both boat and Butts crashing onto the deck of the *Rhode Island*. The next thing he heard was, "Where in hell did he come from?"

One of the rescue boats was sent back to try and find the *Monitor*, but failed. The ironclad was eventually located listing in the, by then, calmer waters, and she was hooked to a towline, with the Philadelphia Navy Yard as the intended destination.

Butts finished his narrative the next day, but his mood was dark and reflective. He had lived while many of his shipmates, most as excited as he was about serving on the *Monitor*, had not.

It was now half past twelve, the night of the 31st of December, 1862. I stood on the forecastle (the bow deck, GVL) *of the* Rhode

Island *watching the red and white lights that hung from the pennant staff above the turret, and which now and then as we perhaps both rise on the seas together, beam across the dark and raging sea, until at last just as the moon had passed below the horizon, t'was lost and the* Monitor, *whose history is still familiar to us all, the victor of the first ironclad conflict, the savior of our naval forces, plunged with a dying struggle at her treacherous foe and was seen no more. The following day we arrived at Hampton Roads. This sad news reached every household and our nation wept. As near as I can now remember, there were thirty eight lives lost and twenty eight saved.*

For Francis Bannister Butts, life after the Civil War was anything but a joy. Even before the war was over, his family received word that his older brother, Edwin, who had risen to the rank of petty officer in the Union navy, had been killed at Vicksburg, Mississippi, on August 17, 1864. He was just twenty-nine years old.

Francis was mustered out of the service on June 17, 1865, after serving nearly four years. On Christmas Day, 1867, he married Helen F. Battey of Scituate. They began life together in Providence, where Francis worked for his father in the hat business. He also worked in the provision and manufacturing fields and, on January 8, 1870, a daughter, Alice Duncan Butts, was born. A son, Frank Horace Butts, was born on May 17, 1873, and was the "apple of his father's eye." They went everywhere together.

Francis was deputy collector of revenue for the federal government in Providence from 1878 until 1887 and, on October 1, 1891, President Benjamin Harrison named him postmaster of the Town of East Providence. However, tragedy would soon bring to an end the world he had come to know and love, a tragedy from which he would not recover.

Frank Horace Butts had been a sickly boy, and his father and mother doted on him. He never attained full health, and on December 10, 1891, he died. Francis had spent considerable time after the war writing about his experiences in combat, and compiling a family history that dated back to the founding fathers of the nation. When young Frank died,

Francis was able to sit down with pen in hand one more time.

Frank H. Butts, was a boy of a most happy and genial disposition and loved by all who knew him. He and his father were companions in all their doings and more than the usual attachments of father and son existed between them. By his death, all hopes and all anticipations are buried in the grave. I have no eulogy to write of him; his dearly loved father and mother will never cease to mourn their loss. My pen here falls from my hand, the name of Butts in this line of the family is lost forever.

Indeed, the family line ended with young Frank's death. Although Butts's daughter, Alice, married Frederick Smith Metcalf, they had no children. They moved to Cleveland, Ohio, where Metcalf was a successful merchant. In 1902, Francis and Helen left East Providence, and moved to Cleveland to join him in business. Francis visited East Providence in August 1905, but took sick and left for his home in Cleveland, where he died on September 8.

Helen moved to Winter Park, Florida, where she passed away on April 12, 1920, fifty-nine years to the day that Fort Sumter was fired upon.

-GVL

The Daughter
of the Regiment

We rarely hear about the heroic women of the Civil War. But there were plenty, and one Rhode Islander – indeed one American — who stands out as unique is Kady Brownell, a true "daughter of the regiment."

From what little we know of her early life, Kady supposedly was born to a French mother and a Scots father, Colonel George Southwell of the British Army, on a battlefield at Caffraria, South Africa, in 1842. The story goes that she was named after Sir James Kady, a friend of her father's. None of this can be verified from public records, but one thing was for sure: Kady quite literally had the army in her blood.

Somehow, Kady ended up in Providence, where she married a machinist, Robert S. Brownell. After the attack on Fort Sumter and Lincoln's call for troops, the nineteen year-old Kady managed to sign up for the 11th Rhode Island Infantry, with her husband, for a three-month enlistment. While it wasn't unusual, early in the war at least, for wives and families to follow men around while they were in the army, and even live in camp, it was illegal for women to actually become soldiers. Rumor has it that Kady – a name indifferent to gender – dressed as a man and signed up. Then, once her comrades found out she was a woman, she became accepted, then respected. Not only that: Her leadership skills were such that she ended up a sergeant in a matter of weeks!

Before her infantry unit went into action, it encamped outside Washington. There Kady practiced with her musket until she became a crack shot. She also became handy with a sword, which she carried as a non-commissioned officer.

Kady also was a color-bearer, carrying the American flag, which made her a prime target for enemy sharpshooters.

In the middle of July, the regiment moved south in the first of several unsuccessful federal drives on Richmond, Virginia, the Confederate capital. Kady carried the flag. Early one hot afternoon, the 11th came under fire near the edge of some woods. Kady reportedly stood there with the flag, amid the heat, blood, and the roar of battle, as minie balls zipped past and artillery shells ripped by overhead. Her own unit fled a few hours later, but it wasn't until a Pennsylvania infantryman grabbed her and pulled her off the line that she, too, retreated, with Confederate troops at their heels. As they ran, the Pennsylvania man fell dead. With his blood all over her, the story goes, Kady found a loose horse, which she rode into Centreville, Virginia, in search of her comrades, especially her husband.

Brownell supposedly ran into none other than Colonel Ambrose Burnside, her commanding officer, who assured her that Robert Brownell was unhurt, and even helped her find him, though one would think he had better things to do. If a major figure like Burnside didn't bat an eyelash that this woman was one of his troops, this incident, if true, lends credence to the stories of the acceptance and respect Kady had among the Rhode Island soldiers.

The three-month enlistment being up, the 11th returned to Providence that August, and Robert and Kady Brownell both mustered out. But that wasn't enough for them! They promptly re-enlisted, this time in the 5th Rhode Island Infantry, where they saw combat under the now-General Burnside once again. This time it was in North Carolina in 1862.

On top of Kady's regular duties, she was now the unit's chief nurse. But soon she was carrying the flag once again. Doing so, she reportedly avoided what could have been a nasty "friendly fire" incident near New Bern, when her unit came face to face with other Union troops in the confusion of battle. Kady ran to the top of a small hill, waving the American flag, heedless of withering fire all around her.

Her husband was wounded that very day, and she helped him and several other injured men to safety. Not only that, but she reportedly rendered the same help to a wounded Confederate officer.

With Robert's permanent injury, he would never fight again, so the couple found themselves back in Providence by the summer of 1862. But Kady kept the flag she had so proudly carried, her sergeant's sword, along with her army discharge, signed by Burnside.

As far as we know, Kady Brownell was the only woman of that era to have U.S. Army discharge papers and to have officially been in combat. In her later years, newspapers made much of her, and she had no problem drawing an army pension.

Here was another first for Rhode Island, and for women's equality!

-PFE

From Peace Dale
to a Confederate prison

"The greatest battle ever fought upon this continent took place yesterday near Manassas Junction."

This report was published in the *Providence Daily Journal* on July 22, 1861. By then, 481 Union soldiers had been listed as killed, 1,011 wounded, and 1,120 missing or captured. Tragically, one Rhode Islander's name was to be listed under all three headings. It was a statistic of a war in which brother fought brother, and about which thousands of stories were to be written after being played out on battlefields in a young nation divided.

This "greatest battle" was the first one to take place at Manassas, Virginia, and it came to be known in the North as the First Battle of Bull Run. It was about 10 o'clock on the morning of July 21 when the Second Rhode Island Regiment became trapped in a wooded area a half mile west of the stream known as Bull Run, and three miles northeast of Manassas Junction. Within five minutes, Confederate forces had inflicted most of the casualties and, after two hours of fighting, it was all over. Union troops had lost the battle.

Corporal Esek B. Smith of Peace Dale, age twenty eight, father of five small children and husband of Lucy Webster Smith, already was on two of those lists: wounded and captured. In less than three weeks, he would be on the third and final list.

Smith was born in South Kingstown on May 19, 1833, and spent his entire life, up to his enlistment in the army, living there. Like many young men of that period, he was a laborer, and worked in the local mill in the Peace Dale section of town.

He married Lucy Adeline Webster on November 9, 1851, at Queen's River Baptist Church in Usquepaug, a hamlet of South Kingstown, in a ceremony performed by the Rev. Ezekiel J. Locke. Esek was eighteen and Lucy sixteen. By the time Smith was mustered into Company E of the Second Rhode Island Regiment of Volunteers, he and Lucy, or Adeline as she was called, had been married for ten years and had five children, ages nine years to eight months.

Esek worked as a weaver at the Peace Dale Woolen Company, and word of the war pitting North against South was everyday conversation during that spring of 1861. One day in May, the mill's overseer, Isaac Rodman, announced to his fellow workers that he was marching off to join the army. Hearing of Rodman's enlistment, and lured by the prospect of $12 cash a month for some excitement, Smith and several other employees went to the Company E recruiter, who was in town, and joined up. Although they signed their names for a three-year hitch, everyone knew the fighting would be over in a few weeks.

The recruiting officer asked Smith, "Are you in good shape?"

"Yes," replied Smith, who proved it by dancing around the room.

The physical examination complete, Smith was appointed a corporal as the Second Rhode Island Regiment wasted no time in getting ready for war.

GOING PUBLIC

On June 7, the full Second Rhode Island Regiment was paraded and reviewed at Exchange Place in Providence, a great distance from South Kingstown in a time before mass transportation. Smith said his goodbyes to his wife and children, and left them for what would be the last time. At Exchange Place, a focal point in the state's capital city, Smith and his colleagues heard a eulogy in memory of the Honorable Stephen A. Douglas, the distinguished senator who had run for president against Abraham Lincoln in 1860, and who had died on June 2.

The following day, the Regiment set up camp at the Dexter

Parade Ground, a mile west of Exchange Place, and by the 12th, under the command of Colonel John S. Rodman, the regiment was beginning to shape itself into a military organization. It was turning out to be a memorable time, as a group of patriotic ladies presented the regiment with U.S. and Rhode Island flags, which they had knitted in honor of these men, who were among the first to respond to Lincoln's call for troops. Those who joined the call-up of volunteers would no doubt sing the strains of the emotional tribute penned in their honor, *We Are Coming, Father Abraham, 300,000 Strong*.

But tributes and memories were far away in June 1861 when, on the 16th, the eloquent voice of the Right Rev. Thomas M. Clark boomed out over the congregation at Grace Church in Providence to those volunteers in attendance, instilling such inspiration in them that they would name their Camp outside Washington after him. Bishop Clark headed the Episcopal Diocese of Rhode Island, no doubt the highest ranking churchman most of the new troops had ever heard preach.

OFF TO WAR

Rhode Island Governor William Sprague had been asked by the Secretary of War to send any volunteers to Washington, where headquarters would be established. On June 19, troops marched from the Dexter Parade Ground to Fox Point, several miles away, where the steamships *Killvon Kull* and *The State of Maine* were waiting to take the Second Rhode Island Regiment, including Company E and Esek Smith, to war.

Slowly the vessels made their way to New York City, and then on to Elizabeth, New Jersey, where the troops disembarked and proceeded by train to Baltimore, Maryland. Marching through that city, they arrived in Washington late on the gray morning of June 22. It had been six days of nonstop travel by land, sea and rail. When the Second arrived at its destination, the men were greeted by the First Rhode Island Regiment, and set up their tents. The combined regiments then were placed under the command of Colonel Ambrose Burnside.

For veterans, life in what amounted to boot camp was monotonous, but it was exciting and novel to the newly arrived soldiers. Days were spent in drills, parades and prayer. There were inspections, reviews, and lessons in war and survival. The troops were becoming accustomed to a new way of living, and they were developing a new spirit of patriotism. Yet even the most bored of the "old timers" could not possibly know that, within days, many of their lives would end on a battlefield.

On July 8, troops camped in the Washington area were formed into five divisions. The Second Regiment was placed into what was called the Second Brigade, Second Division, and commanded by Colonel David Hunter of the regular U.S. Army. To further confuse the newer soldiers, it was announced that the First and Second Rhode Island Regiments would remain under the immediate command of Colonel Burnside.

On July 16, the regiments met for the first time as a brigade, marched down Pennsylvania Avenue and across Long Bridge into Virginia. That night they camped at Annandale and, early on the 17th, resumed marching toward the Southern army.

At 2 a.m. on the 21st, a delayed march began through a forest, where trees had to be cleared. At 9 a.m., the troops reached a good farm road near Sudley Springs, and they came upon residents walking to church in their best clothes. But this was a Sunday when there would be no service in the church. Instead, the little house of worship would soon be filled with the wounded and dying.

Colonel John Slocum climbed a rail fence bordering the corn field near the Mathews House just before 10 a.m. Gunfire was nearby. As Slocum turned to give the command to proceed, bullets ripped into the back and side of his head. Falling mortally wounded, he was carried to the Mathews House, where he died within minutes.

When Esek B. Smith joined Company E, his twenty-two year-old nephew William also enlisted. William saw Slocum fall. He did not see Esek fall, but minutes after Slocum's death, Esek's knee was shattered by Confederate fire.

William later wrote to his mother on Camp Clark stationary.

I am very sorry to say we can't give any account of Esic (sic).
*Don't tell Adeline. I saw many of our regiment shot down. I was
close to Slocum when he was killed. A hard time was had I tell you.
The second regiment, that's the one we are in you know, stood 45
minutes in front of four regiments of rebels before any of the rest
got up to us. I see Esic on the field alighting and have not seen him
since after the fight. I looked everywhere for him but couldn't find
him.*

William would never see his uncle again. Although little
documentation exists, it is likely that the Confederates captured Esek, took him to Sudley Springs Methodist Church in
Manassas, and then to Libby Prison in Richmond, where
Union prisoners of war were kept.

Libby eventually housed mostly officers, but with the first
shots barely fired, Southern forces were not choosy about
where they kept their prisoners. During four years of fighting, 125,000 Union soldiers were housed at various times at
Libby — one of the most notorious POW camps of the war.
According to eyewitnesses, the first prisoners were not
treated as poorly as tales of later incarcerations would describe. It is stated the first to be held at Libby were treated
well, although they were deprived of newspapers, coffee and
sugar, and allowed no visitors.

That the early treatment was good can be attested by the
words of a Dr. Sternberg of the U.S. Army, who managed to
escape capture at Manassas, and travel to safety through the
thick woods. Sternberg learned that the prisoners at Libby
were fed fresh boiled beef and wheat bread, with a small
amount of rice every other day. Perhaps it wasn't a large
amount of food, but it was enough to keep the less severely
wounded, and those taken without injuries, alive.

Esek Smith was not slightly injured. He was seriously
wounded and, without proper food and sanitation, he was
doomed. Smith lingered at Libby until August 6 when, only
six weeks after leaving his wife and young family, he died.
Perhaps Rodman had told him and the others at the mill that
the rebels would run when they heard the sound of gunfire.
But Rodman was dead, too, and so was a young man named

John Clark, also of Company E. All were part of that proud regiment that had encountered 2,000 Confederate troops, who did not run at the sound of gunfire during the first battle of Bull Run.

Smith's widow, Adeline, received three months wages as bounty for her husband's death. Smith's monument stands at Oak Dell Cemetery in Peace Dale, not far from the mill where he worked and the small farm where he lived. It cannot be determined if his body is actually under the stone because recordkeeping was not good in the early, hectic days of the Civil War.

In some accounts of Smith's death, it was not reported until September. The *Providence Daily Journal* listed him as wounded on August 16, ten days after he died. Was he buried at Richmond? Was he transported back to Rhode Island for burial by boat or by train? No words have ever been written pinpointing his final resting place.

Esek Smith will forever be listed as one of the first casualties of the Civil War. Today one is able to walk along Mathews Hill and the Sudley Springs National Battlefield. There is the Stone House and the Sudley Springs Methodist Church. And there is the memory of Esek B. Smith and thousands like him on both sides, one to wear the blue and the other the gray, in what was to become known as First Bull Run or First Manassas.

Lives in Peace Dale eventually returned to normal. Other young men from town volunteered, fought and returned. Some fought and died. In 1865, the war was over.

Lucy Adeline Smith married twice more, and lived until 1923. She is buried at Windham Cemetery in Windham, Connecticut. Nephew William E. Smith, who searched for and failed to find Esek at Bull Run, died in 1896 and was laid to rest not far from his young uncle's stone at Oak Dell.

                                                                    -GVL

You decide!

NORTH VS. SOUTH

In 1861, there were plenty of opinions in Rhode Island about whether the South was right or wrong in trying to gain its independence. Despite what our grade-school textbooks might say, it's not a simple question. We Northerners often scratch our heads about why some Southerners take the "War of Northern Aggression" so seriously even today. But stories have come down in Southern families about Union troops burning their farms, stealing their cattle or killing or abusing their ancestors. That's an experience the North didn't have. Was it unjust, or did the "Rebels" deserve it?

Abraham Lincoln did the right thing in fighting to keep the South in the Union

• The South started the Civil War by attacking Fort Sumter, which was federal property, after South Carolina seceded. Lincoln was just doing his job by protecting government property from illegal seizure.

• The war wasn't just about the right of a state to secede; it was about moral issues and human rights. Foremost was the odious institution of slavery, already outlawed in most of the civilized world. Also to be considered were the rights of those many Southerners who wanted to remain U.S. citizens. Lincoln's job was to defend them, and he did it.

• The Southern states were wrong in seceding. The Articles of Confederation, which they signed in 1781, talked clearly of "perpetual union."

• Lincoln could see the "big picture." Had the Union not fought and been preserved, North America would have split into perpetually hostile factions, like Europe at the time, and everyone's peace, freedom and prosperity would have suffered. Lincoln truly saved America from a terrible fate.

• The very idea that slavery would have been allowed to

continue, or even expand, under an independent Confederate States of America, is unthinkable. Lincoln is deservedly called "the Great Emancipator." Without his decisive action, who knows how long slavery would have continued.

• Sure, Lincoln had to take extraordinary measures in extraordinary times, sometimes on thin constitutional ice. But if he hadn't, where would America be today? Besides, other presidents have done more questionable things when America was in grave danger. Franklin D. Roosevelt approved putting many Japanese-Americans in concentration camps during World War II, a grave wrong that only recently has been officially acknowledged by the government.

Abraham Lincoln was wrong in fighting to keep the South in the Union

• Dragging the South back into the Union at gunpoint would hardly have squared with the beliefs of the nation's founders, who violently separated the American colonies from Great Britain. The whole point of the United States of America was supposed to be individual rights and self-determination. Slavery or not, Southern states had every right to leave the Union. After all, they joined freely, and there was nothing in the Constitution or the law that said they couldn't secede.

• Lincoln may have had the best of intentions, but he had no legal right to fight the war. In bold violation of the Constitution, while boldly claiming to uphold it, Lincoln suspended civil liberties, and had thousands of suspected "traitors" (those who rejected his interpretation of the Constitution) jailed without formal charges, trials or lawyers. He even arrested dozens of state legislators in Maryland, which nearly seceded, and the mayor of Baltimore.

• When U.S. Supreme Court Chief Justice Roger Taney objected to Lincoln's abuse of power, the president threatened to arrest him, too. Lincoln ignored a Supreme Court order to release detainee John Merryman.

• Lincoln had no right to wage war against American citizens in the South or against state governments. By doing so, he *de facto* recognized Confederate independence.

• Lincoln can be called the founder of "big government."

With the precedents he set for federal power, in violation of the Constitution's 10th Amendment, federal power has grown far beyond what the nation's founders intended.

• As for slavery, it was dying anyway. Some 250,000 slaves were freed in the years before the Civil War.

-PFE

Chapter Nine

The World Moves
⚓ to Rhode Island ⚓

"This country is filling up with thousands and millions of voters, and you must educate them to keep them from our throats."

So said the renowned poet and philosopher Ralph Waldo Emerson in the 1870s, and it was one of the nicer things native-born Americans were saying about immigrants from just about everywhere who had started to pour into the country beginning in the 1840s. But, in the words of the great Al Jolson, Emerson hadn't "seen nothin' yet." Driven out of their native lands by economic, political and natural disasters of every description, this human avalanche grew steadily. By the 1910s, it far exceeded the capacity of the country to properly absorb it. Finally, an alarmed federal government drastically curtailed the influx, beginning in 1921.

Many immigrants had made a beeline for Rhode Island. This was largely because, as the most industrialized state in the Union, this was where the jobs were. Most new arrivals were uneducated and unskilled, but the Yankee mill owners saw them as ideal — and cheap — tenders of the textile machines, and doers of any simple job no-one else wanted. Rhode Island's industrialists did everything they could to attract able-bodied immigrants to the state, encouraging the opening of Providence as an official port of entry in 1911. For the next decade, the Fabre Steamship Line carried thousands upon thousands of newcomers to Rhode Island, mostly from southern Europe and primarily from Italy. By the 1920s, Rhode Island had the highest percentage of immigrants in the country. This was still the case in 1950. By 2000, however, the title had long since passed to California.

As far as immigration was concerned, the East Bay area was by no means a microcosm of Rhode Island. The primary immigrants there were Irish and French Canadians, during and after the 1870s. They found employment mostly in the mills of Bristol and Warren, and in Barrington's brickyards.

Emerson's comments about foreigners as a vast horde of new voters wasn't true in Rhode Island because even naturalized immigrants couldn't vote unless they owned property, and even this small concession wasn't granted until the 1880s. The education called for by the poet took its good old time catching up with the immigrants too.

Even though the august among them initially tried to get immigrants to settle here, most native-born Rhode Islanders didn't trust the new arrivals for a number of reasons. One was that fundamental principle of human nature that no amount of legislation or politically-correct dogma is going to change: a simple uneasiness about people who are different, until we get to know them personally and take them into our "tribe." Some anthropologists believe that this tendency, manifested as tribalism at best and racism at worst, is a survival instinct held over from our remote, hunter-gatherer ancestors.

Regardless of how they were received here, each immigrant group has its own poignant story, and each had an easier or harder time being accepted, depending somewhat on whether or not it "struck out" on the three "pitches" of looks, language and religion. The uneasiness of the native-born was strengthened by the natural tendency of the immigrants to form their own social and cultural organizations. For many years, immigrants kept largely within their own enclaves. This helped ease the blow of having been transplanted to a country as alien to them as they were to it. But it also made the natives wonder what the immigrants were up to, and where their true loyalties lay.

A key reason most natives, especially the old-line, Protestant Yankees, looked askance at their strange new neighbors was that the vast majority of immigrants were Roman Catholics. This already-implanted bias eventually became the springboard for a venomous anti-immigrant and anti-Catholic backlash that slowly grew, and is not entirely dead even today. One wonders what the natives of that time would have thought could they see Rhode Island in the 21st century, with a higher percentage of Roman Catholics than any other state in the nation. As of 1990, they made up more than 63 percent of the total population. This turnabout in the state's religious orientation represents what is probably the greatest revolution ever wrought here.

Given the atmosphere (at least officially) of across-the-board equality in our own time, it's hard to imagine such bigotry as was freely displayed in legislation, in the press, and in society generally during the decades immediately before and after the turn of the 20th century. But it's vital to remember that these were not our own times. Since the trauma of the Civil War, Rhode Island and the rest of the country had settled into an American "civil religion" deeply rooted in Protestantism, individualism and nationalism. Because Roman Catholics were viewed as a monolithic community owing loyalty to the pope, that "Italian prince" and "antichrist" who supposedly dictated everything the "superstitious" and "ignorant" immigrants did and thought, the whole immigrant phenomenon was viewed as a direct threat to the American way of life.

Most natives sincerely believed that, unless the ethnics were ruled with an iron hand, the pope would end up controlling the United States through the immigrant vote. Even many Americans of African descent, who had been around virtually as long as the Yankees, started getting alarmed when immigrants began competing for many of the "better" jobs and tenements that had long been the province of this unique ethnic group.

The immigrants were by no means the most tolerant lot

either, especially when it came to each other. Each community imported its own foibles and bickerings, both internal and external. Blood being thicker than water, their common religion didn't spare them the strains of inter-ethnic battles brought from the Old World, or of bitter competition for housing and jobs in the New. While the more liberal among the natives operated a few organizations to help new arrivals, immigrants usually could expect little succor from the existing population, and none from the government. All had to rely upon family and friends who were already here, and on the church, charities and immigrant-aid societies founded mostly by their own ethnic groups.

The Irish were the first major immigrant population, and they were a large ethnic community in Rhode Island well into the 1980s. The Irish migration began as far back as the 1820s, but dropped sharply around 1900. As workers, they were a big part of the state's industrial dynamo. Most of the strong backs for such big-time public works projects as the Blackstone Canal, the building of Fort Adams in Newport, and the construction of the first railroads into Providence in the 1830s were Irish. These sons and daughters of Erin were the first to plunge headlong into the jungle of native tribalism here, and to experience what all other ethnics would face to one degree or another. But they, at least, looked like everybody else and spoke English. But when they "stepped up to the bat," their tenacious Roman Catholicism was a big "strike one" in the eyes of the natives, and it more than made up for their positive features.

In the 1840s and 1850s, young people from the fields and farms of Quebec Province started streaming into the Blackstone Valley, the Pawtuxet Valley and Providence. The draw, of course, was the textile industry. Things really picked up for the French Canadians when they helped fill the state's worker shortage during the Civil War, when most of the Yankee and Irish boys headed for the front.

In the 1880s, the French Canadians were the biggest immigrant group in Rhode Island. Their migration continued with gusto until the 1920's, when the textile industry was fading from the Rhode Island scene. While they looked like everybody else, they had two strikes against them: They clung just as tightly to Roman Catholicism as did the Irish, and they didn't speak English. But they came through, and in the 1990s were the third or fourth largest ethnic group in the state, numbering over 180,000.

Among the least known of the immigrants who slipped in during the late 19th century were those from England, Scotland and Wales, who also headed for the textile mills, so much like the ones in Great Britain. Compared with the other groups, the British hit a home run: Not only were they ethnic "WASPS," but they tended to be better educated, or at least more skilled as workers. Surprisingly, the British ranked third among all the immigrant groups moving to Rhode Island during the early 1880's, with newcomers from English Canada jostling other ethnics for fourth place.

Many historians have ignored the British migration, but its impact was major because they brought just the right skills from their homeland to help Rhode Island industry. Many Britons ended up as factory foremen and technicians, bosses to less fortunate ethnics who would come after them. A few even became mill owners. Including the descendants of the original English settlers, there probably were some 200,000 Rhode Islanders of British ancestry in 2000. They represented a well-dispersed and low-key ethnic group; one that was the chief of the immigrants in seniority and influence, if not in size.

Aside from African-Americans, who took plenty of abuse even from the immigrants, the first major group to have all three strikes against it was the Italians. They started landing in force in the late 1880s, and their numbers ballooned until 1924, when the discriminatory National Origins Quota Act pulled the deck out from under them. Not only did they speak a foreign tongue and adhere to Roman Catholicism, but many of them tended to look a little different because they were darker-skinned. The odds of success for the Italians were that of a snowball's in Hades, but their hard work and tenacity paid off. Today, descendants of Italian immigrants are a major influence in the state's business and politics, and they make up about twenty percent of Rhode Island's population.

In their long immigrant career, society gave the Portuguese two strikes just for religion. The first arrivals from that country, who fled to Newport during the 17th and 18th centuries to escape persecution by Christians, were Sephardic Jews. It was these Portuguese who founded the famous Touro Synagogue, the oldest active synagogue in North America.

The more modern group of Portuguese, which began arriving in the mid-19th century, were Roman Catholics, and they settled over a much wider area. Their main influx continued until 1934, when the Fabre steamship line went belly-up, but there still were Portuguese immigrating to Rhode Island and southeastern Massachusetts as the 21st century dawned.

The Poles weren't far behind, and their immigration history is extensive and quite remarkable. There were Poles here during the Revolutionary War, and several of them fought with distinction in the Battle of Rhode Island. Another small group landed in the 1830s, but the major influx started in the 1890s, prompted by the chances for factory work. The same 1924 law that choked Italian immigration hit the Poles hard too. But Poland started contributing new Rhode Islanders once again in the mid-1960s.

Other prominent groups who helped flesh out Rhode Island's varied quilt of citizenry have included Cape Verdeans, Germans, Swedes, Jews of many nationalities, Russians, Pakistanis, Greeks, Ukrainians, Armenians, Chinese, Lithuanians, Japanese, Indians, Caribbean Islanders, Africans from various countries, and Arabs (both Muslim and Christian).

One of the few positive effects of the Great Depression of the 1930s was that native-born and immigrant alike often found themselves in the same economic boat, and a sinking one at that. Standing in the same bread lines, the rival groups got to know each other a little better, and the walls may have started to weaken. During and after World War II, when the immigrants were starting to give way to their Americanized children, most groups had worked their way into the mainstream of Rhode Island life, taking their places in business and politics alongside the children of the now much more liberal Yankee families. Today, scions of the great immigrant influx usually are distinguishable only by their last names.

The parade of those who seek better lives in Roger Williams's "noble experiment" is by no means over. Enormous numbers of Spanish-speaking people from other parts of the Americas led a flood of immigration that was still going on as the 21st century began. Hispanics of many nationalities poured into Rhode Island in the 1990s, displacing all other newcomers as the state's largest minority by 2000, outstripping in numbers even the African-Americans.

A member of the Narragansett Tribe once quipped to the author that there is a beautiful "poetic justice" in this influx, as most Hispanics have Native American ancestors, albeit mostly of Central or South American tribes.

In the same period, we were joined by a large number of Southeast Asians, fleeing turmoil in their own homelands. Many could tell inspiring, if harrowing, tales of escapes from communist death squads and other terrors Americans can scarcely imagine.

Life was no piece of cake for the immigrant of the early 2000s, but at least the state and various private agencies provided programs to help them settle in by aiding in that all-important quest for housing and jobs. As with all the immigrant groups, the new ones faced a certain amount of prejudice. By the 21st century, though, the three strikes had largely changed to staying power, hard work and courage. And there's still plenty of opportunity to strike out.

Realizing that the world is really a small and delicate place has helped today's Rhode Islanders of all backgrounds live together somewhat better. Along with other Americans, turning their eyes outward toward the wider world and even outer space, in both actual experience and popular literature, probably hasn't hurt either. After all, once one has come to grips with the Klingons and the furry denizens of the Planet of the Apes, the immigrant family down the street hardly seems all that threatening.

-PFE

The Immigrants
Find a Friend

Immigrants had a tough time in 19th century Rhode Island, whether they were American citizens or not. Even after they were naturalized, they couldn't vote unless they owned property. The man who finally improved this situation, at least at the state level, was Augustus O. Bourn of Bristol. Bourn wasn't an immigrant himself. He wasn't a grassroots agitator either, but, of all things, a wealthy rubber-products manufacturer.

Bourn was born into an old Yankee family on October 1, 1834, and moved right into his father's rubber business as soon as he was old enough. In 1864, he founded the National Rubber Company, and he served as state senator from Bristol from 1876 to 1883, then as governor until 1885. As a senator again in 1888, Bourn introduced what became known as the "Bourn Amendment," which allowed immigrant citizens to vote in national and state elections on the same basis as natives by taking away the requirement that they own a certain amount of property.

Maybe it was his interest in other nations that prompted his broad-minded attitude toward people of varying backgrounds. Like all industrialists, of course, he was interested in labor that was plentiful and cheap. In any case, Bourn was appointed American consul-general in Italy in 1889, and held the job until 1893. He traveled extensively in Europe, as well as in Cuba and Mexico. Bourn also was fluent in French, German and Spanish. He is remembered as a true friend to Rhode Island immigrants at a time when they needed every friend they could get.

-PFE

Two Early
African–American Pioneers

Among all Rhode Island's ethnic groups, the African-Americans' experience has been unique. They can't be called immigrants in the classic sense, since most of their ancestors were dragged here in chains. And they suffered the least acceptance because they were so obviously different.

One man who overcame awesome obstacles to establish himself in this hostile society was Thomas Howland, whose position as a tavern owner in the Providence of the 1840s and 1850s gave him more money than most of his fellows. Not only was Howland successful as an entrepreneur, but he also became the first African-American elected to public office in Providence when, in 1856, he became warden of the Third Ward. Despite this honor, race prejudice affected him deeply and destructively. He once remarked bitterly to a friend that he wouldn't have minded being "skinned alive, for then, at least, I'd be white."

By 1857, Howland was so frustrated that he became an immigrant himself — to Liberia, a West African nation founded in 1822 as a home for freed American slaves. In a final, horrible insult from his native country, he was refused a U.S. passport for the trip, partly because of the recent "Dred Scott Decision," in which the U.S. Supreme Court ruled that slaves were property, not U.S. citizens. The *Providence Journal* stated at the time:

Thomas Howland, a very respectable colored man…of this city, has decided to try his fortune in Liberia. His wife and daughter accompany him; the latter proposes to engage in teaching; for which she has qualified herself in our public schools. Mr. Howland applied, through a notary, to the State Department at Washington, and the application was sent back with the following answer, without date or signature; the officials seeming to regard it as an insult that a man born on American soil, a citizen and a voter...should have the presumption to ask for a certificate of nationality....

Another 19th century African-American leader in Rhode Island was George T. Downing. Born in New York in 1819, Downing started out as a restaurant owner and caterer in Newport and Providence in the 1840s. Later, he built a luxury hotel in Newport called the Sea Girt House. Downing's primary fame, though, comes from his outstanding leadership in the effort to desegregate Rhode Island's schools. State law didn't say that schools had to be segregated, but they were anyway in Providence, Newport and Bristol, where most African-Americans lived. Downing's battle lasted from 1855 to 1866, when he finally achieved victory.

In 1863, during the Civil War, the great African-American orator and abolitionist Frederick Douglass recommended Downing as a brigade quartermaster for one of the "colored regiments" then being raised by the Union. Being in his mid 40s by then, Downing never served, but he assisted in recruiting troops.

He died in Newport in 1903.

-PFE

Rhode Island's
First Frenchman

On steamy summer days, when northern Rhode Islanders inch along Route 4 in East Greenwich on their way to the beaches, they pass beneath Frenchtown Road. The village remembered in this name isn't even a memory for most local people, but it was the site of the first settlement by French immigrants to Rhode Island.

They came a very long time ago — in 1685, to be exact — and were natives not of Canada but of France. Also unlike most of their cousins of today, the people of Frenchtown were not Roman Catholics but Huguenots, members of a small but potent French Protestant movement. These immigrants were one of several groups that fled France to escape persecution by the Roman Catholics.

Pierre Ayrault, a doctor, was the leader of this small expedition of about twenty-five families, most of whom had been farmers or merchants. They bought land in East Greenwich from the controversial "Narragansett Proprietors," a bunch of hot-shot Massachusetts businessmen who were that century's answer to New York developers. Early in 1687, the Huguenots got on with building their little village. They had brought lots of grape vines and apple cuttings with them, so they planted vineyards and orchards too. For awhile, everything was great.

Then the Frenchmen really got welcomed to Rhode Island — by getting dragged into one of the endless political debacles that spat and raged up and down the colony in that era. It seems that the General Assembly recognized the Narragansett Proprietors only as a front organization for extending Massachusetts power over areas claimed by Rhode Island. Of course, they ruled the land sale to the Frenchmen illicit. As sauce for the goose, it seemed that the General Assembly had already granted that land to some English settlers almost ten years before, as a reward to veterans of King Philip's War.

These Englishmen lived in East Greenwich already, and trouble started when they cut a field whose hay the Huguenots needed. The colonial government told the two groups to divide the hay equally, but this hardly helped the situation. As tempers rose, several French homes were looted, the Huguenot church was destroyed, and arson did in some of their crops.

By 1692, most of the Frenchmen had had it, and they left for merrier climes.

One of the few who stayed was Dr. Ayrault, who kept his house, and managed to secure 200 acres. He wrote that he was bound and determined to "keep my settlement and bear all outrage." The last recorded trouble that he had occurred in 1700, when an angry crowd broke into his house in the middle of the night, and dragged him and his son out into the street. But after Ayrault complained to the governor, he had no more trouble, and was able to live peacefully on the land he had worked so hard to keep.

The faithful remnant of Frenchtown gradually came to be accepted by other Rhode Islanders, and several moved to Newport. In 1699, Ayrault and his friend Gabriel Bernon were the first signers of a petition to found Trinity Episcopal Church in that city. Bernon later became a founder of the Cathedral of St. John in Providence, seat of the Episcopal Diocese of Rhode Island. His grave is beside the famous spring at the Roger Williams National Memorial. Secure in death if not in life, his memory abides at the site that embodies Williams's principle of welcoming all those oppressed for the sake of conscience.

-PFE

The Unexpected
Italian

The story of Guiseppe Carlo Maurani, the first Italian to settle in Rhode Island, would keep even the most ardent adventure buff on the edge of his seat.

In 1760, when he was twelve years old, Guiseppe and a buddy got into their little sailboat, and headed out of Villafranca, Italy, for a trip to the island of Sardinia, an ambitious expedition for two young boys. Neither of them ever got there. Somewhere off the Italian coast, a British warship apparently mistook them for deserters, grabbed them, and the two young Italians suddenly found themselves sailors in the service of His Majesty King George III.

Two years later, the ship appeared in the harbor of New London, Connecticut. When the captain decided to send a boat ashore to get fresh water, Maurani got himself assigned to the boat crew. As soon as his foot touched land, he started running, and he didn't stop until he got to Rhode Island. Local farmers hid him until search parties from the ship gave up and left. Maurani settled in with his benefactors, and learned the art of farming, first in Westerly and then in Barrington. In 1772, Maurani married a Barrington woman, changed his name to Joseph Charles Mauran, and blended in with everybody else as a typical Rhode Island farmer.

When the American Revolution began, Mauran was front and center. In March 1776, he was given command of the Rhode Island navy gunboat *Spitfire*, with a crew of about sixty men. It must have been with exquisite pleasure that he started harassing the Royal Navy on Narragansett Bay. When the British attacked and burned the American warship *Wash-*

ington at Warren in 1778, then marched southward to attack Bristol, Mauran and his men followed them with a cannon, got around them, and held them off long enough to save the town from being burned.

Toward the end of the revolution, Mauran commanded his own privateer, *The Weazle*, with a license from the governor of Rhode Island. He kept working as a sea captain after the war, and for most of the rest of his life. Finally, the little boy from Italy ended his eventful life on his Barrington farm, in 1813, just before his sixty-fifth birthday.

At the time of this writing, Mauran's descendants owned and operated the Providence Steamboat Company, whose tug-boats guide cargo ships in and out of the Port of Providence.

-PFE

A Leader Among
the Early Jewish Refugees

Few peoples have had to wade through so many tough times as the Jews. One of the toughest was the Spanish Inquisition, which started in 1478 and went on, believe it or not, until 1834. During much of this period, Jewish families in Spain and Portugal had to convert to Roman Catholicism or face expulsion from their countries, or worse.

Many Jews converted officially and were baptized, but remained secret adherents to Judaism. One of these was Don Duarte Lopez, who immigrated to Newport from Portugal, via New York, in 1752. As soon as he got to Rhode Island, whose policy of religious toleration had made his heart pound, he at once began to openly practice his ancestral faith again. Duarte immediately changed his name to Aaron Lopez, and he even remarried his wife in a Jewish ceremony.

Like the Quakers, the Jews worked miracles for the economies of Newport and Rhode Island. They were able to get into successful merchant connections with their fellows in other big trading areas, and business boomed.

Moses Lopez, Aaron's brother, already was a Newport merchant, and he took Aaron into the business soon after the latter got to town. The Jewish communities in both Newport and New York were impressed with Aaron's abilities and his personality. Particularly known for his honesty, Aaron Lopez got plenty of credit from other merchants, and was soon barreling down the road to business fortune on his own.

Aaron started small, buying and selling candles made from whale spermaceti, and by shipping soap to New York. But his fame soon spread to England, and his business grew with it. Before long, he was building ships of his own, got involved in the lucrative slave and molasses trades, and started in big-time whaling in the 1770s. On the eve of the American Revolution, Aaron Lopez was the richest man in Newport.

Meanwhile, he was helping to found Congregation Yeshvat Yisrael in Newport, better known today as the Touro Synagogue, the first in America. Lopez's myriad business contacts gave him sources for financial aid for the building project, completed in 1763.

The revolution brought an end to many things, including the power of Newport's commercial interests. It devastated Lopez's business, but he got along through most of the war from his outpost in Worcester, Massachusetts. He never had time to rebuild things after independence came. On his way to Providence from Worcester in 1782, Aaron Lopez suffered a tragic and most inappropriate death, drowning in Scott Pond in Lincoln when his carriage was overturned by a panicky horse.

-PFE

You decide!

MASS IMMIGRATION

In the "politically correct" atmosphere at the turn of the 21st century, immigration could be a touchy subject. Politicians were especially wary when talking about it so they wouldn't be branded as racists or xenophobes. But the fact is that mass immigration (large numbers of immigrants arriving in the same period) from outside the United States profoundly affected Rhode Island society from at least the 1840s onward. Immigration rates in 2000 were as high as they had ever been. Immigration advocates praised the influx of new blood as just as good for America in the 21st century as it had been in the 19th and 20th. Immigration critics said it was too many all at once, and pointed to how terrorists had used the U.S. immigration system to infiltrate the country before the attacks of September 11, 2001. What do you think?

Mass immigration has been good for Rhode Island

• America always has been "a nation of immigrants," and Rhode Island certainly has been a state of immigrants. The overwhelming majority of those who came here were deserving people looking for a better life for themselves and their families, were willing to work hard, became loyal Americans, and enriched America's economy and society. Many of them were more grateful to be here than many native-born Americans.

• Immigration was the most obvious source of diversity.

Diversity breeds tolerance. And tolerance helps different kinds of people live together in peace and prosperity. Without diversity and the tolerance it brings, we end up with civil and societal disasters like Northern Ireland, the Middle East and Kosovo. Diversity, and therefore immigration, made America more tolerant, more peaceful, and ultimately stronger and more prosperous.

• After the terror attacks of September 11, 2001, America's immigration standards got tougher. Most immigrants didn't come here and live on welfare. Many were highly educated, and moved right into high-paying jobs. Others started or brought their own businesses, and soon prospered.

• By 1990, native-born Americans no longer wanted to be sanitation workers, domestic help, or do other menial tasks. These jobs gave immigrants with low skills a foothold, and a chance to get started in America. Their employers would have told you they were good workers.

• In many ways, American culture at the turn of the 21st century had become sterile and society divided. It can be argued that all we had in common was the American flag and consumerism. Most immigrants came from older, more mature societies. More often than not, they brought with them cultural depth and strong family values that promised to help make America a better country.

Mass immigration has been bad for Rhode Island

• America in general and Rhode Island in particular had too many people as it was. As the 21st century began, there was a housing shortage of crisis proportions, there was too much traffic for our infrastructure, school budgets were severely strained, and the population boom was taking a severe toll on our environment, especially Narragansett Bay. Mass immigration accounted for half Rhode Island's population growth between 1990 and 2000. And, according to the U.S. Census Bureau's figures, immigration at levels current at that time would double America's population within sixty years.

• Even without the overpopulation problem, there were too many immigrants too quickly. Many swelled the ranks of those without health insurance, and they were forming a distinct – perhaps permanent – under class. They competed with Americans for scarce jobs and even scarcer housing, and cost us a fortune in everything from translations of driving manuals to taxpayer-funded health care to housing subsidies.

• The most important single characteristic of a strong,

prosperous nation is unity. America as a "nation of immigrants" was a romantic, 19th-century notion that often encouraged people to come here and remain disunited from the rest of us. We needed to be a nation of *Americans* of many ethnic backgrounds who stood shoulder to shoulder and hand in hand. We could not be a united country if immigrants came here and remained foreigners, huddling in their own ethnic communities, and clinging to their languages and cultures to the exclusion of ours.

• Immigrants who were highly educated and could hold their own in America's 21st-century economy were in the minority. Many immigrants were low-income, ending up with menial jobs that barely supported them, and many certainly weren't able to get off the ground economically. Many certainly "picked themselves up by their bootstraps," starting businesses and pooling resources, but others ended up with some sort of public assistance.

• In order to survive economically, many immigrants and their extended families lived together in overcrowded houses or apartments, creating health and zoning problems.

• *Illegal* immigration was another problem, and nobody resented it more than immigrants who did the work, obeyed the law, and moved to America properly. Among other dangers to American society, illegal immigrants were not properly cleared for criminal records and diseases before they took up residence among us.

• Some immigrants would tell you to your face that they had no respect for America, had no intention of becoming Americans, and were here simply to make money, then send it out of the country to their families, or take it back home themselves.

-PFE

Chapter Ten

America's
 # First Resort

Rhode Island doesn't call itself the "Ocean State" for nothing. For centuries uncounted, Narragansett Bay and the North Atlantic Ocean were the nucleus of life for practically everybody who lived here. Indeed, 181 of Rhode Island's 1,248 square miles are under water. Most modern Rhode Islanders don't have to catch their supper at the nearest cove, or sail out beneath the Newport Bridge into the great beyond in search of foreign trade. But sea and Bay still intimately affect us. They have much to do with the climate we live in, and they provide a great deal of the atmosphere and mystique that help make us proud of Rhode Island.

They also make for tourism, Rhode Island's second largest industry, which sustained 39,000 jobs and some $3.6 billion in sales in 2000. Tourism also is one of the state's oldest activities, reaching back long before traffic jams on Route 4, time-share condominiums, or Newport's mansions. As a matter of fact, Rhode Island was practically America's first vacation resort in the modern sense of the term, and Newport in particular was certainly the first and foremost summer watering hole for the nation's wealthy. This was true to a lesser degree in Westerly, Jamestown, Little Compton, Block Island and Narragansett. In addition, Rhode Island was almost the first place where the average working guy could take his family and get away from the city for a few hours or a few days. Towns along the Bay, particularly Warwick, provided amusement parks and other recreation spots that came to be the getaway places for the working class.

All these great ideas started hatching in the early 1720s, when it apparently dawned on some planter in the British West Indies that he could escape northward to get out of the summer heat. He and thousands like him started as far back as that to pick Rhode Island because of the mild, healthy climate, beautiful scenery, and ease of access by sea. Pretty soon, Newport and the surrounding area became a gathering place for the upper crust from the West Indies, Georgia, the Carolinas, Virginia and Philadelphia. By the 1770s, this cosmopolitan mixture made Newport hop during the summer months. Stodgy entertainment laws and early hours in other cities made Newport seem like Las Vegas.

When the American Revolution demolished Newport's maritime commerce, it was tourism that kept the city from sinking into the shallows as just another coastal village. In the 1780s, Southerners from Savannah and Charleston started coming to town again. In 1783, George Washington told his nephew to come to Newport because it would be good for his health. Needless to say, providing bed, board and entertainment for the increasing summer throngs started becoming big business.

After the economic setbacks caused by the Embargo Act and the War of 1812, Newport tourism took off once again. But it was the stimulus provided by the age of industry that brought Rhode Island's golden age as America's — and its own — favorite resort.

Despite the injustice and other evils coughed up by the 19th century factory system, it did start providing people with some leisure time during "off" hours. The ruling classes, including factory owners and managers, found that they had the time and money for more leisure pursuits. Even the workers and other lesser folk discovered that they enjoyed getting away from their hot, dingy tenements on their one free day — Sunday. By the middle of the century, rich and poor alike were starting to flock to their favorite shore points for outings and picnics.

By the 1840s, Newport in particular was seeing the first of many building booms. Before this, vacationers had stayed in boarding houses or rented cottages. But now the great luxury hotels — the Atlantic, the Ocean House, the Fillmore and the Bellevue — had started their rise to fame.

Richer summer residents began erecting their awesome "cottages." George Noble Jones of Savannah built "Kingscote" in 1839, and other Southern gentry constructed their summer mansions nearby. In the 1850s, developers Alfred Smith and Joseph Bailey carved up well known areas of Bellevue Avenue and Ocean Drive. By the time the Civil War occurred, big shots from New York, Boston and other areas had discovered Newport. After the war, the rich dove with gusto into the orgy of elegance that was to solidify the Newport mystique. This heyday of high society was especially pronounced in the 1890s and is best known today for the advent of "cottages" like Ocher Court (1892), Marble House (1892), Belcourt Castle (1894), the Breakers (1895) and Cross Ways (1899).

These places were the scenes of such things as parties costing $200,000 or more, banquets on horseback, dinner parties for pedigree dogs, and wing-dings with precious stones as party favors. By the turn of the 20th century, Newport's list of summer visitors was bedight not only with America's rich but with presidents, foreign heads of state, royalty and nobility.

As the 20th century progressed, a number of factors combined to start forcing this lifestyle into decline. It was pretty much done in by the Great Depression of the 1930s, when many of the rich lost their shirts, and by the coming of things like personal income taxes under President Franklin D. Roosevelt.

Yet Newport remains a haven for the rich as well as for the rest of us. Its position as the "yachting capital of the world" and other unique factors now attract affluent visitors from all over the place. Though it's usually tasteful and unobtrusive, one still can detect a certain pride of class among many summer residents from Boston, New York, Europe and elsewhere. Today, though, Newport is for everybody.

While Newport was turning into fantasyland, there was plenty of recreational growth going on elsewhere in Rhode Island. Toward the end of the 1800s, from the head of the Bay at Providence, there slowly spread down both shores a line of picnic groves, amusement parks, shore dinner halls, hotels and beaches. People got there in all sorts of conveyances that sprang up for the purpose: local railroads, steamboat lines and, beginning in the 1890s, electric trolley-car systems.

Thus could the working man and his family get out of the cities and northern mill towns for their own share of weekend relaxation. On the East Bay shore, they headed for places like Riverside, Pomham, Vue de L'Eau, Silver Spring, Camp White or Crescent Park. On the west side, Turtle Cove, Mark Rock, Riverview, Narragansett Pier, Bayside and (believe it or not) Field's Point were high spots. Another popular West Bay destination was Rocky Point, with its nationally famous shore dinner hall, which still drew crowds well into the 1990s.

Later, in the 1870s, places like Oakland Beach and Buttonwoods in Warwick, Cold Spring Beach in Wickford, and several spots in Jamestown became popular.

Riding high on the tide of summer fame were critters like the quahog which, along with his various aquatic brethren, stimulated the venerable Rhode Island institution known as the clambake. This delightful activity had originally been learned from the Indians, but was now much in demand by tourists. Most hotels along the Bay threw weekly clambakes, ripe with quahogs, lobsters, fish, sweet corn, buckwursts and oceans of melted butter. These amazing feasts were presided over by expert old-timers known as "bakemasters," only a few of whom were left by 2000.

Both shores of the Bay enjoyed their own building sprees, and many year-round homes near the shore today were once summer cottages for the middle class and upper-class fringers who didn't quite rate Newport.

Recreational boating became a big pastime, especially after the Civil War. Not only did wealthy yacht owners set course for Newport, but the resorts along the Bay nearly all rented boats, so that practically everybody could get in on the fun. When the automobile became readily available to most people after World War I, the local tourist market really came into its own. Today, Massachusetts, Connecticut, New York, and other license plates are numerous at Rhode Island's resorts and beaches.

Unlike many of Rhode Island's past glories discussed in this book, its age of tourism was far from over as the 21st century got going. With the state government's aggressive campaign to boost Rhode Island's image, and the tendency of many Americans to stay in the country on account of the international terror situation, the throngs of tourists couldn't help but swell to proportions unknown even in the 1890s.

"Rhode Island, America's First Resort," a phrase obligingly plucked by tourism officials from the 1985-1986 series of articles on which this book is based, was as apt in 2000 as ever.

-PFE

Newport's Gilded Age

Many of us have gazed wistfully through the gates of a mansion along Ocean Drive, and imagined ourselves a rich summer visitor in the dazzling days of the 1890s. But there were many aspects of that much-touted life that would make any red-blooded, modern Rhode Islander run in the other direction.

For one thing, all the opulence was accompanied by a strict and rather glum code of dress, behavior and social pecking order. It really didn't matter all that much how rich you were: Unless you watched yourself every minute, wormed your way into the right circles, belonged to the right family, and got invited to the right parties by the right fat cats, you wouldn't have had much of a social life. Old connections, business associations, and common prep-school memories had a great deal to do with it too.

This was especially true if you were a woman. Many of the men tried to keep out of the worst of the social politicking, but women couldn't. Many of us would like to be rich so we could get out of the "jungle" and "rat race," but among Newport's elite, you would probably have had to kick, bite and scratch just to be among the "in-crowd" on your summer vacation.

Except for the glamour that currently hovers around Euro royalty, most of us aren't impressed by titles anymore. But among the "cottage" crowd of the 1890s, everyone wanted a noble title. Wealthy matrons would go to ridiculous lengths to fix up their daughters with the European princes, dukes, counts or what-have-you who sometimes breezed through the

Newport social circuit.

Today's run-of-the-mill Rhode Islander would have been looked down upon as a pest or worse. One writer who extolled Newport's wealthy during the 1890s sniffed, "The appalling excursionist from Providence and Pawtucket, with his and her paper bags and odor of peanuts and ginger-pop, infests the squares, the cliffs, the beach, and awakens echoes with enjoyment."

But there were some things in the Newport of that era (besides the money) that we could have used more of at the turn of the 21st century — like plenty of civility and good manners. One magazine writer in 1894 said that a pleasingly exaggerated sense of this permeated all of Newport.

"The clerks in their shops along Thames Street betray the influence in their deportment," wrote W.C. Brownell in *Scribner's Magazine*. "School-children, even, treat each other with noticeably more decorousness than elsewhere."

By the 20th century, however, the overdone social rules in summer Newport had started to become ends in themselves, and many realized that it was getting difficult to have any fun. These mores finally died, along with the seemingly bottomless riches that brought about such habits in the first place. So, despite its good aspects and romance, it was not a world most of us would have liked to live in.

-PFE

The Luxury Steamships
of Narragansett Bay

Rhode Island never would have become a target for tourists if people had no way to get here. Steamships were a major part of this Narragansett Bay success story until relatively recent years. Oddly, it took awhile for the steamboat to catch on here after it became a practical way to transport passengers and cargo.

It wasn't until the summer of 1821 that the famous vessel *Robert Fulton* churned up the Bay from its home port of New York on an excursion trip. But within a few years, regular routes had been established between New York, Newport, Providence and Boston. Local routes soon were in operation too. In no time, rich and poor alike were able to get to and from Rhode Island's high spots on any number of regular steamers. Some of them were amazingly elegant, and fares were sometimes ludicrously cheap on account of bloodthirsty competition for the enormous New York passenger business.

The President, one of the famous steamships from the 1830s and 1840s, for example, had thirty-four staterooms, elegant lounge and dining areas, and berths for 150 passengers. Later ships of the renowned Fall River Line made previous vessels look like garbage scows. The 1880s, for example, saw the likes of the *Bristol* and the *Providence*, each with 240 staterooms, accommodations for 1,200 passengers, a Grand Salon in true Victorian style, and the best chefs the company could find.

Steamships of the 1820s, powered by a paddle wheel on each side, were a bit clumsy, traveling at about sixteen miles an hour, tops. In 1835, the 205-foot *Lexington*, one of the Bay's most famous steamers, made the Providence-New York run in eleven and a half hours, smashing all previous speed records. By the end of the 19th century, when paddle wheels had been replaced by modern screw propellers, you could leave New York in the evening and be in Newport the following morning.

By 1900, excursion boats were carrying 1,250,000 passengers a year on Narragansett Bay. But the steamers' glory was not to last far into the 20th century. The coming of mass transit in the form of the electric street-railway lines that had crisscrossed Rhode Island and the rest of the eastern seaboard by 1910 sent the steamship companies into a long decline.

The automobile finished them off in the 1930s. Even the great Fall River Line died an ignoble death in 1937, a victim of the Great Depression, labor trouble, and dwindling passenger lists.

-PFE

Chapter Eleven

Rhode Island Gets Wheels

Rhode Islanders have made it through all sorts of revolutions, sometimes just barely. Upheavals military, political, religious, social and industrial all have roared across the Independent State. But none has had such a profound personal impact on every man, woman and child as the revolution in transportation that opened the 20th century. It changed the basics of where and how people of all classes could live, and it eventually gave birth to the modern suburbanite, commuter, and all-around "upwardly mobile professional."

There probably are none left among us who have even vague memories of Rhode Island before the coming of asphalt roads, automobiles, and mass transit in any modern form. Given today's large population, suburban development, and transportation links to everywhere, it seems impossible to imagine that much of Rhode Island was a sleepy backwater before the 20th century. Outside the humming industrial centers of greater Providence, and some of the bigger resorts and mill towns, the state consisted largely of sparsely populated farming country traversed by rutted wagon roads. People stayed close to their own doors and workplaces pretty much because they had no choice. Any trip to Providence or Newport, for example, was long, bone-rattling, and undertaken only for very good reason.

The coming of the steam railroads during the 1830s was revolutionary in itself, providing a relatively quick way to get people and cargo from one place to another. But these were not meant as cheap forms of local transportation, and they did next to nothing for the average Rhode Islander. The first real stirrings of the revolution started rumbling out of Canal Street in Providence in March 1864. This was the month that the Providence, Pawtucket and Central Falls Railroad began operating its "horsecar" system in and around the city. Horsecars were small, coach-like vehicles pulled along rails by horses.

The only public transportation before this had been stage coaches and horse-drawn omnibuses, most of which were owned by the people who drove them. On land at least, these new "horse railroads" were the first organized, corporate effort to get Rhode Islanders rolling "en masse" and on a timetable. And since the rails were solid and well laid, horsecars were immune from ruts, mudholes, and other roadway menaces that slowed the coaches and omnibuses. Most people were delighted with this cheap, relatively efficient system for getting around town, plodding as it was. Entrepreneurs, smelling big bucks in the new business of mass transit, established as many as seven horse railroads in the state after the Civil War.

Not everyone was overjoyed at all this, however. A newspaper report talked about one Providence neighborhood where people complained of "...the frightful racket made by the tramp of the horses and the grinding of the wheels and the tinkling of the bells of some sixty or seventy cars, which in the course of sixteen or seventeen consecutive hours roll by their dwellings daily." Had these folks known that Interstate 95 would someday pass quite nearby, they might have counted their blessings.

It wasn't long before horsecar lines like the Union Railroad in Providence teamed up with resorts like Rocky Point and Crescent Park for their mutual profit. The horse railroads and their successors, the electric streetcar lines, would advertise the parks, and very often contributed their own personnel to build and maintain amusements to make the resorts more attractive. The parks, meanwhile, would encourage people to come by sponsoring all sorts of concerts, dances, clambakes, and other drawing cards. Of course, people had to get there by public transportation, gleefully stuffing themselves into the horsecars and, later, the streetcars or "trolleys" by the tens of thousands, all for a chance to get away for awhile.

While all this was under way, the proliferating horsecar lines were beating the bushes for an alternate source of power to their hoofed hayburners. In 1887, the small Woonsocket Street Railway started experimenting with electricity in the form of primitive storage batteries, and a clumsy system of double overhead wires. These wires had the unnerving habit of breaking, then crashing through the roof of the ex-horsecar to dangle over the instantly vacated seats. Incredibly, nobody ever got killed. The vehicle worked, at least, so the experiment was considered a success. But company officials were disconcerted to find that people thought of the electric streetcar more as a novelty than as a serious way to travel. Most passengers would pay simply to ride back and forth on the short, single-stop run on South Main Street.

By 1890, though, second thoughts about the equipment, and complaints from the fire department that the overhead wires were a hazard, caused the Woonsocket Street Railway to pull the plug on the project. One Union Railroad official grumped that electric streetcars would never catch on in New England. Had he tried, he couldn't have been more wrong.

The distinction of having the first regular electric streetcar line in Rhode Island fell to Newport. This was ironic, since people in the "City by the Sea" had battled frantically — and with success — to keep horse railroads out. On August 1, 1889, the Newport Street Railway put some hand-picked guests aboard a "single-truck" (one set of wheels and one motor) Thomson Houston electric car for the first trip on what would become the busy "Cross-town" or "Beach" route. This car used the more practical, current-collecting pole running up to a single overhead wire (hence the nickname "trolley" car). Onlookers were awed as the streetcar stopped halfway down a hill, reversed direction, and climbed effortlessly back up again, to thunderous applause.

Thus began Rhode Island's love affair with the trolley car. Throughout the 1890s, a bevy of transit companies started sending hundreds upon hundreds of miles of streetcar and interurban-trolley lines across Rhode Island. These eventually linked up with what can only be described as an awesome transit system that was developing throughout the eastern half of the country.

Some statistics from the Union Railroad show how quick was this local transformation to electricity. In 1892, when it started to electrify, this particular line had 1,700 horses, 302 horsecars and twenty-seven trolleys. Five years later, it had zero horses, zero horsecars and 435 trolleys. By 1898, the Union Railroad employed over 1,000 motormen (trolley drivers) and conductors, and collected over 40 million fares. On an average day, Providence-area trolleys carried an estimated 250,000 people. This was roughly the population of the city at the time.

Most of the capital for this tremendous change came from a syndicate based in New Jersey, and headed by Nelson W. Aldrich, Rhode Island's senior U.S. senator. Aldrich and his partners knew that fortunes were to be made, and they poured out huge sums to finance the costly switch. But with big growth came big problems. The worst of these were caused by the fact that there were too many little street railways, all engaged in bitter competition, with most struggling financially despite a booming business. Also, increasingly impersonal management and deteriorating working conditions led to serious labor trouble.

After a violent carmen's strike in 1902, the big Union Railroad was combined with several utility interests to emerge as the Rhode Island Company (RICO). It wasn't long before big-time New York millionaire J.P. Morgan, the most powerful director of the important New York, New Haven and Hartford Railroad, was hot on RICO's trail. In the first years of the century, Morgan set out to buy up every southern New England steam railroad, trolley line and steamship company he could get his hands on. His enormous conglomerate acquired RICO in 1906. Aldrich and his business associates found themselves $15 million richer, Morgan got his monopoly on Rhode Island public transportation, and the average Rhode Islander saw that he was poised on the threshold of an entirely new world.

People on every level of society suddenly discovered that they no longer had to live in the hot, crowded urban areas to be close to their work. They could move to the suburbs, and commute to work on the trolleys. People also discovered the joys of traveling to another city to shop and have fun, thus further stimulating the state's economy. For the first time, large numbers of ordinary people from every corner of the state started mingling with each other regularly.

Believe it or not, there was even a subway system proposed for greater Providence. In 1914, RICO suggested to the city that such a system be built to help solve the abominable traffic congestion caused by 20th century vehicles on 18th century streets. But since neither RICO nor the city was in a position to build it, the idea got derailed in the planning stage. The heyday of the trolleys in Rhode Island lasted until about 1920.

But another sound that had started at about the turn of the century got louder and louder until it finally drowned out the clanging and grinding of the streetcars. This was, of course, the putt-putt of the "horseless carriage."

If you like to complain about Rhode Island's roads of today, you should have been around in the 19th century. After pressure from, of all things, bicycle riders, the state started sprucing up the roads, beginning in the 1890s. The first asphalt roads were paved in 1895, and this practice spread rapidly around the state. Naturally this encouraged ownership of the increasingly available automobile.

Providence's first automobile appeared in 1898. Owned and built by A.T. Cross (yes, the pen company), it was steam-driven, and it created a big stir. Its four-horsepower engine sent it bombing through the streets at ten miles-per-hour. Amazingly, these steam-powered cars were more popular around here than gasoline models during the first decade of the century. Had they been as popular everywhere else, Providence might conceivably have become what Detroit is today!

In 1904, there were 767 automobiles in Rhode Island. In 1921, thanks to assembly-line production and affordable prices, there were 43,662 cars, 64,118 licensed drivers, 3,450 accidents (many of these with trolleys) and ninety-eight deaths on the highway. As cars multiplied, so did buses, foresightedly put on the roads by the United Electric Railways Company after it took over the bankrupt RICO in 1919. Growing numbers of trucks added yet more problems to an already pandemoniac traffic situation in every city in the state.

The automobile just accelerated the changes in lifestyle already started by the trolleys. The author has observed elsewhere that the car-in-every-garage phenomenon contributed to the decline in community feeling in the state's urban neighborhoods, mill towns, and rural villages alike. The reason: It was such a ferociously "individual" vehicle. People could now go virtually wherever they liked, whenever they liked, with whomever they liked, and they didn't have to travel on a crowded trolley or bus.

In any event, competition from gasoline-powered vehicles brought about diminishing trolley use after 1923. The streetcar companies, always in a precarious position anyway, gradually eliminated the long interurban lines and, by the 1930s, only intra-city service, and a few lines to resorts, were left. World War II gave the streetcars a temporary reprieve because of strict gasoline rationing, but automobiles made a smashing comeback after 1945.

On May 14, 1948, Rhode Island's last trolley car made its last run in Providence, up Butler Avenue to Swan Point. United Electric Railways had to add several other cars to the run to accommodate all the grief-stricken trolley fans.

Between 1931 and 1955, some "trackless trolleys" operated in Providence and Pawtucket. These were electric buses that drew power from overhead wires, using double trolley poles. But these met their demise because gasoline and diesel buses proved more efficient in the long haul. In 1951, United Electric Railways became the United Transit Company. Ridership figures for this period were miserable, but so was the bus fleet. As financial problems, deteriorating service, and labor troubles multiplied for the company, the General Assembly started wondering about establishing some sort of statewide transit authority.

On July 1, 1966, the Rhode Island Public Transit Authority (RIPTA) emerged from the legislative shell. It inherited a horrific situation. Ridership was at an all-time low, the buses were a disgrace, and employee morale was abysmal. Aside from the Transit Line Bus Company in Newport, and Bonanza Bus Lines, Rhode Island's bus service had pretty much dwindled to greater Providence.

In the years leading into the 21st century, RIPTA had its ups and downs, but overall picked public transit up by its bootstraps. Service generally was efficient, buses clean and pleasant, and riders could go to most any high spot in the state for a reasonable fare.

As for automobiles, it's certainly needless to say that their popularity and all-pervasive presence grew to mammoth dimensions. Rhode Islanders, like most Americans, are hopelessly in love with their cars. They fuss and fume over them just as our forbears did over their horses, and buy and sell them in much the same ways too. The "go-anywhere-vehicle" envisioned by Henry Ford became a complete reality in Rhode Island with the advent of interstate highways, namely routes 95, 195 and 295, in the 1960s and 1970s. Not only did these roads speed automobile travel and trucking, they opened up vast, formerly rural areas to development, further changing our landscape and lifestyle.

Despite what might be called progress, there are so many cars (often three or more per family), trucks, SUVs, RVs and variations of every description that we routinely sweat in traffic jams, especially if we commute to work. But, hey! We're all mobile! The transportation revolution, despite a few dead ends, was truly total.

-PFE

Around Rhode Island
in a Trolley Car

While today's RIPTA buses are their direct descendants, not many people realize that in the twenty years between 1905 and 1925, you could board an electric trolley ear at Exchange Place in Providence (the hub of Rhode Island's transportation network) and be taken not only all over the city and suburbs, but to practically any other major point. The longer trips often required making connections, but many trolleys ran direct and express.

In today's terms, travel on the electric interurban lines was practically free. In 1911, for example, a trolley trip from Providence to Worcester cost eighty cents. (Of course, it took four hours, forty five minutes to get there.) You also could ride to Fall River (thirty cents — one hour, fifteen minutes), Narragansett Pier (seventy cents — two hours, ten minutes], Danielson, Connecticut (sixty five cents — two hours, forty seven minutes) or Newport (fifty five cents — one hour, fifty five minutes).

From Providence, you could make trolley connections to northern New England, Boston, New York, Washington, or virtually any other major point in the eastern or central United States. Unless you rode an express car, the trip probably would be inordinately long because the interurban lines sometimes ran down the middle of major highways, and would stop at every one-horse town.

Trolley travel was the technological wonder of its day. Between 1895 and the mid-1910s, when automobiles still weren't all that available to the average working person, many people from out-of-the-way places were able to travel for the first time in their lives, while city people had the easy and welcome novelty of getting out into the country. Rhode Islanders even had an affectionate name for United Electric Railways (UER) — "Uncle UE."

Streetcars that served within Providence, Newport and other Rhode Island cities usually weren't all that comfortable for any long ride. Seats generally were wooden and without cushions. The cars themselves were noisy, with groaning electric motors, hissing and thumping air brakes, and the "clickety-clack" of the rails. In later years, there were automobile horns and shouting motorists during the all-too-frequent auto-trolley accidents and close calls. By contrast, the interurban trolleys, while still somewhat noisy, often were quite plush in comparison with their city-street cousins. They usually were faster, too, because they sometimes traversed long stretches of open country on their way to more distant locales.

Before takeovers, conglomerations and bankruptcies molded most of the trolley lines into the Rhode Island Company (RICO) and its successor, the UER, there were local trolley companies of all sorts. Among these were the Newport and Fall River Street Railway, the Providence and Taunton Street Railway, the Providence and Fall River Street Railway, the Seaview Electric Railway (probably the most scenic and popular line, running from East Greenwich to Narragansett, Wakefield and Peace Dale), the Pawcatuck Valley Street Railway (Westerly to Watch Hill), the Providence and Danielson Street Railway, the Providence and Burrillville Street Railway (the main interurban between Woonsocket and the capital until 1907), and the Columbian Street Railway (a short line between Woonsocket and the North Smithfield area).

Believe it or not, there were plenty of others, many with headquarters in Connecticut or Massachusetts, but with service into Rhode Island. If you wanted to go pretty much anywhere in Little Rhody, you could bet that somebody ran a trolley line through it or near it.

Along with passenger transportation, many trolley companies offered other services. Some operated cargo trolleys or freight trains pulled by electric engines to serve industrial

One of the author's sons stands at the controls of an electric trolley car at the Seashore Trolley Museum, Kennebunkport, Maine. Trolleys like these once took passengers virtually anywhere in Rhode Island.

-Photo by Paul F. Eno

customers along their routes. Since roads weren't plowed during the winter in the early days of the trolley era, the street-railway companies had their own trolley snow plows, which would billow their way down the tracks in the early hours of wintry days. Many old timers in Rhode Island can tell hair-raising stories about their fathers, desperate to get some-where in the family Model-T, driving down the only plowed part of the road — the trolley tracks — praying that a trolley wouldn't come barreling around the next bend.

Several lines ran what amounted to rolling post offices, to serve people in rural villages who didn't have a more con-ventional way to send and receive mail. In addition, the Provi-dence and Danielson offered "The Oregon," a trolley funeral car that could be chartered for these or less somber occa-sions. Not having today's morbid "hang-ups" about death, many groups chartered the car for outings and picnics.

Urban trolley companies sponsored social events of all kinds at local amusement parks, and they attracted hordes. Natu-rally people had to ride the trolleys to get to the events. In addition, groups often chartered city trolleys much as they do buses today.

During the heyday of the trolley in Rhode Island, the street-car lines put on open, or "bloomer," cars during hot weather. These open-air trolleys were especially popular on runs to Narragansett Bay and ocean-resort spots. A delightful de-scription of a pleasant summer trolley trip in Rhode Island (this one between Providence and Chepachet) comes down to us in a letter by the distinguished Providence author H.P. Lovecraft, one of the founders of modern fantasy and sci-ence fiction. In September 1923, Lovecraft and a friend went to Chepachet in search of a rumored "Dark Swamp" that they thought might inspire a story.

We took a lunch and boarded the 10:55 a.m. car for Chepachet, the nearest Providence-connected village to our objective; speed-ing through some of the quaintest countryside conceivable.... Chepachet itself, which we reached in a little over an hour, is a veritable bucolic poem.... The return route (from Pascoag, PFE) led through some idyllic regions and frequent, pleasing vistas of winding river, verdant plain and steepled hamlet; so that we truly regretted our arrival at the smoky suburbs that presaged Provi-dence.

By the close of the 1940s, the trolleys had disappeared from the Rhode Island scene, having given way to buses and the automobile. Many feel that the state lost something very special when the trolleys departed. Most trolleys were junked, being run up to Auburn, Massachusetts, to be burned, and the metal parts sold for scrap. Some were sold to trolley companies in third-world nations, where rumor has it that a few of these long-lived, maintenance-easy vehicles operate today.

The UER also sold a number of streetcar bodies to companies and individuals, to be reincarnated as tool sheds, chicken coops, utility buildings, cabins and even diners. Happily, at least five Rhode Island trolleys met with a more worthy fate. In 2000, three of them were alive and well at the Shoreline Trolley Museum in Branford, Connecticut. These included an 1893 RICO car and two UER work cars. Two more local veterans still operated at the Seashore Trolley Museum in Kennebunkport, Maine: car #4175 of the Newport and Fall River Street Railway, built in 1913, and snow plow #16, built in 1905 for RICO.

While the romantic days of the trolley usually are considered "gone forever," this is not necessarily the case. The gasoline crisis of the late 1970s and early 1980s, along with the "sticker shock" fuel prices at the beginning of the 21st century, shook public officials into the realization that public transit of the electric variety was an important alternative that demanded reconsideration. Many rued the day when most of the old streetcar rails were torn up, unable to be brought back into service with more up-to-date vehicles.

Nevertheless, modern trolleys (usually referred to as "LRVs" or "light rail vehicles") still operate in many cities, including Boston, Philadelphia, Los Angeles and others. New Orleans still has a few lines with vintage trolleys that never went out of service. In the 1980s, an LRV line was considered for Aquidneck Island, to help ease traffic congestion .

While trolleys probably will never return to Rhode Island in profusion, we may yet hear the groan of the electric motors in our countryside.

-PFE

Annie Smith Peck:
'Higher Than Lingbergh'

There are many intriguing monuments in Providence's North Burial Ground.

There is one for Al Martin, who died at the Alamo, and whose remains may or may not be here. Supposedly, Mexican General Santa Ana gathered the bodies of the men he had killed at the Alamo and piled them in the courtyard before setting them on fire.

The stone of Stephen Hopkins is here too. He signed the Declaration of Independence. If you look long enough, or do it the easy way and ask at the office, you will be able to find the small stone of Sarah Helen Whitman, apple of the eye of Edgar Allan Poe, and a resident of Benefit Street in Providence. Poe spent considerable time in the capital city, tossing 'em down at the Hotel Earl on South Main Street, where the Washington Insurance building now stands, before making his way to Helen's home to woo her in vain. An intolerant Mrs. Whitman finally broke off the would-be romance after seeing Poe in his cups once too often.

Early Rhode Island governors and Providence mayors also rest in North Burial Ground, as does General William Barton, whose capture of the British General Richard Prescott helped turn the tide in favor of the American forces in the Revolutionary War.

Then there is the bullet, rising out of the cluster of older headstones , marking the final resting place of Dr. George B. Peck, educator and scientist. The bullet is visible from most parts of the cemetery, and that makes it easy to find the slab lying next to it. On that long, thin stone is the quote, "You have brought uncommon glory to women of all time." The remark was made by Dr. John H. Finlay as a tribute to Annie Smith Peck at the celebration of her eightieth birthday.

Who was Annie Smith Peck? Why was such praise applied to her?

Annie Smith Peck was a local girl, born on October 19, 1850, in a two-story house built by her grandfather at 865 North Main Street, across from the cemetery. She grew up with three brothers, two older and one younger. Her family on her mother's side traced its roots to Roger Williams, founder of Providence.

Although Peck gained worldwide acclaim when she reached the top of Mount Huascaran in Peru, she already had made her presence felt wherever she lived and worked, whether in the Providence school system, or in faraway places like Greece and Germany, where she excelled in languages and music.

What is now Rhode Island College was once known as The Rhode Island Normal School, where teachers were trained, and Peck was a graduate of its first class, in 1872. Her father and brothers had studied at Brown University, and she wanted to continue the family tradition, but no woman had ever applied, much less attended, the all-male institution. Ezekiel G. Robinson, head of the school, would not hear of it.

"Women are not encouraged to seek higher education," he said, flatly turning down her attempt to enroll.

That rejection set the tone of Peck's life of accomplishment. Before it was over, she would be in a position to boast, "Lindbergh, I am told, has not been as high in his famous *Spirit of St. Louis* as I have on my two feet."

As if to thumb her nose at Brown University, Peck registered at the University of Michigan where, as part of a class of scholars, she excelled, receiving her bachelor of arts degree with highest honors. Three years later, she was awarded a master of arts degree for proficiency in Latin and Greek. By 1884, Peck was a world traveler, had studied music in Germany, and was the first woman to attend the American School of Classical Studies in Athens, Greece. Her list of "firsts" became long, but the best and most notable events were yet to come, even though they also were physically and mentally painful: Peck became a renowned mountain climber.

While in Athens, Peck found that climbing was more than healthy, it was fun. She climbed Mount Hymettus and Mount Pentelius, near Athens, and the 12,000-foot Gross Glockner in Tyrol. But it wasn't until she was forty years old that she began climbing mountains in earnest. Once she had scaled the Matterhorn in 1890, she knew she had to go higher.

"I began climbing mountains because I like walking, especially among hills, and I wanted to climb something enough to take hold of with my hands," Peck explained. "For this reason, I enjoy rock mountains more than snow."

She had adventure in her blood, adding, "I became a suffragist *(someone who worked for women's right to vote GVL)* in my teens, when it was unfashionable."

She once told a newspaperman, "I was sure I would live to be fifty or sixty. I thought I could help the (suffrage) cause by adding what one woman might to show the equality of the sexes."

When she first saw the Matterhorn, Peck knew she would never be happy until she climbed to its peak. While the 15,000-foot ascent was perilous, she tossed the threat aside, quipping, "The streets of New York I consider more dangerous."

She conquered the Matterhorn, but considered it child's play compared with Peru's Huascaran. All the aggravation and personal suffering Peck had known up to that point did not prepare her for the ascent of Mount Huascaran. Four times she tried, and four times she failed, not for want of ability and desire, but because of the sheer cowardice of her guides and other so-called helpers.

Before she was able to conquer the Peruvian mountain, Peck mastered California's Mount Shasta in 1894, the Matterhorn in Switzerland in 1895, and Nameless Rock Mountain in Peru in 1906, among others. She made two attempts to scale Mount Huascaran in 1904, and two more in 1906. In the spring of 1908, Mrs. Anne Woerishoffer, a well-to-do woman from New York City, wired Peck, advising her that she would fund another expedition to Peru and another try at Mount Huascaran. On June 27, 1908, Peck sailed from New York, leaving the home she had established in Manhattan, and headed for Peru.

Providence native Annie Smith Peck, ready for her
ascent of Peru's Mount Huascaran in 1908.

-Collection of Susan Heuck Allen

Well supplied, and accompanied by a team of Swiss guides
and Indian helpers who proved to be adequate, Peck was
ready to climb again on August 6. She was well insulated
against the cold, writing that she wore "three suits of light-

weight woolen underwear, two pairs of tights, canvas knickerbockers, two flannel waists, a little cardigan jacket, two sweaters and four pair of woolen stockings." The American Museum of Natural History in New York had given her an Inuit suit that had belonged to Admiral Robert E. Peary, the famed polar explorer. Unfortunately, it was lost along with other necessities, including a stove, when they fell into a crevasse.

Despite the hardships, Peck reached the north peak of Mount Huascaran on September 1, 1908, accompanied by her Swiss porters, Gabriel and Rudolf, and four Indian guides. She had succeeded in climbing higher than any woman in the world, and she was fifty-eight years old!

Upon completing the descent, Rudolf required immediate medical attention because he was suffering from severe frostbite. As a result, his left hand, one finger of his right hand, and half of one foot had to be amputated. Peck, needing no medical attention, was angry with Rudolf for refusing to wear extra socks and mittens, though she made certain he received excellent care before she left Peru.

Annie Smith Peck was more than a mountain climber, though her feats in that area gained her worldwide fame. In 1910, when she was sixty, she climbed Mount Coropuna in Peru, carrying a banner for women's suffrage, given to her by the Joan of Arc Women's Suffrage League. She also wrote about her adventures, producing a short book with the long title *Search for the Apex of America; High Mountain Climbing in Peru and Bolivia, Including the Conquest of Huascaran with some Observations on the Country and People Below*.

When she was eighty, Peck took a 20,000 mile trip by air to get a "bird's-eye view" of the mountains she had climbed throughout the world. She wrote about that experience in another book, *Flying Over South America, 20,000 Miles by Air*, published in 1932.

Although she suffered terribly during her years of mountain climbing, facing numerous difficulties and poverty, her efforts did not remain unappreciated by the government of Peru. In honor of her conquest of the north peak of Mount Huascaran, the Lima Geographical Society renamed it

"Cumbre Ana Peck." She also was named a fellow of the Royal Geographical Society, a member of the Society of Women Geographers, and of the Academy of Political and Social Science, along with Pi Gamma Mu.

Peck was outspoken on virtually any subject, such as equality with men.

"I see no reason why women should care to equal men in brawn and muscle. If any do, and have special enjoyment, it is quite proper for them to undertake strenuous tasks." But she was quick to tell listeners that she was five-feet, seven-inches tall and wore size 5½ AA shoes.

In 1925, Peck, who came from an old Rhode Island Baptist family, became embroiled in a publicized battle with Dr. Harry Emerson Fosdick, a modernist minister. While she was living in Manhattan, Peck attended the Park Avenue Baptist Church, owned by the Rockefellers, and served as a trustee. Dr. Fosdick was hired as minister, but Annie voted against his calling, thus preventing a unanimous vote of support. She disapproved of his belief that Baptists should no longer be immersed in water when being baptized.

"In Providence, Baptists are liberal," she complained. "There is no excuse for a Baptist Church unless immersion is the form of baptism practiced."

Word of the controversy surrounding Peck reached the administration of President Warren G. Harding, and apparently was not well received. Though she denied reports to the contrary, it was said she was seeking the appointment as U.S. minister (ambassador) to Guatemala.

She commented, "Although I have no expectation of being offered the post, I may be better qualified than some of the ministers who have been appointed in the past."

Her appointment never materialized.

However, she continued to receive acclaim for her mountain-climbing exploits, in addition to her considerable scholastic achievements. In 1922, the National League of Women Voters was asked to name the twelve greatest living women in the United States, and Peck was included in the list.

In celebration of her eighty-fourth birthday, Peck received the good wishes of the Peruvian ambassador in Washington,

M. De Freyrey Santander, as well as those of the director general of the Pan American Union, who said, "Miss Peck's name is an 'open sesame' throughout Peru. Her memory is cherished as that of one who contributed to make known inaccessible parts of the land where she achieved fame."

Peck continued to climb until the end of her life. On her last ascent, she reached the top of Mount Madison in the White Mountains of New Hampshire, a height of 5,362 feet. As late as January 1935, she climbed the road to the Acropolis in Athens, Greece, in her final accomplishment.

She spent her remaining months in her apartment at the Hotel Monterey in New York City. On July 1, 1935, she became critically ill, and had to cancel her plans to spend the summer in Asbury Park, New Jersey. A few weeks later, on July 18, she died in her apartment. She was eighty-four years old.

Honoring her wishes, her body was cremated, and her ashes placed beneath a flat stone, near the graves of her parents and her brother, George. She was survived by her younger brother, William, with whom she stayed when in Rhode Island. He had recently completed a long career as principal of Classical High School in Providence.

The name of Annie Smith Peck may not be remembered by many today, but her life can be put in clearer perspective with the words of no less than famed aviatrix Amelia Earhart: "I felt myself an upstart beside her."

-GVL

Annie Smith Peck in later life.

-Collection of Susan Heuck Allen

Chapter Twelve

The Twentieth Century Roars In

Some people complain that we Rhode Islanders are a suspicious lot who don't take easily to new ideas or change. If that were true, it wouldn't be any wonder: The 20th century brought so many catastrophes, economic and otherwise, that we must hardly know how to act without them.

The century opened auspiciously enough. Providence was the center of an industrial wonderland, the transportation revolution was starting to open up the wide world to everyone, and America, having won an overseas empire in a brief war with Spain in 1898, was at peace again. But before many years had passed, it became apparent that things in Rhode Island weren't quite as peachy as they seemed. This usually is blamed on the state's leaders, both industrial and political (they tended to be one and the same). They failed to recognize that the world and national economies were changing, and that revolutionary steps were required if Rhode Island was to adapt.

William H. Caunce, president of Brown University, summed it up in 1913. "We cannot graze upon the past and become fat. We cannot live on inherited wealth, inherited traditions, inherited memories when we should be getting together to create new wealth, to establish new traditions and memories which posterity may cherish."

Few listened. As demand for goods made in Rhode Island declined (things like metal products and textiles were starting to be produced more cheaply elsewhere), the state's economy started to crumble.

In 1914, meanwhile, World War I erupted in Europe. As with most Americans, Rhode Islanders strongly supported the British and French against the Germans and Austro-Hungarians. Whether or not they knew what the fighting was about, people at that time generally had a naive, romantic picture of war, which it took all the horrors of world conflict to dispel. Even before America entered the war against Germany in April 1917, anti-German hysteria flared up all over Rhode Island, fanned by John R. Rathom, editor of the *Providence Journal*. He brought national attention to the paper by running all sorts of exaggerated or fabricated stories about German atrocities, and plots for sabotage or subversion within the United States.

After war was declared, Rhode Islanders climbed over each other to enlist, to buy war bonds, and to join home-front support organizations. Many opponents of the war were arrested, and a campaign against all German influences passed through Rhode Island like a very nasty storm. The state made all teachers take a loyalty oath. Even instruction in the German language, and its greatest literature, vanished from Rhode Island classrooms. In short, patriotism went haywire.

When the war ended in November 1918, the paranoia did not. The Russian Revolution of the precious year had scared the dickens out of the western democracies, so the communist movement now became the enemy. These fears were certainly justified to a degree, since everybody knew it was the avowed purpose of Moscow and the "Communist International" to export violent revolution to workers all over the world, though these efforts always had mixed results in developed nations. Indeed, there were a few labor agitators in Rhode Island and elsewhere who tried to stir up unrest and Bolshevik-style revolution. But Rhode Island's workers, dissatisfied as they were with working conditions, were as solidly patriotic as anyone.

By 1920, the "Red Scare" had a lock-tight grip on the state. Afraid that incoming immigrants might be foreign rabble-rousers in disguise, the Americanization effort was stepped up. In January alone, more than a dozen people in Rhode Island were arrested as suspected radicals. In Providence, a city ordinance forbade the carrying of red flags in any procession.

As Rhode Islanders were peeking under every rock for communists, the state's economy was falling down around our ears. In a real way, the Great Depression began in Rhode Island long before the stock market crash of 1929. As wars always do, World War I had brought plenty of jobs, higher wages and temporary economic relief for the state. But when peace returned, so did the problems.

The 1920s came storming into the Ocean State with high wages, falling prices, railroad cargo rates that were up to 113 percent higher than elsewhere, and soaring costs for foreign cotton imports. These factors conspired to all but wreck Rhode Island's industry, especially the textile business. If you'd told people at the turn of the century that the state's enormous B.B. and R. Knight "Fruit of the Loom" empire would be sold at a loss some twenty years later, they would have thought you needed professional help.

When some textile manufacturers tried to survive by cutting wages by forty to fifty percent in 1921 and 1922, they brought down upon themselves the wrath of increasingly powerful labor unions. But the mill owners deserved what they got: Instead of modernizing their plants or using cheaper synthetic materials, they clung to the ways of the past in management, manufacturing, and sales techniques. There were violent strikes by textile workers in 1922 and 1924, and other strikes throughout the decade threatened to turn bloody. But it was a lost cause: The textile industry was fleeing to the South, where labor, taxes, and just about everything else were cheaper.

Those in charge made half-hearted efforts to improve things by talking about economic-development funds and efforts to attract new industry. But it was too late. On "Black Thursday," October 24, 1929, and the week that followed, the bottom fell out of the stock market. Confidence in the system melted; virtually no buyers could be found for any stock. Since all sorts of people in all classes of society had played the "bull market," usually on "margin," a kind of credit, millions lost their shirts.

While today's global economy certainly has its ups and downs, only those old enough to remember the Great Depression have any true idea of what it was like when things really did go to hell in a bucket. The stock market crash generated a rolling domino reaction over the next few years. Huge numbers of banks failed because people couldn't pay their loans, depositors panicked and withdrew their money, and there was no federal insurance to protect savings. Many utilities and transportation systems collapsed, and business and industry contracted. Prices plummeted, but since staggering numbers of people lost their jobs, and had their savings obliterated in bank failures, low prices didn't do them much good. In these days before Social Security and unemployment insurance, the mass suffering simply went on and on for years.

In Rhode Island, almost eighty percent of the cotton mills had closed by 1937. Forty percent of the state's textile workers, over fort-seven percent of the jewelry workers, and thirty-eight percent of the iron and steel workers lost their jobs. The lucky few who had jobs often had to be satisfied with part-time work, and precious little of that.

With 115,000 Rhode Islanders out of work, frightening numbers of people had to swallow their pride, and stand in bread and soup lines to keep from starving. Some folks along the Bay and the South County coast had to fish, lobster and quahog just to get enough to eat, never mind make a living. In the once thriving summer rookeries like Oakland Beach and Conimicut in Warwick, middle-class summer-home owners had to sell out at Depression prices. Near-penniless families fleeing the worse destitution in the cities often moved in, and turned cottages into year-round homes.

The Great Depression didn't maul everyone. Those who had managed to stay rich still summered in Newport, and many old-line families kept their College Hill mansions. While municipal budgets were cut, public employees, including teachers, generally kept their jobs. So did most railroad workers and utility employees.

In 1932, amidst this unprecedented mess, people went to the polls and threw the fiscally conservative Republicans out of office. Franklin D. Roosevelt became president of the United States, and Theodore Francis Green became governor of Rhode Island. To have a Democratic governor and, a few years later, a Democrat-dominated General Assembly was a political revolution. The firm, almost morbid, grip the old-line Republicans had had on the state for decades finally was broken.

As for the economic debacle, help finally came in the form of Roosevelt's "New Deal," with federal relief funds eventually pouring into the state. These were used to create training programs, new jobs, and many public-works and civic-improvement projects. New federal job programs like the Works Progress Administration (WPA), the Civilian Conservation Corps (CCC), and the Public Works Administration (PWA) were like a miracle drug for a dying patient. They provided jobs and, just as importantly, hope. Other federal programs helped with rents and mortgages, and housing projects started in profusion.

Many of the parks, sidewalks, public buildings, and other facilities we take for granted today were built during the Depression with federal job funds, usually organized and administered by the WPA. In Warwick, for example, Hangar #1 and the Air National Guard Hangar at Green State Airport were built with WPA and PWA money in 1938 and 1940, respectively.

One could argue that it was the introduction of socialism without "Red revolution," a smart move by Roosevelt, who reportedly quipped that if he didn't take radical steps to bring the country out of the Depression, he might be the last president of the United States. One also could argue that his "New Deal" was the final death blow to pure capitalism, and the enthronement of the tax-heavy welfare state.

It was the New Deal that established the Social Security Administration, along with the first federal job, health, housing and education programs, including food stamps. The

Democrats also lit fires under the states to establish unemployment benefits and workers' compensation plans. Of course, this all had to be paid for by somebody. Unfortunately, it was by Washington's going on a spending binge that hasn't ended to this day. But what was the alternative?

Traditionally, social relief had been the job of private charities like the Salvation Army and the Red Cross. The Depression, however, sent these organizations reeling because of the ocean of people who suddenly needed help. The New Deal was a milestone in social history. For the first time, government felt it had to act in the name of plain humanity, not to mention fear of an uprising, a real possibility under the dire circumstances. Patriotism notwithstanding, no nation is more than a few meals away from a revolution.

By the end of the 1930s, confidence was on the rise, and people started to feel that maybe things would get better. But Rhode Island still had the highest per capita unemployment rate in the nation in 1939, primarily because its industrial base had been suffering for twenty years. It was to take the combined efforts of Adolf Hitler and Emperor Hirohito to drag Rhode Island up out of the Great Depression.

The Second World War changed things in Rhode Island so dramatically that it's hard to imagine for people who didn't see it with their own eyes. For today's individualistic, perhaps spoiled, generations, the atmosphere of total mobilization and cooperation in that era would also be difficult to picture. There was almost no dissent during the war, either, not only because the United States had been attacked first, but because the threat to the country from the Axis powers was so obvious, immediate and overwhelming. Rhode Island became not only an armed camp but a throbbing industrial center for defense goods.

The war had been raging in Europe since September 1939, but the United States was officially neutral until the Japanese attacked Pearl Harbor, Hawaii, on December 7, 1941. Nonetheless, defense contracts started flowing into Rhode Island as early as June 1940. Much of the $115 million in defense work went to the state's gasping textile industry, which was tailor-made for producing things like military uniforms and accessories. Also, weapons, rubber products, lifesaving gear, and all manner of other equipment poured out of Rhode Island's reopened factories.

At long last, anyone who wanted a job had one and, for the first time, women entered the work force in large numbers, primarily because most of the young, able-bodied men had joined the armed forces. Large-scale shipbuilding even returned to the upper Bay and expanded elsewhere. At Field's Point in Providence, the Rheem (later the Walsh-Kaiser) Shipyard, launched its first wartime vessel, a merchant ship ironically named after arch-Quaker William Coddington, in November 1942. The Herreshoff Yard in Bristol built high-powered wooden patrol torpedo (PT) boats that gave many a pleasure boater heart failure as they roared across the Bay on test runs at fifty miles an hour. The little Warren Shipyard even pitched in with wooden picket boats used for coastal patrols.

The Navy had recognized the practical and strategic value of Narragansett Bay since the Civil War, when the U.S. Naval Academy had moved to Newport for the duration. As World War II approached, the Navy, and Army too, injected millions of dollars into Rhode Island to beef up already existing bases, airstrips, piers, housing, and supply facilities, and to build new ones.

These humming military installations included the awesome Quonset Point Naval Air Station in North Kingstown (the largest in the East), other naval aviation facilities at Westerly and Charlestown, the Naval Construction Battalion ("Seabees") Training Center at Davisville, the Army Air Corps pilot training center at Hillsgrove in Warwick (where Green State Airport is today), and, of course, the vast training, storage and ship-berthing facilities at Newport itself. Among the latter were the Anti-Aircraft Training Center, the Motor Torpedo Boat Squadrons Training Center, the Naval Torpedo Station on Goat Island (the nation's chief manufacturing center for torpedoes), and storage facilities for ammunition and high explosives, on Gould and Prudence Islands.

To defend all this, the Navy mined all the approaches to

Narragansett Bay, and installed anti-submarine nets in the Bay's passages. This wasn't overcaution: German U-boats sank nine merchant vessels off New England in the first seven months of 1942.

What today are the quaint forts at the mouth of the Bay all were manned by as many as 10,000 personnel during the war. Historic Fort Adams in Newport was the headquarters for Rhode Island's coastal defense. Formidable coastal gun emplacements were built at strategic locations, and innocent-looking beach cottages often were outposts for spotters, who constantly watched the seaward horizon for enemy craft. The remains of some of the gun emplacements still can be seen at places like Beavertail State Park in Jamestown.

In 1942, Rhode Island was declared first a "military district" and then a "vital war zone." The authority of the Army superseded that of the civil government. Hundreds of thousands of military and civilian personnel trained, worked and lived at these myriad facilities. There was a nightmarish housing shortage for civilian employees, and the famous "Quonset Hut," produced by two factories at Davisville, proved a partial answer to this problem — all over the world. On the other hand, the presence of so many free-spending soldiers and sailors created a golden age for retail business, especially in Newport.

Rhode Island's World War II story is filled with fascinating but little-known anecdotes. For example, a top secret radio-monitoring station at Chopmist Hill in Scituate eavesdropped on enemy transmissions from all over the world. So important was the work that there were federal officials in the late 20th century who told the author that the war might have been lost if it weren't for this station.

By the end of the conflict, Rhode Island was the center of an ambitious "re-education" program for German prisoners of war. Even before this, a few dozen of them had been in Rhode Island, working in a secret anti-Nazi indoctrination program aimed at the 370,000 German POWs in the United States. This program helped find and cultivate democratic-minded Germans for positions of responsibility in postwar Germany.

Few people realize that the last battle of the naval war in

the Atlantic took place between Point Judith and Block Island. Twenty-eight hours before Germany's official surrender in May 1945, the U-853, which had either not received or simply ignored the German High Command's recall order, torpedoed and sank the coal ship *Black Point* three miles off Point Judith. Twelve crewmen died. The Navy and Coast Guard went into action right away, hunting down the U-boat, and destroying it the next day near Block Island.

Just as at the end of World War I, the same old problems returned to haunt Little Rhody after the surrender of Japan in August 1945. The Great Depression was over, but so was the honeymoon.

-PFE

The Tragedy
of Henrietta Drummond

"I am having a wonderful time here, and it will be a trip to remember."

Henrietta Isabel Drummond, Pawtucket nurse, member of the Rhode Island Chapter of the American Red Cross, was writing to her mother from aboard a ship making its way across the Atlantic to France during the waning days of World War I. She had recently finished her training at Camp Wadsworth, South Carolina, and eagerly awaited the role she would play in saving lives as an American Red Cross nurse at Army Base Hospital #68 in Nevers, France.

Unfortunately, it was the last word Jean Drummond would ever receive from her daughter. Within days of her excited letter, Henrietta Drummond would be dead at Army Base Hospital #68, the victim of a blood infection called septicemia. She was twenty-five years old, and the only nurse from Rhode Island to make the supreme sacrifice during the "War to End All Wars."

In the middle of a busy square at Main Street and Mineral Spring Avenue in Pawtucket stands a granite monument with the inscription, a quote from poet John Greenleaf Whittier, "She laid with him the dead as she turned to sooth the living and bind the wounds that bled."

It was a warm Sunday afternoon on September 26, 1937, when that monument was dedicated to Henrietta Isabel Drummond by an American Legion Post bearing her name, the only post in the United States named after a woman. Some 10,000 people, including 1,000 marching men, turned out to see Henrietta's sister Helen pull the cloth veil from the monument, atop which was an illuminated torch held by a hand much like that of the Statue of Liberty. Each dignitary who spoke lauded the young nurse, who had graduated from St. Joseph's Hospital in Providence in 1917, and who had died doing as much for her country as any man with a rifle in a trench had done, according to the day's keynote speaker, Francis B. Condon, chief justice of the Rhode Island Supreme Court.

In July 1987, the Henrietta I. Drummond American Legion Post #50 turned in its charter and ceased to exist. Today, few people remember the young, dark-haired woman who left the security of her home in Pawtucket to participate in the "Great War" and help preserve that security for others. This is both her story and a reason never to forget who Henrietta Drummond was, and what she lived and died for.

Henrietta Drummond was a fun-loving girl who, according to one classmate, danced on a table during a school party at St. Joseph's Hospital School of Nursing.

After she joined the Red Cross, Drummond was stationed at Headquarters, 71st Infantry, New York National Guard, at Park Avenue and 24th Street, New York City. During that time, she wrote a song, sung to the tune of *Tramp Tramp Tramp The Boys Are Marching*, a popular tune during World War I. It was called *The Song of Base Hospital Unit No. 88*, and it surfaced in the late 20th century with the discovery of a letter sent to Drummond's brother, William, shortly after her death by Lieutenant Ervin W. Reid of the U.S. Army. William Drummond, who lived at 252 West 22nd Street, New York, had visited Reid in December, about eight weeks after learning of his sister's death. He was pleased to discover that she wrote the unit song.

TRAMP TRAMP TRAMP, OUR UNIT'S COMING!
Tramp! Tramp! Tramp!
The girls are marching
Here we come one hundred strong,
With Old Glory at the front,
We will make old Kaiser grunt
With a push he never, never had before.

Tramp! Tramp! Tramp!
Our unit's coming,
Cheer up, Allies, we'll be there
We are nurses full of pep,
Germany will lose its rep,
When Unit 68 gets over there.
Tramp! Tramp! Tramp!
Sixty-eight is coming,
Coming o'er the deep blue sea,
Sixty eight will do its best,
To put Kaiser Bill at rest,
And we'll all come marching home across the sea.

Drummond was one of ten graduate nurses who received diplomas from St. Joseph's Hospital School of Nursing in May 1917. She joined the Red Cross at Providence in June, and was assigned to the Army Nurses Division of the American Expeditionary Force. She knew exactly what she wanted to do and, after training, Henrietta would do it. She would go to France and help in the war effort. That training was conducted at Spartanburg, South Carolina. She returned home from active duty just twice, at Christmas and in July 1918, to attend the funeral of her father, who had died suddenly of a heart attack.

During the Great War, two types of hospitals operated in France. One was part of the U.S. Army's evacuation system, where facilities were named American Red Cross One, Two, Three, and so on, depending on how many were in operation. Army officers commanded them, with Red Cross personnel handling the daily duties. The second type of hospital was for French and American soldiers, connected with the French evacuation system, run independently by the Red Cross for wounded allied troops. Both classes of hospitals provided more than 8,000 beds, and donations to the Red Cross allowed several chateaux to be run for those men, who were convalescing after surgery or from the effects of poison gas.

On September 16, Drummond and other staff of Army Base Hospital #68 left New York for France aboard the *Balmoral Castle*, stopping in Glasgow, Scotland, on the 29th, proceeding to Southhampton, England, and finally to Nevers, France, on October 4th.

In six days, Drummond was dead of what was described as typhoid fever or Spanish influenza. A Protestant funeral was held on Columbus Day, October 12, 1918, two days after her demise. By all accounts, it was impressive. There were thirty-two soldiers, followed by a military band, which led the casket to a burying ground that had been established for officers and nurses near the base hospital. According to one nurse, more than 200 people, mostly soldiers and nurses, attended the afternoon service, after which Drummond's body was buried beneath a large stone cross.

Nurse Katherine Magrath praised Drummond by telling her sister Helen, "The officers and enlisted men of the company deeply sympathize with you in your bereavement. Divine Providence decreed that she should be taken before she had done much of what she came over here to do. However, we hope you feel as we do, that she is none the less a heroine, for she has given as much for the sake of her country, she had made the supreme sacrifice."

Magrath noted at the end of the letter that Drummond had carried a war-risk insurance policy of $10,000.

If services for Henrietta Drummond were impressive in Nevers, France, they were extraordinary when her body was returned to Pawtucket in December 1920. The casket was drawn on a flag-draped caisson from the George E. Brown Funeral Parlor on Mineral Spring Avenue to Park Place Congregational Church, a half-mile away, as thousands of people lined the sidewalks. Uniformed veterans were on hand as a guard of honor lifted the casket from the caisson and carried it into the church, where a simple service was conducted.

Park Place Pastor Henry B. Kirkland told the standing-room-only congregation that Drummond sacrificed her life on an errand of patriotism for her country. Someone sang *Lead Kindly Light* and *Beautiful Tale of Somewhere*. The congregation then joined in *America*, and *Taps* was sounded. The service was over, and Henrietta Drummond's final journey began with a three-mile ride from the church to Moshassuck Cemetery, where she was laid to rest beneath a stone bearing

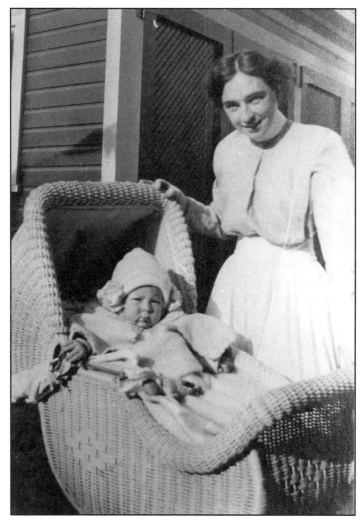

Henrietta Drummond visits with her niece in
Cumberland before leaving for France in 1918.

-Collection of the Author

the symbol of the Red Cross.

The Henrietta I. Drummond American Legion Post #50 and
Auxiliary were created in 1920, shortly after her body was
returned from France. During its lifetime, the post and auxiliary were responsible for many community efforts, the most

celebrated being money raised for the benefit of a young Pawtucket boy badly burned in a fire. Jimmy Beaucage nearly lost his life, but thanks to the money raised by the Drummond legionnaires and their auxiliary, the enormous medical expenses were eased. Countless dinners raised thousands of dollars over the years, as did dances, bake sales and rummage sales.

But like the soldiers who marched with Henrietta Drummond's casket in 1918, time also marched on, and membership in the post began to dwindle. Many of its members were veterans of World Wars I and II. Like the young girl who stepped off a boat in Nevers, France, the post bearing her name was doomed. By the early 1980s, membership had fallen from a peak of 1,560 to 21, and the charter was turned in to the state American Legion headquarters.

There may no longer be a Henrietta I. Drummond Post #50, but there will always be the memory of a young nurse from Pawtucket who never knew a husband, children, retirement or old age. The young nurse who sacrificed it all to place a soothing hand on those who needed one, and who died just four weeks before the 11th hour of the 11th day of the 11th month in 1918, when the war ended "over there."

What no one could see then was the other wars to be fought and other Red Cross nurses who would go to the aid of victims. Henrietta Drummond would no doubt have been among the first to volunteer, and to give her all to do as much for the war effort as any soldier in any foxhole, and to help bring peace on earth once and for all.

-GVL

Rhode Island's
Greatest Lover

Not far from the serene pond and fountain at Swan Point Cemetery in Providence is a small headstone with a very arresting epitaph. Like the man whose grave it marks, the stone is conservative, unimposing and somewhat off the beaten path.

It says simply: "I am Providence."

Such was the self-description of the man who, among all the brave and loyal Rhode Islanders we have met in this book, can, in terms of sheer passion, arguably be called Providence's, and Rhode Island's, greatest lover. Howard Phillips Lovecraft, who lived from 1890 to 1937, was a storyteller: a writer whose tales of horror, fantasy and science fiction form a foundation on which much of modern literature in those genres is built. Virtually unknown to the general public in his own time, Lovecraft's work was widely reprinted in the 1960s, and has been surging in popularity around the world ever since.

Opinions about Lovecraft's stories differ to an unbelievable degree: a Spanish authority, Jose Luis Garcia, once called Lovecraft one of the ten greatest writers of all time. Others have said that his work is worthless. No matter what one feels, it cannot be denied that most of his stories are highly original and of significant literary importance. As for Lovecraft the man: He embodied, in the words of a biographer, "more contradictions than one would think could be crammed into a single human being."

For example, Lovecraft is bitterly criticized today for the racist and xenophobic statements he made for all but the last years of his life. Yet, he married a Russian Jew whom he loved deeply and praised to high heaven, and he had a loyal circle of literary friends of many backgrounds. Also, Lovecraft is chuckled at today by those who read his letters posing as an elderly gentleman (while only in his 30s) and as an 18th century country squire. But H.P.L. himself never took this as seriously as some of his critics do, and he greatly enjoyed laughing at himself. Nearly everyone who met him was impressed by his erudition, sharp mind, gentle spirit and quick wit.

There is little question that the greatest practical force in Lovecraft's life was his passion for the 1,248 square miles surrounding and including Narragansett Bay. Born in his grandfather's rambling house, on the site of what is now an apartment complex on the corner of Elmgrove Avenue and Angell Street on Providence's East Side, Lovecraft lived on College Hill for most of his life.

In 1924, just before his marriage to fellow writer Sonia Haft Greene, Lovecraft made his sole attempt to live somewhere else. That New York City is uninhabitable has long been a cliché, but the principle was compounded in Lovecraft's case. So homesick did he become that his work, marriage and mental health practically collapsed. Finally, relatives convinced him that he ought to give in and come home. His description of his return to Providence in April 1926 is filled with rapture:

....the train sped on, and I experienced silent convulsions of joy in returning step by step to a waking and tri-dimensional life. New Haven — New London — and then quaint Mystic.... Then at last a still subtler magick filled the air — nobler roofs and steeples...WESTERLY.... intoxication followed — Kingston — East Greenwich with its steep Georgian alleys climbing up from the railway — Apponaug and its ancient roofs — Auburn — just outside the city limits — I fumble with bags and wraps in a desperate effort to appear calm — THEN — a delirious marble dome outside the window — a hissing of air brakes — a slackening of speed — surges of ecstasy and dropping of clouds from my eyes and mind — HOME — UNION STATION – PROVIDENCE!

The grave of Howard Phillips Lovecraft at Swan Point
Cemetery, Providence. Flowers and other tokens from
admirers frequently appear there.

-Photo by Paul F. Eno

Lovecraft constantly led friends and literary visitors on tours of the city's colonial attractions, on which he doted. A born tour guide, he often would stop and regale them with, "Where but in Providence could you find...?"

It should be understood that Lovecraft was a creature who thrived almost entirely on atmosphere, which Providence's colonial riches provide in abundance. So, his love affair was with the city — particularly College Hill — and not with the people, whom he considered incidental to the general scene. He was nearly as passionate about the rest of the state, especially Foster (whence came his maternal Phillips ancestors), western Coventry and Chepachet. Like most people who have never had to do chores on a farm, Lovecraft rhapsodized about grassroots rural life there.

Lovecraft would have been ecstatic about the restoration of the Benefit Street area on College Hill, which took place beginning in the 1960s, but would have had conniptions if he had seen the gobbling up of once rural lands by condominiums and housing developments in the late 20th century.

In honor of Lovecraft's 100th birthday, in August 1990, fans, scholars and writers gathered at Brown University for the Lovecraft Centennial Conference. While there, they dedicated a memorial to him on the lawn of the John Hay Library, which houses much Lovecraft memorabilia, including some original manuscripts.

H.P. Lovecraft, as eccentric as he was, was an honest, upright man by all accounts. And surely the thing he was most honest about was his undying love for Rhode Island and Providence Plantations and his hometown. He wrote:

"I am Providence, and Providence is myself – together, indissolubly as one, we stand thro' the ages...!"

-PFE

The Day
Nature Went Crazy

Most normal people don't sit around waiting for natural disasters. Most people don't even think about them in terms of their own lives. Perhaps this is a psychological defense mechanism, but it also may be responsible for a lack of preparedness, and the shock that accompany the rare but all too possible natural events that forever change — or take — people's lives.

This was a lesson learned in August 1986, when three tornadoes, albeit minor ones, hit Rhode Island in two days. Happily, nobody was killed. But true catastrophes are not uncommon in Rhode Island's long geological history. While New England averages two earthquakes a year of magnitude 3.0 or above on the Richter Scale, real disasters have been few during mankind's relatively brief span here. By the 20th century, there hadn't been such a thing in so long that, as is the case today, most people were pretty smug about the power of nature. Natural disasters were things that happened somewhere else.

The summer of 1938 had been very pleasant. The latest war scare in Europe was over, and President Franklin D. Roosevelt's "New Deal" programs were easing the suffering caused by the Great Depression. People generally felt better than they had in years.

The intermittent showers began on Wednesday, September 14. No-one paid much attention as the rain stretched on into Saturday. But that night, it became torrential. When it kept up for four straight days, people started to puzzle over such pain-in-the-neck weather. By Tuesday, the 20th, the ground was so saturated that it couldn't hold any more water. By then, people were starting to get scared. On Tuesday morning, flood warnings were issued for Rhode Island's river valleys. On Tuesday night, the Blackstone, Pawtuxet and other rivers already were rising over their banks, forcing many people in the lowlands to leave their homes in the middle of the night. That night, concerned authorities got word that some of the state's earthen dams were beginning to fail. They had plenty of reason to be worried: The worst natural disaster in Rhode Island history was about to descend upon them.

On Wednesday, hurricane warnings finally were issued, but no-one paid much attention because hurricanes happened in Florida, not Rhode Island. Toward midday, people along Narragansett Bay and the South County coastline became frightened when the incoming tide didn't stop coming in. Shortly before 3 p.m., there was a sudden rise in the water level everywhere. The dreaded "storm surge" that precedes every major hurricane slammed into the Rhode Island coast in the form of a thirty-foot tidal wave.

Crashing in from the southeast at nearly 100 miles an hour, it swept the beaches clean of buildings, boats, motor vehicles and people at Napatree Point, Misquamicut and Quonochontaug. At Charlestown alone, fifty people died in a matter of minutes. The tidal wave rolled on inland. After the storm, survivors stared in disbelief at whole houses, cottages, cars, trucks and bodies that had been carried more than a mile from shore.

Rolling madly up Narragansett Bay, the surge cleared beaches all along the way, then smashed into Providence right in the middle of the rush hour. People in cars, buses and trolley cars found water suddenly rising around them to thirteen feet above flood stage. Some never lived to tell the tale.

The hurricane itself howled into Rhode Island packing winds of up to 175 miles per hour. Its power was so great that brick factory walls collapsed, people were picked up and hurled about, and cars were sent cart-wheeling. Newport's Ocean Drive crumbled into the sea. Yacht clubs along the Bay vanished. Church steeples all over the state crashed to the ground. Millions of magnificent trees were lost forever, especially in western Rhode Island.

The worst destruction took place in the first half-hour after the hurricane's landfall. When it finally passed, it went north, dissipating slowly over the saturated ground, to wreak havoc in Massachusetts, and onward into Vermont and New Hampshire, finally dying over the forests of southern Quebec.

Dazed people emerged from wherever they had found shelter, to see death and destruction all around them. Many found boats, cars or other gifts of the storm in their yards. Others found their own homes destroyed, and family members dead or missing. It was Wednesday evening before the National Guard, the Red Cross, and other emergency agencies could get into action. During the forty-eight hours following the disaster, state health authorities inoculated thousands of people against typhoid. Thousands of workers from the WPA, the CCC, and other "New Deal" agencies were rushed into Rhode Island to help with the immense cleanup.

If nothing else can be said for the Hurricane of 1938, it got rid of beachfront shanties, old docks, and run-down buildings everywhere, and it gave Rhode Island the kick it needed to start some long overdue "urban renewal." The only fortunate thing about the destruction of hundreds of thousands of acres of woodland was that there was plenty of lumber available to rebuild the state.

People dealt with the hurricane as best they could. In those days, because of the relatively primitive state of weather forecasting and hurricane watching, there was very little warning possible before such a disaster. Today's weather satellites and highly organized weather-forecasting agencies would preclude the total lack of readiness on the part of Rhode Islanders. Hurricane Gloria in 1985, for example, would have had much graver consequences were it not for these modern factors. As we saw that year: When it comes to nature, anything can happen.

-PFE

Robert Toner
and the 'Lady Be Good'

Each day, thousands of vehicles travel Robert Toner Boulevard in North Attleboro, Massachusetts. Who was Robert Toner, and why is there a street named after him? There is a monument at Toner Boulevard and North Street dedicated to Lieutenant Robert F. Toner. It holds part of the answer, but there is a lot more to the story.

Robert Francis Toner was born in Woonsocket in July, 1915. His mother was a young woman named Nolan, and she apparently had no intention of keeping her baby. The little boy whose life was to end in mystery began life the same way.

Although it was a well kept family secret, discussed only by adults in hushed words, baby Robert, as he eventually was named, actually was dropped off at the home of Frank Toner on a warm Sunday afternoon by his mother, who said she was going on a picnic. Obviously, she was a family acquaintance at the very least, but her exact relationship to Frank Toner was never revealed.

Frank's sister, Gertrude Emerson, already had children, but she took the baby, adopted him and gave him her brother's name.

Frank Toner was North Attleboro's first police chief and, until his appointment, had been known as "the sheriff." In 1915, he also was one of the best loved citizens of the area, and he served as superintendent of moth control and as town forester.

George Elliot was a police officer in those days.

"Frank Toner kept his horses in our barn," Elliott remembered. "Frank and my grandfather were two of the original police officers in town. Toner used to come down about three times a week and ride. He was a great rider."

Toner's namesake and cousin, Frank, of Scituate, recalled at the age of 95 how the chief helped young people.

"Kids do crazy things, and he helped them out of scrapes. I used to go and sit with him in his office and just talk."

Chief Toner donated time, equipment and material to make certain that young people always had a first-rate playground. Behind the present Town Hall in North Attleboro is the Frank Toner Building, used by the Public Works Department to store equipment that keeps the town ballfields in playing shape.

Young Bob attended the newly opened St. Mary's School in North Attleboro, then went to St. John's Prep School in Danvers, Massachusetts, entering North Attleboro High School in 1932, graduating in 1934. He excelled at football. Bob had a rugged look, with a mop of blond hair and a winning smile that attracted the young ladies in town. One of them was Peg Mullen.

"We did different fun things in those days. We went to May basket parties and the June Box, as well as dances," she recalled.

Bob Toner was known as a "cool" guy. When not playing football, he worked in his uncle's garage on Washington Street.

"Bob was a good looking and happy young man, always smiling at everybody," Mullen said. "We all liked him; he was very sociable. That's why I would invite him to the dances at my college. He would come to my dormitory with a corsage, and take me out."

She also remembered having to parade Bob by Miss Polk, the dean of women, who liked him right away.

"He could charm anybody."

A boyhood friend, George Cunningham, who later operated the North Attleboro Museum, where Toner memorabilia was on display, echoed those thoughts.

"Everybody, particularly girls, liked Bob," Cunningham said. "He was always doing something for somebody."

In 1936, when Bob Toner was 21, his role model, the man whose name he carried so proudly, died. Chief Frank Toner

Woonsocket native Robert Toner in Royal Canadian Air Force blue, 1941.

-Collection of the Author

had gone to his office in the Odd Fellows Building on North Washington Street, where police headquarters was located, sat down at his desk, and suffered a heart attack. Patrolman John Brown, on duty at the time, took him home in a police car. Dr. D.J. Kiely was called, but it was too late. Cousin Frank Toner remembered the funeral.

"The whole town of North Attleboro went to that funeral. The church was full, and the streets were lined with people as the funeral procession went down Washington Street. It was tremendous."

Jeanette Emerson, Bob Toner's sister-in-law, recalled Chief Toner going to schools at Christmas time to distribute candy.

"He was a very, very good-hearted person who helped people quite a bit. He would send them food and even radios."

Emerson thought that Bob got much of his personality from Frank Toner.

In 1941, before the United States was involved in World War II, Bob Toner couldn't wait to fight. Canada was already at war with the Axis powers. So Toner, along with many other young Americans, enlisted in the Royal Canadian Air Force. The young Woonsocket native received his pilot's wings on May 14, 1942. By then, of course, the Japanese had attacked Pearl Harbor, and America was in the war. Toner soon traded in his checked cap for the khaki and leather of the U.S. Army Air Corps, which was in desperate need of pilots.

In letters that survive, Bob wrote from his 376 Bomb Group, 514 Bomber Squadron, of enemy planes constantly shooting at him from all directions. He longed to be home with his family.

Although World War II would last another two years, the North African Campaign was all but won. By April 1943, a small, German-controlled area in Northern Tunisia remained. Allied desert airstrips were acting as important bases for extending the battle into Sicily and Italy. The base for the new and highly touted B-24 Liberators, specifically the 376 Bomb Group, was in Soluch, about 300 miles from the Egyptian-Libyan border.

On April 4, an air attack was begun on Naples Harbor, 700 miles to the Northwest. The newest B-24 D Liberator was named "Lady Be Good" for good luck, after a popular song. It had a nine-man crew. The co-pilot was Second Lieutenant Robert F. Toner.

From all indications, the bombing raid did not go very well, mainly on account of clouds of sand thrown up earlier by departing aircraft. When the Lady Be Good finally reached its target area over Naples, it was too dark to drop bombs, and the crew turned back. By 11:30 p.m., all twenty-four planes that had left on the mission had returned to base, except the Lady Be Good. What happened will forever be a matter for debate, but one thing is certain: She never made it back.

At this time in the war, the Germans were broadcasting false radio signals to throw off allied planes. American and British forces had not been in North Africa long, and Germany still held some key areas along the coast. For some reason, the Lady Be Good kept flying past its base, and was some 300 miles off course. Perhaps it was the German signals, but a more likely theory is put forth by Frank Tedesco, who flew B-24 Liberators during World War II.

"Somehow (the plane's crew) got disoriented. In those days we used a system of orientation that used coded signals from a source. What you would have to do, and it was very difficult, was listen very carefully. You turned down the volume on your radio, and you heard a dot-dash or a dash-dot. If it got dimmer and dimmer, you knew you were going away from the station. You then made a procedure turn-around, came back on the same heading to pick up that signal and see if it increased in volume.

"Somehow or other, they got turned around and lost the signal. I've flown over the desert out there and came up through North Africa and into Italy in the B-24's, and it's desolate. There are no landmarks you can pick up. So there's nothing you can identify to find out where you are."

It was learned later that, out of gas and in danger of crashing, the Lady Be Good had to be abandoned. The pilot, Lt. William Hatton, would have told his crew members to bail out, and reassemble at the site of the crash. There was plenty of drinking water, cigarettes and rations on board, allowing them to survive until help arrived. They jumped, but the Lady Be Good kept going for miles before crashing into the desert. Her tail broke off, but otherwise the plane remained in livable condition. It was April 4, 1943. Sometime during that night, Robert Toner began writing in his diary.

Peg Mullen recalled, "It was at St. Mary's that we were told by the sisters to write in a diary. When I taught at North Attleboro Junior High School, I always had the children come into class each morning and write three lines on what they did the day before. I would tell them: 'There are two people I want to tell you about who wrote diaries and who amounted to something. Maybe some of you will, too. One was Anne Frank and the other was Bob Toner.' They were all hepped up about writing, and it started at St. Mary's."

Toner and his crew were in the desert, never thinking they would die there. This is what he wrote in his diary, a final record of those last days.

Sunday April 4. Got lost returning. Out of gas. Jumped. Landed in desert at two A.M. no one hurt. Can't find John.

"John" was Second Lieutenant John Woravka of Cleveland, Ohio. There was a reason John could not be found. His parachute had failed to open, and he was killed instantly when he hit the ground.

During the day, the temperature rose to 135 degrees. At night, it fell to freezing. The area was so remote that not even nomads brought their camels there. The nearest water hole was 160 miles away, at an oasis. The crew did not know where the Lady Be Good went down, but they saw tracks in the sand that apparently had been there since February 1941, when the Free French had attacked an Italian outpost. Believing those tracks led to civilization, the Lady Be Good crew began following them. What they could not know was that civilization was 440 miles away.

Eventually, they cut strips from their parachutes, and left them behind as markers for what they thought would be a search party. They discarded their heavy flight jackets as well. Toner continued to write in his diary.

Monday April 5. Started walking Northeast. Still no John. A few rations, half a canteen of water, one capful a day. Sunny, fairly warm. Good breeze from the Northwest. Night very cold. No sleep. Rested and walked.

Under ordinary circumstances, a man walking across the desert in 135-degree heat could last no more than a day without water. However, for these well trained fliers, survival methods were no doubt followed to the letter. They traveled at night to avoid the sweltering heat of the day, when they rested under the shade of their parachutes.

Tuesday April 6. Rested at 11:30. Sun very warm. No breeze. Spent PM in hell. Rested until 3:30 PM. Walked, rested all night. 15 minutes on five minutes off.

Wednesday April 7. Same routine. Everyone getting weak. Can't get very far. Prayers all the time. Again, PM very warm. Hell. Everyone can't sleep.

Thursday April 8. Hit sand dunes. Very miserable. Good wind. Continuous blowing of sand. Everyone now very weak. Thought Sam and Moore were all done. LaMotte eyes are gone. Everyone else bad. Still going Northwest.

The references to "Sam" and "Moore" were Staff Sergeants Samuel Adams of Illinois and Vernon Moore of Ohio. The "LaMotte" was Technical Sergeant Robert LaMotte of Michigan.

Friday April 9. Shelley, Rip and Moore separate try to go for help. Rest of us all very weak. Eyes bad. Not any travel. Still very little water. Temperature about 35 degrees. No wind. No shelter. One parachute left.

The name "Shelley," written by a very weak Toner, was Staff Sergeant Guy Shelley of Pennsylvania. "Rip" was Technical Sergeant Harold Ripslinger of Michigan.

Saturday April 10. Still having prayer meetings for help. No sign of anything. Couple of birds. Good wind from North. Really

The 'Lady Be Good' as she was found in the desert in 1959.

-Courtesy of U.S. Navy

weak now. Can't walk. Pain all over. Nights cold. No sleep.

Sunday April 11. Still waiting for help, still praying. Eyes bad. Lost all our weight. Aching all over. Could make it if we had water. Just enough left to put our tongue to. Have hopes for help very soon.

At this point, researchers theorize that Toner and his crew had about a day to live. They had traveled more than eighty-five miles from their landing site, and were nowhere near the plane. The Lady Be Good would have saved their lives because she carried drinking water.

Monday April 12. No hope yet. Very cold night.

This was the final entry in Robert Toner's diary. Did he die on the 12th? Did he last another day, but was too weak to write? No one will ever know.

When Toner and his crew failed to return to their base at Soluch (now known as Qaryat Suluq), the Army Air Corps began an aerial reconnaissance over the sea toward Naples. It was believed the Lady Be Good went down in the Mediterranean, but a two-day search revealed no sign of the plane. Families were notified and, a year later, when there was still no trace, the crew was declared missing in action and presumed dead. There also had been a one-year search by the Army's mortuary team, which had found the trail left by the men when they cut their parachutes to leave markings for rescuers. The Army simply gave up.

Ten years after the Lady Be Good disappeared, an oil-exploration project began in Libya for British Petroleum, Occidental, Esso and Mobil. The exploration was carried out in the Libyan desert, and went smoothly for five years. A pilot looking for oil-bearing rock strata spotted a plane lying on the desert floor 385 miles south of Tobruk. The information was given to survey parties exploring near the site. In November, the wreck was spotted again, but because there were no bodies seen in the immediate area, and because of the remote location, nothing was done, and the plane was forgotten.

In February 1959, a survey team decided to finally land next to the plane and check it. What they found would prove to be one of the greatest aviation stories ever told. The Lady Be Good was in good shape, except that the fuselage had broken in half upon impact in 1943. Inside were clothing, still hanging up, life rafts, a can of water, charts and maps, all in good condition. A check of military records indicated that it was indeed the Lady Be Good, missing since 1943. Every one of the nine crew had been declared dead long before.

When the investigators returned to the U.S. Air Force base in Wiesbaden, Germany, they prepared a news release for the Associated Press (AP), and the world finaly learned what had happened to the Lady Be Good.

The AP reported that a special team of investigators had been charged with looking into the wartime crash of an American Liberator bomber in the Libyan desert sixteen years before. The discovery had presented one of the greatest air mysteries of modern times.

Every daily newspaper in the country jumped on the story and, for the first time in many years, the memory of Robert Toner was stirred up in North Attleboro. The Lady Be Good had been found, but not the bodies. Following the story, which appeared in major magazines and a CBS television documentary, it seemed the Lady Be Good saga again died down.

Oil exploration in the Libyan desert continued, however, and on February 11, 1960, the remains of five men were discovered eighty-five miles north-northwest of the crash site, and along the southern part of the Sand Sea. Sensing death, the men had formed a human cross. One of them was Robert F. Toner. He was wrapped in a rolled up pair of coveralls, with his diary, describing the final days of these brave men. Also found at the site was a ring Toner had worn, as well as a second lieutenant's insignia and many articles of clothing.

The "John" whom Toner had written about was indeed John Woravka, who had died instantly when his parachute failed to open. Three other bodies were discovered a short time later. The body of the ninth crew member, Staff Sergeant Vernon Moore, was never found. The remains of those who had been discovered were flown to Frankfurt, Germany, for formal identification, then were returned to their hometowns for burial. One man, Second Lieutenant D.P. Hayes, was buried in Arlington National Cemetery.

Robert F. Toner was coming home for the first time since 1942, and many of the same family and friends who said goodbye to him when he left to serve the cause of freedom would be there to welcome him home in somber ceremonies. His body arrived at T.F. Green Airport in Warwick on March 23, 1960, two weeks short of seventeen years since he had disappeared. It was taken to the John Diamond Funeral Home on North Washington Street in North Attleboro, where the family was offered the opportunity to view the skeletal remains. They declined. The body was taken to St. Mary's Church, where Rev. Edward Booth conducted a Solemn High Requiem Mass.

The casket was driven through town, accompanied by Company A, Second Battalion, 60th Infantry, from Fort Devens, Massachusetts. A color guard carried Toner's unit colors. St. Mary's Cemetery had been prepared for Toner's arrival, and a grave stood open next to that of Police Chief Frank Toner. John Thomson, superintendent of the cemetery at the time of this writing, recalled his father-in-law and predecessor saying that Bob Toner's was one of the most memorable burials he had witnessed. There was a twenty-one gun salute, and the color guard stayed until the last bit of earth had been put over the grave.

In 1964, a stone was placed at Toner Boulevard and North Street, with the story of Toner's fate engraved on it. The Lady Be Good stayed on the floor of the Libyan desert for fifty-one years. On August 1, 1994, a ten-day recovery mission was mounted by the Antiquities Department at Cyrene, Libya, to retrieve the Lady Be Good for an International Military Museum planned for Tobruk, at the site of German General Erwin Rommel's headquarters in World War II. The remains of the plane, which had been stripped of all instruments, radios and propellers, was loaded onto trucks in sections and driven to Tobruk.

It has always been assumed that the Lady Be Good ran out of fuel over the desert and simply floated to rest after its crew had bailed out. In 1968, the number-two engine was recovered, and examined by the Royal Air Force. Remarkably, a fragment of enemy cannon shot was discovered lodged in the engine, enough to cause serious trouble and contribute to the plane becoming disabled.

It was another mystery that never would have been found if Robert Francis Toner had not kept a diary. Today, his diary, ring and other artifacts can be found in the North Attleboro Museum, donated by his family, who wanted to share him with the world. School children had recreated the crash of the Lady Be Good with models, also on display.

The United States built more than 18,500 B-24 Liberators. One is still flying.

-GVL

How Rhode Island
Almost Became the
Center of the World

The least known chapters in history often are the most astonishing. Virtually all Rhode Islanders today would look at you as though you had ten heads if you told them that North Scituate almost became home to the United Nations in 1946. But it's true, and the reason is more amazing yet.

It seems that in a large, rambling farmhouse near the summit of Chopmist Hill in that town, there occurred one of the most vital operations of World War II — an activity so secret that some of the information about it is still classified. According to the few unclassified records, scanty postwar newspaper accounts, and officials of the Federal Communications Commission (FCC) who spoke with the author in the 1980s, this farmhouse was the site of the most important of the 150 radio-monitoring stations operated during the war by the FCC's Radio Intelligence Division (RID).

The official story, given to the local press at the end of the war, was that the site was so important because it was the only known place in North America where radio signals of virtually any strength from all over the world could be intercepted.

This remarkable story has its beginnings several years before American entry into the war, with a man named Thomas B. Cave, who was to become the key figure in the operation. This tall, intense Bostonian was a top agent of the RID. Before his death in 1983 at the age of eighty one, Cave, who lived in retirement at Holmes Beach, Florida, was still reluctant to talk about what took place on the then-isolated Rhode Island hilltop. It was Cave who found the site, commanded the station during the war, and put together the official story afterwards. Before he died, he admitted that it was not the receptivity of the location, but the advanced, secret radio equipment used there that made Chopmist Hill's place in history. Though reception was remarkably good, "it was ninety-nine percent know-how" that created such success between 1941 and 1945.

What is known for certain is this: Listening in on enemy spies on virtually every continent, many of whom no other Allied station could pick up, agents at Chopmist Hill were able to crack foreign and domestic spy rings, save hundreds of thousands of Allied lives in battle by eavesdropping on enemy plans in advance, and bring about a number of dramatic land and sea rescues.

No local resident knew what the heavily guarded farmhouse was being used for, and even the forty or so RID employees there had little idea of the magnitude of what they were doing. Only Cave and his superiors in Washington knew.

In 1940, Cave had been sent to scour the hills of southern New England for a suitable site for a monitoring station to link up with the one at Bar Harbor, Maine, for direction-finding purposes. When Cave stumbled on it, the William A. Suddard farm seemed just what the RID needed. It had a fourteen-room house and several spacious buildings. And it was secluded, had 183 acres, and was up for lease. Cave pounced on it and, before long, discreet but steady work was under way, aimed at turning the farm into a virtual mini-city, with every available space used for housing equipment and agents.

At first, the U.S. Army brass were skeptical about the radio reception Cave claimed he could get at Chopmist Hill. He replied that his station could pinpoint the location of any transmitter in the country within fifteen minutes. Actually, it took only seven minutes for Cave and his men to locate the test station the Army secretly set up in the Pentagon itself! The brass were convinced. Once fully established, the station picked up virtually everything in good weather and bad: station to station broadcasts in Germany, messages beamed to Berlin from spies in Africa and the Americas, and German U-boat communications from all over the Atlantic. Japanese movements were no secret either, thanks to the men at Chopmist Hill.

Cave's boss, George E. Sterling, eighty-eight years of age when the author spoke with him in the mid-1980s, said then that he still couldn't understand how the United States was caught napping at Pearl Harbor on December 7, 1941, since messages indicating the attack was imminent had been intercepted at Scituate for months. Also intercepted every three weeks "like clockwork," said Cave, were messages from a Japanese submarine that lay off Tokyo Bay, and reported to the Imperial High Command every foreign vessel that entered or left.

At Chopmist Hill itself, RID monitors worked in six rooms that bulged with equipment and hummed with activity around the clock, keeping tabs on some 400 enemy transmitters that were secretly (so their users thought) on the air every day. The monitors even ferreted out low-frequency transmissions that were hidden under more powerful commercial signals abroad. Messages intercepted at Scituate were instantaneously sent to Washington by teletype for decoding, and provided crucial information for top Allied leaders on a daily basis. Teletype links were maintained with Westover Army Airfield in Massachusetts, Hillsgrove Army Airfield in Warwick, Quonset Naval Air Station in North Kingstown, the Air-Sea Rescue Service in New Hampshire, and the Army's Transatlantic Transport Command in Maine.

The entire property was dotted with utility poles on which 85,000 feet of antenna wire was strung. To avoid suspicion, the poles were never higher than the treetops, and were virtually invisible, both from the air and from much of the surrounding terrain. Agents bivouacked in a bunk house about 1,000 feet behind the farmhouse, and two other wooden structures (called "doghouses" by the men) enclosed high-frequency direction finders. There was even a concrete blockhouse containing an emergency generator. Armed guards patrolled the property day and night, and brilliant floodlights discouraged the approach of the curious during the hours of darkness.

Roads leading to the site bore signs with the sobering message: "In the event of an enemy attack on Rhode Island, this highway will be closed to all save military vehicles." Nobody could even visit the place except on official business, and only then if escorted up the main road by Rhode Island State Police.

One of the most secret aspects of Chopmist Hill's mission was its daily contact with British Security Coordination (BSC), to which all interceptions related to British home defense and battlefield operations were given, even before America's official involvement in the war. According to Sterling, the men at Scituate also were given special assignments on behalf of the British in monitoring frequencies that couldn't be picked up in Britain. These included listening in on special diplomatic frequencies and German weather reports broadcast from central Europe. The latter would be used by the British in planning bombing missions to Germany.

The British had their own "Chopmist Hill" at a place called Bletchley Park, about fifty miles north of London, where, in 1940, they broke the German code with a machine that was codenamed "Ultra." Kept secret until 1974, Ultra is generally acknowledged as the single most important intelligence operation of the war. More vague, and still quite secret, is Scituate's involvement in the Ultra operation. Was there a twin Ultra machine in Washington to which Scituate fed information that Bletchley Park couldn't pick up? If not, how were interceptions in the secret German code translated? We may have to wait quite a while to find out, since 2049 is the declassification date for Chopmist Hill's more sensitive information, according to FCC officials.

One instance in which Scituate and Bletchley Park both took a hand was during the fierce desert warfare in North Africa in 1942, when German General Erwin Rommel's elite Afrika Corps was pitted against the British Eighth Army and its assisting Commonwealth forces under General Sir Bernard Montgomery. It was Hitler's plan to smash the Allied forces in North Africa, then drive through the Middle East, and link up with the Japanese on the shores of the Indian Ocean. Thanks to good radio intelligence in America and Britain, this never happened.

The blockhouse that housed the generator at the Chopmist Hill radio-monitoring station, as it appeared in the mid-1980s. A 1940s-era car still sat forlornly behind it.

-Photo by Paul F. Eno

While the official story is that Bletchley Park did most of the work intercepting enemy transmissions, reception at Chopmist Hill was so good that Cave and his men were able to listen in on inter-tank transmissions between Rommel and his commanders! Thanks to good intelligence and good strategy, the Afrika Corps was effectively destroyed that November. All through Rommel's retreat from the front at El Alamein, Cave kept calling the Narragansett Electric Co. to send crews to Chopmist Hill to move antenna poles, sometimes only a few feet at a time. Since these were full-sized utility poles sunk nine feet into the ground, it was heavy work.

Narragansett Electric crewmen like Charlie Weinert thought the people at the Chopmist Hill farm were crazy. He had no idea that he was helping to defeat Rommel by moving antennas to follow German tanks across North Africa.

"If I'd known that" he said after the war when the story was made public, "I'd have dug poles all the way to Cairo!"

On another occasion, Chopmist Hill saved the British luxury liner *Queen Mary*, loaded with 10,000 Allied troops, from a pack of U-boats that was after her. It seems that on her way to Australia, this gem of Britain's merchant fleet had docked at Rio de Janeiro, Brazil, to take on fuel and supplies. German spies there somehow got hold of charts showing the *Queen Mary's* course, relaying word to comrades in Africa. Orders were broadcast to a German U-boat "wolf pack" in the mid-Atlantic to pursue and sink her. Chopmist Hill got the word as soon as the German navy did, of course. The warning was passed to London. Cave and his men had prevented a major tragedy: The ship's course was changed, and she made it safely to Australia.

The interception of such coded transmissions by spies was the most important part of Chopmist Hill's day-to-day work. Monitors there discovered numerous enemy transmitters in Europe, South America, Africa, and within the United States. Ever wonder why there were virtually no successful acts of sabotage by enemy agents in the continental United States during the war? You can give a good deal of the credit to Thomas B. Cave and the RID monitors at Chopmist Hill.

The men at Scituate discovered so many enemy transmitters no-one else could find that Allied commanders soon were breathing down Cave's neck for more and more information. Cave estimated that ninety-nine percent of all secret German communications intercepted by the United States in the course of the war were picked up at Chopmist Hill.

"The Germans were very clever," he told the author.

But Wilhelm Hoettl, a German intelligence area chief, might have said the same thing about Cave had he known of his work. During Hoettl's interrogation by American intelligence officers in June 1945, the German said that his people had not been able to set up a single, lasting wireless station anywhere in the United States. Something always gave them away. Most of the time, it was the RID at Chopmist Hill.

Elaborating on the cleverness of the foe, Cave explained how a German agent in, say, South America would send the first few letters of a message, then, hours later, a few more letters on another frequency, and so on.

"Sometimes we learned that an agent had two transmitters (of different frequencies) in the same room. He'd use one, then switch to the other," said Cave.

Several hundred enemy agents operating in the United States were detected by Chopmist Hill as soon as they went on the air. Some were pinpointed, and rounded up by the FBI, while others were allowed to continue operating briefly so that their sources and contacts could be traced. Even the broadcasts of American agents operating in enemy territory were monitored to help insure that they could be warned in the event of discovery.

A major sideline at Chopmist Hill was land and sea rescue. Among those whose lives were saved were twenty-two wounded soldiers whose plane went down in the wilds of Labrador, and the popular actress Kay Francis, whose plane ditched near Florida on the way back from a USO show in Europe.

The way the monitors located a spy, a ship or a downed plane is relatively simple if you know a bit of math. Inside each of the "doghouses" with the direction finders was a wheel. The operator would turn the wheel, rotating an antenna on top of the structure and listening for the "null" or point of weakest reception from the sender. A dial under the wheel would tell him the direction his antenna was pointing, providing a right-angle bearing on the sender. This information was transmitted to Washington at once, where bearings from one or more other land or sea stations that could pick up the signal were plotted. The intersection of the two or more lines gave the location of the target.

There were two direction finders at Scituate, though, and locations were very often found simply by using them, especially in the case of ships or submarines. In this situation, plottings were made from both the Scituate signal and that of the source the target was broadcasting to or receiving from. Thanks to Chopmist Hill and this original technique, the U.S. Navy and Coast Guard were able to mop up U-boat activity in the Caribbean early in the war.

When World War II ended in victory for the Allies in 1945, almost no-one realized that Chopmist Hill had done much to achieve it. On November 21, 1945, a reporter from the *Providence Journal* was allowed to visit the mysterious Scituate farmhouse. The story as released by Cave appeared, with photos, over the following two days. Steering away from the secret equipment and techniques used at the station, Cave attributed the great success of his work to "a peculiar advantage of terrain and atmospheric surroundings."

E. Merle Glunt of Mount Union, Pennsylvania, an intercept analyst for the RID during World War II, and the division's "unofficial historian" when the author spoke with him in the 1980s, attributed Chopmist Hill's success very largely to the personal expertise and "first class" organizational ability of Cave himself. After the war, Cave and a few of his men stayed on at Chopmist Hill to continue monitoring the air waves, this time for nothing more exciting than illegal domestic broadcasting.

It was shortly after the remarkable story of the wartime work at Scituate became public that the United Nations accepted Congress's invitation to establish its headquarters somewhere in the United States. An irrepressible Scituate town councilman named George E. Matteson, whose interests ranged from politics to cartography, persuaded the Scituate Town Council to invite the U.N. to settle on Chopmist Hill, based on what was believed to be the site's phenomenal potential for ease in international communication.

After he saw the invitation and learned what had gone on at Scituate, Dr. Stoyan Gavrilovic of Yugoslavia, chairman of the U.N. committee searching for a headquarters site, presented the information to his colleagues. The skeptical diplomats decided to visit the site an January 23, 1946.

"I remember the busload of them coming up," Cave recalled. "They came in and I let them listen to some of the things we could pick up."

Each committee member was astonished to hear local broadcasts coming from his own country as he sat at a console at the farmhouse. Then they realized that Chopmist Hill was indeed a "possible site," Dr. Gavrilovic later told the press.

"The site meets most of the technical points," he said, noting that the miles of unbroken woodland offered "ample room" for the airport and large buildings that would be required. "It is good," he said. Other members of the committee agreed that Chopmist Hill was "one of the top sites yet seen in New England, and probably in the United States...."

It was one week later to the day that the committee announced its decision: U.N. headquarters would be built in New York City, on land that had just been donated to the organization. Rhode Island had lost out because of two primary factors: the donation of the New York land, and the lack of immediate access to the site by water. The U.N. would have had to buy the Scituate land at about $60 per acre. New York represented a great deal more convenience and much less expense. If the decision had gone otherwise, one can only imagine what Rhode Island would be like today!

So the green hills of Scituate remained quiet. The FCC stayed on at Chopmist Hill until 1950, when the property was turned over to the State Council of Defense of Rhode Island, later renamed the Rhode Island Office of Civil Preparedness, which made its headquarters there until its move to Providence in 1965.

It was in 1968 that Frederick Leeder acquired the property at auction. Its 183 acres had long been carved up, but five of them, and most of the buildings, were left. The farmhouse, its story virtually forgotten even locally, was home for the Leeders in the 1980s, when this story was being researched. Leeder, at the time a rescue lieutenant with the Chopmist Hill Volunteer Fire Department, was pleased with the price he paid, but baffled by the hundreds of old utility poles that stood all about the place.

"I cut down nineteen poles in the immediate vicinity of the house, just to make fence posts," Leeder said, adding that he only gradually learned the house's history from following up local sources. He and others were intensely interested in preserving the property, and they wanted to see it placed on the National Register of Historic Places, but much of the original site had already become residential subdivisions.

The blockhouse that housed the station's emergency generator became the Leeders' hay barn. The wartime warning signs that stood at the ends of nearby roads served to board up the windows of the old pump house. In the basement, over the washing machine, could still be seen the old conduit, filled with frayed teletype cables that once carried the peril of the world. And everywhere outside were poles and the remnants of poles. With dates ranging from 1938 to 1943 carved into their aged wood, they still dotted what was left of the scrubby woods and fields on the east side of Chopmist Hill.

As though a vague echo of what once took place there, there stood a single, modern, steel antenna, anchored in concrete hard by the Leeders' driveway. Owned by the state, it beamed and received emergency messages for police vehicles and ambulances, and stood ready for use by the civil defense network. It remained there in 2004, when the site still was not listed on the National Register, nor commemorated in any other official way.

Reception isn't as good as it used to be on Chopmist Hill. There are new houses all around, and lots of people use cellular telephones and other electronic devices. But somehow, the crackle of static and the nervous little beeps of code that echoed within those farmhouse walls from the far corners of the globe will never wholly cease... not while there are those who remember what might have been lost if Thomas B. Cave and men like him had not been there so many years ago.

-PFE

Chapter Thirteen

Coming
 # Full Circle

You know what the fellow said: "The more things change, the more they stay the same."

No period saw such wholesale change in Rhode Island than the fifty-five years between the end of World War II and the turn of the millennium. Everything shifted: the economy, the people, the politics, even the countryside. The "post-industrial" economy of service and high-technology industries replaced manufacturing as king of the dollar. By 2001, new waves of foreign immigration had brought major population and social change, and population shifts transformed the state's very landscape. Housing was scarce, and you needed a telescope to look at both prices and rents.

Behind it all, however, this still was Rhode Island and Providence Plantations, with the same exciting dramas playing out: new ideas, political hijinks, colorful characters, and news events that wouldn't happen anywhere else in the modern world. But, as always in Rhode Island, the positive won out in the end, even though it may have taken its time doing it. It was a time of great abuses, but also a time of great reform.

Just how much Rhode Island changed in the latter half of the 20th century can't really be appreciated without thinking about the depths from which it started in the years just after

1945. World War II hauled the state out of the Great Depression with a deluge of defense manufacturing and other war-related activities. After the war, however, familiar bugbears that had started haunting the state as early as the turn of the century returned in their same ghastly forms.

Foremost among these was the ever-leaking balloon of the textile industry. Patched up for awhile by Uncle Sam's defense contracts during the war, the industry started deflating again soon afterward. Strong unions insisted on closed shops and the same high wartime wages. Mill owners simply refused to meet these demands, and many mills closed, throwing thousands out of work. Fifteen mills gave up the ghost between 1945 and 1953 alone, and textile jobs took a dive of seventy-five percent between the end of the war and 1982.

During the same years, factory workers in general were almost as harried: Rhode Island's manufacturing jobs fell from fifty-two percent of all jobs to thirty-two percent. Many large firms, like the former industrial titans Nicholson File and American Screw Company, either were sold to international conglomerates or moved away. By 2001, only one of Rhode Island's ancient industrial giants, Brown and Sharpe, still existed in anything like its original form.

The Korean War and increased defense manufacturing perked things up a bit for some sectors of Rhode Island industry from 1950 to 1953, but this didn't last. Basically, the state's industrial base continued to crawl along through the '50s and '60s in the same more or less depressed condition. To some extent, though, this slump was slowed by the continued growth of the jewelry industry, which by the 1990s was the state's largest industrial employer. But jewelry here has had a speckled history: Fads and public whim give it plenty of ups and downs. Working conditions, job security and wages often were substandard, and that persisted in some shops into the 21st century.

One bright spot was that the Navy remained in Rhode Island after World War II, and it was the state's largest single employer for nearly thirty years thereafter. Though forces were reduced to peacetime strength, the Navy still retained a $200 million annual payroll here. So it was with horror that

Rhode Islanders learned in 1973 that President Richard Nixon had approved a plan to yank the Atlantic Fleet out of Newport, and its support facilities out of Quonset Point - Davisville in North Kingstown.

Ostensibly, this was part of an effort to cut back military spending and consolidate forces as the Vietnam War wound down. But some people grumbled that it was one of Nixon's ways of punishing New England because he had won every state but Massachusetts in the 1972 election. Whatever the president's motive, this move was a bloodbath for Rhode Island's economy. Almost overnight, more than 16,000 civilians lost their jobs, real-estate prices in many areas of Newport and Washington Counties plummeted, schools closed, and a vast source of retail business dried up. When it was over, 30,000 people had left Rhode Island.

One thing that kept the noose from tightening completely around Rhode Island's economic neck was the continuance — and eventual increase — of defense contracts after the Big Pullout. The Electric Boat Division of General Dynamics moved to a new submarine hull plant at Quonset Point, and consistently employed thousands of people there. Firms like Raytheon Signal Division and, until it closed in 1992, the Robert Derecktor Shipyard in Middletown did a great deal of work for the military. Smaller firms around the state got contracts of their own for items ranging from tools to uniform insignia.

Throughout the late 20th century, nevertheless, Rhode Island had the image of an anti-business state run by corrupt politicians, a land of strong labor unions, and a haven for organized crime, factors that contributed to slow business growth and an unwillingness by out-of-state companies to move here. From time to time during this period, the state government and private industry put together commissions and systems for statewide economic planning and for attracting industry. But diverse circumstances, such as the state's relatively unskilled work force, astronomical rates for workers' compensation insurance, an aging population, municipal unwillingness to go along with statewide planning, and the granting of unemployment benefits to strikers, all had negative effects on these efforts.

Some of these problems gradually were eliminated, beginning in the 1980s, through legislation and new job-training programs. One especially ambitious plan proposed in 1983 was the Greenhouse Compact, a $750 million effort proposed by the Rhode Island Strategic Development Commission for lighting a fire under a state economy that was "dead in the water." The sweeping program was intended to create 60,000 new and higher-paying jobs by 1990, and use tax and bond money to help current industries survive, and to establish new ones. With traditional contrariness, however, Rhode Islanders soundly defeated the Greenhouse Compact referendum that November.

But beyond all the plans, hopes and general ups and downs, circumstances bigger than proposals and commissions were getting ready to turn the economy around. All along, more and more of the slack left behind by the decline in manufacturing had been taken up by two phenomena: the spread of service industries like banks, colleges and health institutions, and by the ever-fatter payrolls of state and municipal governments. The latter started with the New Deal programs of the 1930s and, stuffed by patronage jobs and federally-funded social projects, generally lasted until the recessions of the '70s and '80s.

Another key economic factor was construction of the interstate highway system in the 1960s. This opened vast areas of rural Rhode Island to development, and allowed for the long-distance commute from here to Boston or wherever. By the time the recession of the early 1980s ended, Rhode Island laws had become more business-friendly, "high tech" industries ruled nearby Massachusetts, and Rhode Island real estate had become solid gold. Things started to turn in a more prosperous direction.

It wasn't happy times for all, however. Hard-hit during the '80s and '90s were many industrial workers. Laid off, they waited for better days to get their jobs back. Even when boom times started returning, many of the industrial jobs never did because Rhode Island's old economy was gone, apparently forever. In a state where, by 2000, the state itself was the largest employer, restaurants and tourism were the largest private industries, and housing costs were at Jupiter and headed for Pluto, many basic economic problems stubbornly persisted.

There was, of course, the age-old cavalcade of bizarre events and equally bizarre characters. This parade was led by not-quite-role-model politicians, business leaders, and organized-crime bosses who never seemed to "get it" when it came to the fact that, in the "information age," you couldn't keep a secret: Sooner or later, everybody found out everything.

Some would say that the quintessential Rhode Island debacle of this kind took place at the beginning of 1991, when a bank president named Joseph Mollicone Jr. disappeared with nearly $13 million from his Heritage Loan & Investment Company in Providence. Not only was it the state's worst financial scandal of the 20th century, but it brought down the Rhode Island Share and Deposit Indemnity Corporation (RISDIC), which turned out to be insolvent. In the first act after his inauguration that year, Governor Bruce G. Sundlun closed forty-four RISDIC-insured banks and credit unions. Nearly every Rhode Islander was affected in some way, and some 300,000 people lost some or all of their savings.

Mollicone, who had been holed up in Las Vegas, eventually turned himself in, pled guilty, and landed behind bars. Most private victims eventually were "made whole" in ensuing years as the state cleared up the mess. But unresolved legal and financial issues from the crisis persisted well into the 21st century.

Among the other scandals that took place during this period were the state pension scams and early-retirement deals that started emerging in the 1970s, with some former state employees claiming far more years of service than they actually had put in, and the General Assembly letting them – sometimes helping them – get away with it. One state senator claimed what amounted to seventy-nine years of state and municipal service – when he retired at the age of fifty one. The state pension system allowed many of these darlings credit for time spent doing union work, moonlighting, and time served – or not served – in the armed forces. Furious voters shut down the old pension system in a 1994 referendum.

Another embarrassment was a scandal at the Rhode Island Housing and Mortgage Finance Corporation. In 1985, news broke that the fund, which was supposed to guarantee mortgages for first-time, working-class home buyers, was low because politically connected people were getting financing at the expense of ordinary folks. Eventually, twenty-five people were indicted for misuse of public funds, and other crimes.

In the worst of a parade of judicial dishonors in the '80s and '90s, state Supreme Court Chief Justice Joseph A. Bevilacqua dodged impending impeachment by resigning in 1986 amid a probe that alleged his misuse of staffers and public money.

Then there were the mayors. Hijinks involving bribes from city contractors and other mischief landed Pawtucket Mayor Brian Sarault in the slammer in 1991. And the late '90s saw the beginnings of the "Operation Plunderdome" federal investigation of Providence City Hall, which eventually landed the city's legendary and colorful mayor, Vincent A. Cianci, in the "big house" too. Providence was rife with shenanigans. People got paid for city jobs they never showed up for. One employee ran a pizza parlor on city time. Not even former governors were spared: Edward D. DiPrete went to jail after pleading "no contest" to swapping state contracts for political contributions during his 1985 to 1990 watch.

At times during this period, as in previous eras, corruption was so rampant – even flaunted – that Rhode Island sadly found itself a national laughingstock.

But it's crucial to keep all this in perspective: The "good old days" recounted in our previous chapters weren't really so good because people of this ilk usually got away with their crimes, and even the police looked the other way if the criminals were influential enough. As the 21st century approached, it became harder and harder for corrupt politicians, corporate types, or even mobsters to get away with things. Whether because of the snoopy media, more professionalism in law enforcement and government, or a combination of these and other factors, Rhode Island was far more honest in 2001 than

The new Waterplace Park and the Providence Place Mall as it appeaed in 2004.

-Photo by Paul F. Eno

it had been in 1901.

More obvious to the eye were the sweeping changes wrought by residential development between 1945 and the end of the century. There were slowdowns and there were frenzies, but the march of housing was inexorable. Propelled by soldiers returning from World War II and starting families, the Rhode Island housing boom began in 1945. The fact that the Rhode Island Builders Association was chartered the following year was a dead giveaway that a boom was in the offing.

The long expansion in housing and other development was pioneered by men like Italian immigrant and visionary Nazarene Melocarro who, in the late '40s, took an undeveloped, 233-acre tract off New London Turnpike in Cranston and turned it into the Garden City shopping and residential development. It was the first development of its kind in the state, and it was hailed as a national model of the "planned community," with curving streets, an old-neighborhood feel, and varied shopping within walking distance.

You could have bought a new home there for as little as $15,000, and an existing home elsewhere in Rhode Island for as little as $5,000.

Throughout the 1950s and 1960s, housing developments, some tasteful and well planned and others less so or not at all, sprouted all over Rhode Island's suburbia and a growing "exurbia" – former rural areas that better roads and a willingness to do longer commutes made developable.

An aging population and slower economic times following the Vietnam War led to a slowdown in the 1970s, but by the mid-1980s, home building had taken off again, and it was still going as the 21st century began.

All this residential growth came with a heavy price tag, however. As more of rural Rhode Island was being bulldozed, people realized that they were losing the state's precious open lands forever. Pollution and other environmental crises began to emerge as top issues. It became obvious that Narragansett Bay and the rivers flowing into it were in serious danger because of ever-more polluted runoff from human activities.

There were actual environmental disasters too. For example,

a runaway tugboat and barge ran aground at Moonstone Beach in South Kingstown in January 1996, spilling more than 800,000 gallons of home heating oil into Block Island Sound. It was the worst spill in the state's history, with beach, birds and other wildlife coated with oil. Both the cleanup and the litigation dragged on for years. The incident became known as the "North Cape" disaster because that's what the media dubbed it. Anyone scouring the map of Rhode Island for a North Cape will be frustrated, however. *North Cape* was the name of the barge.

It was in the 1970s that the environment truly emerged as a national priority, once modern man began to realize what every other critter on the planet has always known: We're part of nature, not separate from it. Now, Rhode Island and its new Department of Environmental Management were regulating not just builders, but all property owners and their activities more and more strictly.

Then came the mid-'80s. Like Icarus in the Greek myth, flying too close to the sun, Rhode Island's development highflyers found their wings melting with the heat of financial overextension, high prices and lack of demand. Like the stock market in October 1987, they crashed. It wasn't until the mid-'90s that housing would really pick up again. But by that time, Rhode Island's municipalities were ready. Armed with the state Zoning Enabling Act of 1992, they greeted developers with everything from stricter zoning and planning laws to development-impact fees and caps on the number of building permits that could be issued each year.

To officials, environmentalists and the populace, developers responded that they were people too, were tired of being demonized, and made the not unreasonable assertion that they were simply filling people's need for places to live. They further claimed that it wasn't their own greed driving up costs, it was partially the fault of a worsening housing shortage, increasing government regulation, and municipal growth controls.

By the late '90s, the housing situation was complex and confusing. While the state's population had increased only four and a half percent between 1990 and 2000, there were more and more households. Out-of-state property owners, mainly Boston-area commuters and New York-area vacationers, were driving up real estate costs to the point that native Rhode Islanders often couldn't afford to live in the towns they grew up in. Foreign immigrants were flooding the state in numbers not seen in a century, driving up demand for a shrinking number of rental units.

By 1997, housing costs were increasing twice as fast as personal income. Clearly, a coalition was called for. As of 2001, spearheaded by the Grow Smart Rhode Island organization, a team of groups – builders, environmentalists, state and municipal officials, planners, academics, business leaders, and even banks — was working to balance the state's economic requirements, human needs, and environmental necessities.

But it wasn't just residential development that was changing Rhode Island throughout this period. By the 1950s, America's cities in general and New England's in particular had seen better days. Slime, grime and crime seemed all too present, and the residential and retail exodus from city to suburb only made it worse. The '60s dawned with the cry of "urban renewal" from Washington. Through the next decade in most American cities, this largely meant bulldozing vast areas of historic but dilapidated buildings, and replacing them with boxy, utilitarian piles of glass and steel.

Then, advocates for historic preservation got together with one or two urban planners who actually had paid attention in their college psychology classes. Together, they got the message across to decision makers that people are happier if they have a sense of place. Thus began urban renewal in the true sense: Usable historic buildings were rehabilitated for residential and commercial use rather than being bulldozed. This happy trend continued into the 21st century. By that time, when old buildings had to be replaced, it often was done with "post-modern" architecture (such as the Westin Hotel in Providence), which, if not historic, at least showed some imagination beyond right angles.

Providence was the only city in Rhode Island big enough to be first-line urban renewable. Fortunately, the '60s spared the city the worst of the glass-and-steel craze that devastated Hartford and, to some extent, Worcester. This was largely through the efforts of world-renowned preservationist, author, and lover of Rhode Island Antoinette Downing of Providence, along with her friend Katherine Urquhart Warren of Newport. Both women worked tirelessly to save Providence's and Rhode Island's priceless historical structures, and to have laws passed that would keep them preserved.

Along with the preservation of Newport's colonial treasures and Providence's College Hill, one of the most striking examples of determined conservation took place on Block Island in 1993. Islanders raised $2.3 million to literally move the four-million-pound Southeast Light lighthouse back from Mohegan Bluffs so it wouldn't crumble into the ocean.

Meanwhile, pressure for residential development was bringing pressure for retail development too. First it was the "strip malls" that followed the early housing subdivisions in the '50s and '60s. Then, in the '80s and '90s, as the heat continued on rural areas, especially in South County, battles over "affordable housing" and new subdivisions were punctuated by skirmishes over proposals for new "big box" stores, like Wal-Mart and Home Depot.

One major catalyst for development of any kind was the interstate highways, notably I-95, which cut the state in half beginning in the 1960s. Because people could now drive relatively quickly between Boston, Providence, New London, New Haven and New York, this "Northeast Corridor" became a magnet for development. Communities on or near the highway were in the bullseye. For much of the late 20th century and into the 21st, Westerly, Charlestown, South Kingstown, North Kingstown and East Greenwich, all in the I-95 corridor, were among Rhode Island's fastest-growing communities. It was no different along I-95's great tributary, I-295, a sort of Providence "beltway" that bisected northern and central Rhode Island. In these parts, Cumberland, Lincoln, Smithfield and Cranston led the growth march.

Whether dear old Roger Williams would have laughed or cried we don't know, but "Indian gaming" came to the fore in Rhode Island in the 1990s. Some state and municipal officials, taxpayers, and Narragansett tribal members gazed longingly over the border into nearby Connecticut, where the Mashantucket Pequot Tribe used their reservation's federal status as a semi-sovereign country to erect an enormous casino and resort hotel, raking in millions every month, some of which they simply handed to the State of Connecticut. Things really heated up in 1997, when the Pequots bought over 250 acres in Hopkinton, with an option for 400 more. The Narragansetts, lacking the Pequots' land holdings, still were lobbying for a casino – notably in West Warwick, of all places — as the 21st century approached.

One of the biggest stories of the 1990s was mass immigration, a major factor in Rhode Island's shifting and changing population. Remember our earlier chapter, "The World Comes to Rhode Island"? Well, it came back again as the 20th century wound down. By 2000, an estimated eleven percent of the state's population was foreign-born. This didn't include large numbers of newcomers from Puerto Rico, a U.S. "commonwealth" with a national identity of its own but whose citizens were not legally foreigners.

On the streets of Providence – or practically anywhere else — you could hear languages ranging from Chinese to Farsi to Hindi. But by far the largest foreign-language group was Spanish, with speakers representing every Hispanic nation in the Western Hemisphere. As a matter of fact, many people did double-takes at 2000 U.S. census figures showing that, since 1990, Hispanics (at 8.7 percent of the population) had replaced African-Americans (at 4.5 percent) as Rhode Island's largest minority group.

Signs at banks and other businesses began appearing in English and Spanish, not because the commercial sphere was trying to be liberal, but because there was more and more money to be made from that constituency. Even some immigration advocates thought all this was too much of a good thing. Too many immigrants from one language group, they believed, weren't good for "diversity." Hispanic leaders assured nervous natives and other immigrant groups that their people were here to become Americans, learn English, and fully participate in society. In the meantime, some older Hispanic immigrants were complaining privately that the younger generation, thanks to television and the Internet, didn't want to use Spanish, even at home, and would forget it in a generation or two. One critic of mass immigration quipped that the various ethnic groups would have to learn English just to talk to each other.

As the 21st century got under way, however, Hispanics proved as good as their word: Most took with gusto to being Americans, and many wasted no time in getting educations and job training, moving into the middle class far more quickly than their immigrant predecessors of a century earlier.

As if to cap this period of newness, ambitious restoration plans for downtown Providence took place in the century's final years. Kindled perhaps by an insightful, 1970s study of how traffic moved downtown, carried on by Gerald Howes of the Rhode Island School of Design, the eventual project ended up transforming the central city. The crown jewel was Waterplace Park. Overlooked by the State House, the project involved restoring much of the long-buried cove and promenade, creating a social and cultural center where everything from concerts, arts festivals and shows, to weddings and the famous Waterfire could take place. Other aspects of the downtown resurrection were new restaurants, a new Convention Center, the huge Providence Place Mall, and new apartments and condominiums that typified the residential return to revived cities envisioned by Grow Smart Rhode Island.

We can't help notice the happy irony in the fact that the cove now restored was the very one Roger Williams traversed before landing in what was to become Rhode Island and Providence Plantations. So we have quite literally come full circle.

Despite – or because of – its heroes and villains, Rhode Island has achieved a balance not often found in places of less personality. From Woonsocket to Newport, there is a uniqueness and an independent spirit that surely would have made Roger Williams proud of his, and our, "noble experiment"!

-PFE

You decide!

DEVELOPMENT

Probably the most hot-button issue as Rhode Island approached the 21st century was residential development and "urban sprawl." Most communities, especially smaller towns, complained of a strained infrastructure, overcrowded schools, and overextended budgets for town services. At the same time, what housing there was was extraordinarily expensive. Was there too much development? Not enough? Would the state lose its unique character because of it? What do you think?

Residential development has been good for Rhode Island

• The population was growing, and people had to live somewhere. Decent housing is essential for any healthy society.

• Everyone needs a clean environment and accessible open space to maintain a healthy and attractive quality of life. Development techniques that became common in the 1990s — such as "rural compounds," "conservation development," and "village centers" – encouraged denser housing while preserving open space and small-town atmosphere.

• In the late 1990s, more housing would have eased demand and brought down prices, but communities and government agencies helped keep prices high with overregulation and heavy-handed controls on land use.

• Housing was the anchor that kept the state economy of the 1990s from falling into recession. Without it, other sectors would have suffered, and there would have been serious job losses.

• Development created wealth and assets for families and a firm residential tax base for communities.

• When the 21st century arrived, much of the residential development was taking place by reviving old mill buildings and turning them into attractive apartments and condominiums. This saved many a rural parcel from development.

Residential development has been bad for Rhode Island

• Overdevelopment in the 1990s led to deterioration of the environment, and it severely harmed Rhode Island's uniqueness, especially in what had been rural areas. Communities began to lose their personalities and cohesion, and people began to lose their sense of place.

• Local communities acted too slowly in adopting growth restrictions. By the time they adopted new "comprehensive plans" and tougher zoning rules, much damage had already been done.

• Development techniques that called for denser housing or getting people back into urban areas to live were all fine on paper. But the fact was that most people didn't want to live in denser housing environments, especially those who were more affluent. So developers kept building the "McMansion" subdivisions in rural areas.

• More residential development encouraged more commercial development, with more strip malls and more "big box" stores. This created a need for bigger roads and led to more and more congestion.

-PFE

⚓ Bibliography ⚓

ADAMS, James Truslow. *New England in the Republic 1776-1850*. Boston: Little, Brown and Co., 1926

AHLSTROM, Sydney E. *A Religious History of the American People, Volumes 1 and 2*. Garden City, New York: Image Books, 1975

ALLEN, Everett S. *A Wind to Shake the World: The Story of the 1938 Hurricane*. Boston: Little, Brown and Co., 1976

BALFOUR, David W. and KOUTSOGIANE, Joyce H. Cumberland by the Blackstone: 250 Years of Heritage. Norfolk, Va.: Donning Company, 1997

BAYLES, Richard M. *History of Providence County, Rhode Island* (2 volumes). New York: W.W. Preston & Co., 1891

BRIDENBAUGH, Carl. *Fat Mutton and Liberty of Conscience: Society in Rhode Island 1636-1690*. Providence: Brown University Press, 1974

BUHLE, Paul M. (ed.). *Working Lives: an Oral History of Rhode Island Labor*. Providence: Rhode Island Historical Society, 1987

CONLEY, Patrick T. *Democracy in Decline: Rhode Island's Constitutional Development 1776-1841*. Providence: Rhode Island Historical Society, 1977

CONLEY, Patrick T. *First in War, Last in Peace: Rhode Island and the Constitution, 1786-1790*. Providence: The Rhode Island Bicentennial Foundation and The Rhode Island Publications Society, 1987

CONLEY, Patrick T. and CAMPBELL, Paul R. *Providence, A Pictorial History*. Norfolk, Va.: Donning Company, 1982

ELLIS, Joseph J. After the Revolution, Profiles of Early American Culture. New York: W.W. Norton & Co., 1979

ENO, Paul F. *The Best of Times: 100 Years of the Valley's Home Paper*. West Warwick, R.I.: Community Newspapers of Rhode Island and New River Press, 1992

GALLAGHER, Gary W. (ed.). *The Third Day at Gettysburg & Beyond*. Chapel Hill, North Carolina: The University of North Carolina Press, 1994

HALEY, John Williams. *The Old Stone Bank History of Rhode Island* (3 volumes). Providence: Providence Institution for Savings, 1939

HARPIN, Matthias P. *The High Road to Zion*. West Warwick: Harpin's American Heritage Foundation, 1976

KELLNER, George H. and LEMONS, J. Stanley. *Rhode Island, the Independent State*. Woodland Hills, Calif.: Windsor Publications and the Rhode Island Historical Society, 1982

LIND, *Louise. William Blackstone: Sage of the Wilderness.* Westminster, Maryland: Heritage Books, 1993

McLOUGHLIN, William G. *Rhode Island, A History*. New York: W.W. Norton & Co., 1978

MOLLOY, D. Scott. *Rhode Island Transit Album, Bulletin Number Fifteen*. Boston: Boston Street Railway Association, 1978

MOORE, Christopher. *The Loyalists: Revolution, Exile, Settlement.* Toronto: McClelland & Stewart, 1994

POWELL, Sumner Chilton. *Puritan Village, the Formation of a New England Town*. Garden City, N.Y.: Doubleday & Co., 1963

SOLOMON, Barbara Miller. *Ancestors and Immigrants, a Changing New England Tradition*. New York: John Wiley & Sons, 1956

THOMAS, A.P. *Woonsocket, Highlights of History 1800-1976.* Woonsocket, R.I.: Woonsocket Opera House Society, 1976

WILLIAMS, Catherine. *Biography of Revolutionary Heroes.* Privately published, 1839

PETTAQUAMSCUTT CHAPTER, Daughters of the American Revolution. *Facts and Fancies Concerning North Kingstown, Rhode Island*. Wickford, Rhode Island: Privately Published, 1941

ENO, Paul F. "William Blackstone." *American National Biography.* New York: Oxford University Press, 1999

ENO, Paul F. "R.I. 350" series. Providence: Rhode Island Historical Society: 1985-1986

ENO, Paul F. "Dorr Rebellion 150" series. Providence: Rhode Island Historical Society: 1992-1993

ETULAIN, Richard. "John Cotton and the Anne Hutchinson Controversy." *Rendezvous* 2.2 (1967): 9-18.

GROSSMAN, Lawrence. "George T. Downing and Segregation of Rhode Island Public Schools, 1855-1866." *Rhode Island History.* Providence: The Rhode Island Historical Society. Vol. 36, No.4 (November 1977): 99-105.

HEWITT, J. H. "Mr. Downing and His Oyster House: The Life and Good Works of an African-American Entrepreneur," *New York History* (July 1993): 229-252.

MILLER, John F. "The French in Rhode Island." *Rhode Island Yearbook 1974*: 32-37

WALDEN, George F. "The Battle of Rhode Island." *Rhode Island Yearbook 1974*: 24-27

NEWSPAPERS:

The Providence Journal and Evening Bulletin
The Newport Daily News
The Woonsocket Call
The Pawtucket Times
The Observer
The Pawtuxet Valley Daily Times
The Warwick Beacon
The Westerly Sun
Worcester National Aegis and Transcript

⟨⟩ Acknowledgments ⟨⟩

Every section of this book had many contributors over many years, especially the wonderful, varied and generous people of Rhode Island through the many eras we cover.

A primary and special "thank you" to Albert T. Klyberg, director emeritus of the Rhode Island Historical Society, for bringing the two of us together in the 1997 meeting that resulted in this book.

We also thank Executive Director Bernard P. Fishman and the entire staff of the Rhode Island Historical Society and Library for their practical help and encouragement.

We also acknowledge the invaluable help of the late Princess Redwing of the Narragansett Tribe, Ken Carlson and Gwen Stern of the Rhode Island State Archives, the staff of the Providence Journal Company, the staff of the Providence Public Library, the staff of the Newport Convention and Visitors Bureau, the staff of the North Attleboro (Massachusetts) Museum, the family of Gertrude Emerson, the family of Robert F. Toner, the staffs of North Burial Ground and Swan Point Cemetery (Providence), the staff of the South County Museum (Narragansett), the staff of the Sprague Mansion (Cranston), the Cranston Historical Society, the U.S. Bureau of the Census, the late Thomas B. Cave, and the late George E. Sterling.

Special thanks to David W. Balfour, chairman of the Cumberland Historic District Commission, and Rhode Island author in his own right, for his advice and encouragement.

Many thanks also to Robert Billington, Kevin Klyberg and the administrative and ranger staffs of the John H. Chafee Blackstone River Valley National Heritage Corridor Commission, and to Raymond Bacon and the staff of the Museum of Work and Culture (Woonsocket).

For their generous permission to use photographs and illustrations, our gratitude goes to the Rhode Island Historical Society, the Providence Journal Company, the Casemate Museum (Fort Monroe, Virginia), Susan Heuck Allen, and the U.S. Navy.

Paul has special thanks for the summer intern staff at the Washington office of Congressman Patrick J. Kennedy, who got him into the heavily secured U.S. Capitol on a hot day in August 2003 to take photographs for this book in Statuary Hall and the Rotunda.

Most of all, we thank our longsuffering wives, Jackie Eno and Linda Laxton, for their endless patience, encouragement and support!

-Paul Eno & Glenn Laxton

Index